Japanese
Politics
Today

Japanese Politics Today

Beyond Karaoke Democracy?

Edited by   Purnendra Jain
UNIVERSITY OF ADELAIDE, AUSTRALIA

Takashi Inoguchi
UNITED NATIONS UNIVERSITY, TOKYO

ST. MARTIN'S PRESS
NEW YORK

JAPANESE POLITICS TODAY

Copyright © 1997 by P. Jain, T. Inoguchi and individual contributors

St. Martin's Press, Scholarly and Reference Division, 175
Fifth Avenue, New York, N.Y. 10010

First published in the United States of America in 1997

Printed in Hong Kong

ISBN 0-312-17394-6
ISBN 0-312-17398-9

Library of Congress Cataloging-in-Publication Data
Jain, Purnendra.
    Japanese politics today / Purnendra Jain, Takashi Inoguchi [i.e.
  Inoguchi].
        p.   cm.
Includes bibliographic references and index.
ISBN 0-312-17394-6 (cloth). – ISBN 0-312-17398-9 (paper)
1. Political planning – Japan. 2. Bureaucracy – Japan. 3. Japan –
Politics and government – 1989– I. Inoguchi, Takashi. II Title.
JQ1629.P64J35 1997
320.952–dc21   96–52488
                                                              CIP

Typeset in 10/11pt Plantin by
Typeset Gallery, Malaysia

Contents

Notes on contributors

Takashi Inoguchi, formerly Senior Vice Rector of the United Nations University in Tokyo, is Professor of Political Science at Tokyo University.

Masumi Ishikawa, formerly of the Asahi Shinbun, is currently a Professor at Niigata Kokusai Joho University of Niigata.

Tomoaki Iwai is a Professor in the College of Human Science at Tokiwa University in Mito.

Purnendra Jain is Professor and Head of the Centre for Asian Studies at the University of Adelaide.

Masaaki Kataoka is an Assistant Professor in the School of Public Policy at Keio University.

Junko Kato is an Associate Professor in Politics at the Komaba Campus of Tokyo University.

Akira Kubota is an Associate Professor of Politics at the University of Windsor in Canada.

Minoru Nakano is Professor of Comparative Politics in the Department of Government at Meiji Gakuin University in Tokyo.

Steven R. Reed is Professor of Public Policy at Chuo University in Tokyo

Toru Shinoda is an Associate Professor in the Department of Politics at Waseda University in Tokyo.

J.A.A. Stockwin is Professor and Director of the Nissan Institute of Japanese Studies at Oxford University.

Maureen Todhunter is a researcher in Brisbane.

Acknowledgements

This book has its origins in a workshop on Heisei politics held in Brisbane in July 1995 at the Eighth Biennial Conference of the Japanese Studies Association of Australia, hosted by the University of Queensland. Thanks are due to Alan Rix and Donna Weeks for facilitating the organisation of this workshop. Eight of the ten papers presented there are included in this collection. All eight paper-givers refined and updated their chapters in the light of feedback from the workshop and subsequent developments in Japanese politics. We invited Arthur Stockwin, Toru Shinoda, and Masaaki Kataoka to contribute specific chapters to the volume to broaden the picture that we present here of politics and policy in 1990s Japan. We thank all contributors for their papers and for co-operating readily to fit in with editorial requirements. We also thank Russell Trood, Director of the Centre for the Study of Australia-Asia Relations at Griffith University, and the Japanese Studies Association of Australia; both institutions provided funds to defray some of the expenses of producing this volume. We also owe a debt of appreciation to Maureen Todhunter for her valuable editorial contributions. Finally, we express our gratitude to Peter Debus of Macmillan Education Australia for his interest in our efforts, and for arranging the timely publication of this collection.

A note on conventions

In the Japanese language, family name is placed before given name, and we respect this custom in this book. The names of all authors, including the Japanese contributors, appear with given name followed by family name. The one exception is names of Japanese authors of publications in English, for which we have retained English-language conventions. This includes the names of Japanese contributors to this volume.

Purnendra Jain
Takashi Inoguchi
August 1996

1
Introduction

Takashi Inoguchi and Purnendra C. Jain

The primary features of contemporary Japanese politics until 1993 were relative stability and predictability in both political processes and policy outcomes. This was mainly due to thirty-eight years of uninterrupted one-party domination of the National Diet by the Liberal Democratic Party (LDP), and the firm grip on national administration by the elitist and seemingly all powerful national bureaucracy. Japan's policy-making apparatus, centred on this bureaucracy, facilitated policy effectiveness, while the LDP's well entrenched system of mobilising grassroots political support, especially in rural areas, contributed to a high degree of political stability. The invariably unwavering support for this regime by big business further entrenched centre Right political domination. These features made Japan a leading contender among 'uncommon democracies'. One party predominating under a democratic multi-party parliamentary system was a state of affairs that lasted nearly four decades.[1]

During the long years of LDP rule, from 1955 to 1993, politics and policy processes in Japan in some ways resembled a Kabuki drama. The central legislative body, the Diet, or parliament, played a minor role in drafting and debating policies of national and

2 Japanese Politics Today

international significance. The drama was played out according to a script drafted behind the scenes in Diet committees and party boardrooms.

It is not surprising, then, that Japanese political life rarely made headlines in the international media, except at times when a major political scandal broke, something which was rare until the late 1980s. Even though Prime Ministers changed far more often in Tokyo under the stable LDP regime than in many of the world's national capitals, Japan watchers generally assumed that no drastic political or policy changes were imminent.[2] An apt description of the Japanese political system in which Prime Ministers and Cabinets changed while policy directions remained largely unchanged, is 'karaoke democracy';[3] on a karaoke stage, the visible singers come and go, but the songs remain the same, selected from a limited, rarely changed menu.

While stability and predictability were the two key characteristics of Japanese politics until 1993, the potent circumstances that finally delivered a change in the national government in July that year had in fact been in train for at least two decades prior to that. Some signs of this have been highlighted in chapters in this volume. They include the formation of the New Liberal Club as an LDP splinter group in 1976; the rise of the Socialist leader, Doi Takako, in the late 1980s as a potential Prime Minister; the LDP's loss of its majority in the House of Councillors (upper house) election in 1989; and the seething discontent in the LDP reflected in the establishment of the Japan New Party (*Nihon Shintō*) by LDP renegades in 1992, and further splintering of the party just before the LDP's momentous fall from power. However, it was not until the July 1993 general election that the LDP lost its majority in the House of Representatives (the lower house of the National Diet) and thereby its ability to form a government in its own right. Over the following three years, coalitions became the norm in Japan. Alliances between politicians and parties produced unlikely marriages of convenience, to the point where an LDP/socialist coalition took government in 1994, a relationship that previously would have been unthinkable.

Contemporaneous with these political changes at the party and parliamentary levels, some of the inherent weaknesses of the 'infallible' and elitist national bureaucracy began to be exposed with growing frequency. In recent years the bureaucracy has suffered severe critical onslaught from within and without. In 1995, there were inadequate and belated ministerial responses to a series of national emergencies. These included the Hanshin earthquake, the poisonous gas attacks that led to eleven deaths in Tokyo's subways, and the accident at the Monju nuclear power station. All these intensified public concern over the efficacy of Japan's policy-making machine. The interests of LDP politicians and the bureaucrats, once solid partners in Japan's economic progress, are no longer so closely aligned. In 1996 the Japanese public became even more aggrieved when the media uncovered a number of cases highlighting political ineptitude. These include action, and inaction, by the Ministry of Health and Welfare around 1983–84 allowing unintended transmission of HIV-AIDS infected blood, and the Finance Ministry's failure to act decisively on the 'bad loans' provided by housing loan-related financial institutions during 1991–95. In these cases in particular, an increasingly angry Japanese public were exposed to some of the fundamental weaknesses and incompetence of a national bureaucracy which had once been regarded as virtually infallible. Until the closing years of the LDP regime, the bureaucracy had been seen as the one dependable pillar that would stand even when other leading institutions such as political parties and big business firms were in disarray. The public exposés have shattered a comfortable, reassuring dream.

Increasingly, Japanese politics exhibit signs of a syndrome which has been more or less common in many political systems. It is a syndrome of uncertainty in a transitory era, uncertainty that emanates largely from the consequences of three 'endings' unfolding at beginning of a new millennium: the end of the Cold War; the end of geography; and the end of history.[4] The end of the Cold War means the end of ideologically-driven global bipolar rivalry between the United States and the Soviet Union, something that fundamentally shaped international politics after World War II. The end of geography is symbolised by the increasing insignificance of geographical distance and national boundaries in economic, political and social transactions. The end of history is manifest in the disappearance of a grand ideology organising societies and guiding the minds of people in capitalist democracies. These 'three endings' have reverberated across the world in such a pervasive manner that Japan could not remain isolated from their powerful collective force.

With the so-called end of geography, national security has become more a part of a regional or international co-operative security system; national economies have become parts of the global economy; and national governance can best be conceived of as part of global governance. Autonomous management of national security and economic policies has become increasingly unsustainable. Japan has found that it cannot continue to be a passive beneficiary of security arrangements underpinned by the United States; it cannot continue to sustain its position as a global economic power while maintaining a *keiretsu*-organised domestic economy; and above all, Japan's political economy cannot sustain the politics of complex clientelism in a self-contained policy environment. In short, global economic, political and social forces have permeated Japan much more than is often realised by casual observers of Japanese politics and society. The continuity and predictability that had marked political life under the LDP regime has ended.

These circumstances mean we need to look more carefully at the major institutions and other actors in Japan's political system. We need to consider the motivations and policy options that drive these actors' political behaviour, in order to better understand the politics and the policies of one of the world's strongest economic powers at the dawn of the twenty-first century.

The most important considerations in our minds at the time we were organising this volume were political events leading up to the 1993 election and the policy responses that these produced. We hope that, through this book, readers will quickly develop a comprehensive grasp of these events, their antecedents, and the trends that mark Japanese politics and major policy areas as we move into the latter half of the 1990s.

The book begins with a chapter by Jain on the changing dynamics of party politics. He explains the transition underway in Japan's party politics, especially since mid-1993. He considers the various coalition governments following the defeat of the LDP in the 1993 election, pointing out that the formation of coalitions between socialists and conservatives is not an entirely new phenomenon. As Jain sees it, the end of the Cold War and the collapse of the East-West ideological divide has had a significant impact on party politics in Japan, and he explores this in some detail. From his assessment of past and present trends, Jain concludes that party politics in Japan will inevitably become more policy-based, rather than grounded primarily in pork barrelling, as was the case over most of the forty years from 1955.

In Chapter 3, Masumi Ishikawa examines the reasons for the rising level of voting abstention in Japan's national elections in the 1990s. He denies this is simply a sign of people's lack of interest in national politics, claiming instead that some of this is deliberate, actively expressing disdain for the nation's politicians. In Japan, voter turnout rates at the polls have generally been high, especially when compared to other industrial societies. Yet in the 1993 lower house election, one-third of eligible voters did not cast a vote. Voters had little reason to believe this election would bring an end to corruption in the parliamentary system, whatever contrary messages the mass media had conveyed. In the two years between the July 1993 lower house election and the July 1995 upper house election, voters were unconvinced by the flimsy new garb that parties had donned hoping to win their trust, or at least their vote. More than 55 per cent of the population of eligible voters stayed away from the polls in the 1995 upper house election. There are many questions that remain unanswered, but what is clear, according to Ishikawa, is that this rising abstention level signals an ever deeper political malaise. Politicians have responded by taking bold self-serving steps, forcing voters to recognise that their vote is not enough to flush out the corruption of Japan's electoral system.

In Chapter 4, Minoru Nakano explores the role of the National Diet in the legislative process. This was a domain of major political change after the LDP's fall from government. Nakano's analysis identifies how the legislative process and the power relations within decision-making structures have begun to change. He explores differences and continuities from July 1993 to July 1995, turning first to formal decision-making structures in the legislative system, and then to informal channels of influence. He explains the shift from LDP rule when initiatives came from bureaucrats and the LDP's Policy Affairs Research Council (PARC) to the Hosokawa and Hata coalition governments that pushed for a more open and contested legislative system through various institutional arrangements that move away from *misshitsu seiji* (politics behind closed doors). Nakano notes the minimal success of the coalitions' efforts, due to complex difficulties borne of resentment against Ozawa Ichiro's top-down dictatorial manner. Under the LDP-SDPJ (Social Democratic Party of Japan) coalition, much of the decision-making clout has returned to PARC, with a decline in the influence of *zoku* (policy tribes) and *jitsuryokusha* ('capable' people), due to multiple decision-making routes, stronger public criticism, and fewer individuals who could control parties and bureaucrats. Nakano explains this as a shift from *tatemae seiji* towards *honne seiji*, though the legislative process was still marked by continuing problems arising from trying to maintain unity among coalition members.

In Chapter 5, J.A.A. Stockwin considers the course of political reform during the two years after the fall from government of the LDP. He takes up three concerns: first, that 'reform' was in limbo, in suspended animation. Politicians were uncertain about where political advantage really lies. Conditions were unconducive to bold and comprehensive reform, and leadership pushing for real reform is slow to emerge. Any true political reform was impossible until after lower house elections then due in 1996–97. Second, once an election had been held under the new electoral system, the way is open for reform. According to Stockwin, lower house electoral reform is indispensable for any reform of Japan's political system. He argues that advantages for the Left are still possible (if the Left plays its cards intelligently), while more obvious advantages for the Right are likely. Some of his prognoses are that first, politics will be overwhelmingly the preserve of larger parties, second, the likelihood of intra-party splits is greater for *Shinshintō* than for the LDP; third, that the smaller parties' best chance for influence is under a fairly even 'balance' between the two big parties; and fourth, weakening of party factions will create a more flexible political environment.

Takashi Inoguchi's Chapter 6 then takes on the much-discussed changing status of bureaucracy in Japan. Through several recent well publicised cases — the failed housing loans companies; the bungling within the Ministry of Health and Welfare that is purported to have caused thousands of Japanese to contract HIV-AIDS through untreated blood transfusions; the serious accident at the Monju nuclear power station; and local government bureaucrats entertaining central government bureaucrats to facilitate favour — Inoguchi argues unequivocally that the once 'all-powerful' bureaucracy has lost some of its invincibility. Yet he also argues that the time-tested tenacity of the bureaucracy, which has its origins in the 200-odd samurai-manned bureaucracies of the seventeenth and mid-nineteenth centuries, will die hard, enabling the bureaucracy to remain as a key actor in Japanese politics in terms of defining the framework of policies and agendas for their implementation.

Steven Reed's Chapter 7 examines three specific 'political booms' and their significance for political life and the prospects for democracy in Japan. He argues that each of these booms — the NLC (New Liberal Club) boom of 1976, the Doi boom of 1989 and the Hosokawa boom of 1993 — was produced by the inter-action between an electorate frustrated with the corruption of the conservative regime and the creation of attractive new alternatives. Using data aggregated at both candidate and district levels, Reed's analysis of each of the three booms is guided by a set of key questions, and his conclusions are based firmly on the answers delivered by his data. First, was the apparent trend towards bigger booms real? Second, where did the booms come from? Were they primarily an urban phenomenon or did rural voters also respond to them. Was the geographical distribution of each of the booms similar or did they differ in significant ways? Put more simply, who was upset with the LDP and how upset were they?

In Chapter 8, Akira Kubota examines big business as a key interest group in Japan's political system, focusing on its changing relationship with the LDP. Big business and its peak organisation, *Keidanren*, applied significant pressure to politicians to unify conservative political forces in 1955 and supported (financially and in other ways) the LDP throughout the Cold War period. With growing criticism of rampant corruption within the LDP, Keidanren decided in 1993 to cease acting as an intermediary in collecting corporate donations across all sectors of Japan's big business. Despite weakening of the LDP-big business relationship, Kubota argues that the structure of Japanese society is such that the intimate ties between big business and conservative political forces are unlikely to end in the foreseeable future.

In Chapter 9, Junko Kato extends her earlier work on tax politics to take into account developments after the fall of the LDP government in 1993. She considers consumption tax as a useful indication of power relations between party politicians and bureaucrats. Kato asks why the seven-party coalitions had been so divisive and failed in their tax-reform attempts. She examines how the political milieu after the LDP ouster shaped tax decision-making, and subsequent significant changes in the power relationships between central influence brokers. Her argument is that the tax case reveals that the power of financial bureaucrats is declining, countering the conventional view that bureaucratic power has increased under the coalition governments. Clearly, political instability underlay change as all interested players struggled to maximise their own advantage by promoting fissures, as well as alliances. But propelling these changes was not just instability, nor bureaucratic policy savvy, as had been the case in earlier times. Under the coalition governments, Ministry of Finance bureaucrats could gain clout when leading incumbent politicians sought not only to support bureaucrats' proposals, but also needed to *defend* them inside the coalition. This is why under the tri-partite Murayama administration, which was able to present a more united front that the earlier two coalitions on the tax issue *vis-à-vis* the bureaucrats, the government's position could prevail.

The focus of Shinoda's Chapter 10 is *Rengō*, as a clear illustration of the consequences of the 1990s' political transition for the union movement. After providing a background on the development of labour unions in Japan in the post-war period, Shinoda explains Rengō's debut, the prolonged struggles to unify public and private unions under it, and its moves in the 1990s to establish new goals and approaches, alongside the advent of Local Rengō. He considers its apparent success in forcing reduced work hours, given an environment that was in any case sympathetic to this outcome. Even so, results were not long-lasting. The effect of a non-LDP coalition government was to recreate within Rengō the fissures between Left and Right wing support around the ex-Sōhyō and ex-Dōmei traditional political divides, as each arm struggled to identify where their political advantage might lie. Inertia in Rengō's presidency has compounded problems of disunity and local Rengō have weakened rapidly to become virtually institutionally redundant. Shinoda assesses that Rengō in recent years has made a significant contribution to improving social welfare in a difficult climate of economic recession. He concludes that institutionally, Rengō has moved full circle, from participative democratic strategies to political democratic strategies and back, in its quest to register a strong political voice.

Tomoaki Iwai's Chapter 11 examines the apparent decline in political influence of the agricultural sector. Iwai explains the political influence of both *Zenchū* and *Nōkyō* on the LDP, and the party's long-standing willingness to implement policies suiting the agricultural interests of those two representative bodies. With the LDP defeat in 1993, the agricultural lobby lost political clout, as reflected in the Hosokawa government's move to partially liberalise the nation's rice market. Iwai argues that the sweeping changes in government and in agricultural policy in 1993 dramatically transformed the nature of agricultural politics in Japan. The upheaval forced farmers to reconsider how best to protect their interests, given that former strategies for dealing with an LDP government were now clearly ineffective. Iwai carried out an extensive national survey of farmers' attitudes towards politics, finding that those who were once strong supporters of the LDP are considering alternatives. Some have even expressed interest in forming their own party to represent specific agricultural interests. Nōkyō is reluctant to form its own party, and is concerned about Nōkyō constituents who want to form a new party. Iwai concludes that it faces the difficult prospect of having to reorganise its influence in a way which satisfies both the existing parties and its own membership.

Chapter 12, on local politics, is by Masaaki Kataoka, who examines how the 1993 LDP downfall at the national level set in train structural transformation that has begun to revitalise policies at local level. He explores two parallel developments. The first concerns the changing patterns of competition and alliance between parties at the local level after local assembly members were plunged into a crisis of loyalty. There were pressures to do with holding onto prefectural LDP membership or following Diet patronage at the national level to a new party. These were coupled with changes in party loyalty after the redrawing of electoral boundaries disturbed long-standing political relationships of loyalty and trust between local and national political actors. Kataoka then turns his attention to the wave of populist politics at local level resulting from voters' distrust in existing parties, and their attempts to bring forth a more representative, competitive style of government. He focuses on the surprise outcome of the 1995 gubernatorial election in which voters elected former comedians in the two largest and most influential metropolitan local governments in Japan. Kataoka concludes that more active politicking, realignment, and the wave of populism currently shaping politics at the local level in Japan will continue, flowing from fluid and uncertain conditions at national level.

The volume closes with a chapter by Jain and Todhunter examining the outcomes of the October 1996 general election. This election was an indicator of the functioning of new electoral rules introduced in 1994 as a key part of political reform. It was also, inevitably, the verdict of the Japanese electorate on the coalition governments of the previous tumultuous three years. Yet the election appears not to have ended the political volatility of coalition rule. Jain and Todhunter examine the results of this election, returning the LDP to minority government, but leaving it unable to woo any party or group into an alliance that would secure its majority hold on power, as before July 1993. The authors look carefully at the election data, identifying change and continuity under the new electoral rules. They observe that the claimed goal of the electoral reforms to bring a fairer representation of the people's voice — to curtail corruption and place policy ahead of 'political pork' as key election features — did not really eventuate. The authors close the chapter with prognoses on future possibilities, speculating upon the 'tightrope' confronting the LDP; the prospects of moving towards a political system that will deliver an alteration in the balance between two main ruling parties; and the need for the nation's rulers to move ahead with serious political reforms, now that 'reform' is a powerful political issue with potential to make or break future governments.

The workshop on Japanese politics held at the University of Queensland in July 1995, from which this book has come, included presentations and discussions of key issues on Japan's political landscape in the wake of the July 1993 watershed. These papers have been polished and updated. Other papers have been included in the book to fill out and strengthen the picture. Chapters 1 to 12 were written and revised between 1995 and the early months of 1996. The final chapter was written in November 1996, just after the first general election to be held under new electoral rules.

We recognise that other issues and actors are worthy of treatment. Yet on balance we feel that the central aspects of political life examined in this collection provide readers with strong indications of what has shaped the contours of Japanese political institutions and what processes are in train in this transitory phase of its politics.

All essays in this volume illustrate how, in the mid-1990s, political life in Japan is in the grip of transitory alliances. Uncertainty and the search for alternatives prevail. For this reason, all authors have given their well-informed views about possible future scenarios, while none speak definitively of future prospects. All authors' arguments support our conclusion that political actors of every stripe, and all over the country, are identifying new courses of action and adjusting their own positions, as well as their relationships to each other.

As part of the transition in world affairs since the end of the Cold War in the early 1990s, we can observe mounting external pressures, and internal demands that Japan contributes more fully to the multilateral solution of regional and global problems. Readers will find repeated in all the chapters of this volume that Japanese politics will remain volatile, as the nation's active political players adjust to new power relations, new institutional frameworks and new issues of importance in domestic and international environments.

Notes

1.   See T.J. Pempel (ed.) (1990) *Uncommon Democracies: The One-Party Dominant Regimes*, Ithaca, Cornell University Press.
2.   During the thirty-eight years of LDP rule, Japan produced fifteen Prime Ministers, with an average of two-and-a-half years in office.
3.   See Inoguchi Takashi, *Nihon seiji no mikata* (Analysing Japanese Politics); *Shiten*. NHK Television Program Channel 3, 30 June 1994. Following this, reference to karaoke democracy was made in the *Economist*, 2 July 1994, pp. 23–24, and the *Far Eastern Economic Review*, 4 July 1994, p. 11; Inoguchi Takashi, *Karaoke seiji kara no datshitsu* (Away from karaoke politics). *This is Yomiuri*, February 1995, pp. 62–71.
4.   Inoguchi Takashi (1994) *Sekai hendō no mikata* (Perspectives on Global Change), Tokyo, Chikuma shobo; 'Dialects of World Order: A View from Pacific Asia', in Hans-Henrik Holm and George Sorensen (eds) (1994) *Whose World Order? Uneven Globalisation and the End of the Cold War*, Boulder, Westview Press.

2
Party politics at the crossroads

Purnendra C. Jain

Japan's party politics between 1955 and 1993 was marked by a broad-based conservative ruling party, the Liberal Democratic Party (LDP) and a narrow, ideologically-based, Leftist opposition party, the Japan Socialist Party, more recently known as the Social Democratic Party of Japan (SDPJ). Between these two sat a range of smaller political parties including the religion-based Komeitō, the Right-wing socialist Democratic Socialist Party (DSP) and a variety of breakaway groups. At the far Left of the spectrum, and a long way from being a real contender for government, was the Japan Communist Party (JCP).

The July 1993 lower house elections in Japan may well be regarded as the most significant of all Japanese elections since the establishment of the so-called 1955 system.[1] Although parties had split and realigned at various times under the thirty-eight years of LDP rule, the result of this election changed the old party constellation significantly. First, this election broke the seemingly never-ending rule of a single political party. The LDP lost its lower house majority for the first time in thirty-eight years and thus the ability to rule in its own right. Second, the electoral results provided opportunities for the first time since 1948 to the parties in 'perennial opposition'

11

(the JCP was the only exception) to form a coalition to seize the reins of government. Third, and as a consequence of the first and second, rather stable and predictable party politics turned highly volatile, as reflected in the establishment of three coalition governments in a space of just under twelve months (July 1993 to June 1994) and in the frequent change of Prime Ministers.

My main argument here is that although the volatility of party politics from 1993–95 is reminiscent of the volatility of the 1945–55 decade, the prevailing political instability is unlikely to continue for another decade. As at the end of 1995, with the imminent introduction of a new electoral system for the lower house, it seems certain that Japan is moving towards some kind of a competitive party system. This new system will allow alternative periods of power — a hallmark of liberal democratic polity — although it may take a form that diverges from a typical two-party system as, for example, in Britain and the United States. It is highly unlikely that a single party will rule Japan again for anywhere near as long as the LDP did until 1993, since some key elements in the structure which enabled this system appear to have disappeared. Furthermore, the post-1993 political alignments have demonstrated quite clearly that the once-strong ideological divide is no longer the organising principle for political parties or alliances. While in the mid-1990s a handful of powerful politicians dominates the course of political alliances, it appears that in the long run, substantive domestic and international policy issues rather than ideological cleavages, will become the defining characteristic of party politics in Japan.

I begin this chapter with an outline of party politics in the post-war period. This outline not only sets the context for understanding current political developments, but also serves to highlight the many similarities between post-1993 party politics and early post-war party politics, especially in the pre-1955 period. It reminds us that while post-1993 political developments and party realignments present elements of real change, some are not without precedent, and analysis of Japanese party politics must not overlook continuities with the past. I then turn to consider political changes from 1993 to 1995 and the principal reasons behind them, taking into account both domestic and international circumstances. The third section examines the state of party politics in the middle of the 1990s, especially new party alliances and their 'cherry blossom-like' life span. In this context the introduction of the new lower house electoral system will be discussed, for the advent of the new system is one major factor responsible for transitory party alliances. In the final section I will offer a tentative evaluation of party politics and consider future prospects as the transition now occurring fundamentally reshapes Japan's political system.

The 1945–55 period

The party system that took shape from the end of World War II until 1955 was complex and in constant flux. Complexity was a product of domestic and international circumstances. Between 1945 and 1952, Japan was under Occupation forces, principally from the United States, who had defeated Japan in the Pacific War. Policy changes introduced by the Occupation authorities inevitably impacted on the course of party politics. Universal franchise was introduced, considerably expanding the size of the population eligible to vote. The election system was changed from large districts to medium-sized ones and a number of politicians were purged and depurged. Under these conditions, new parties emerged, realigned, and in many cases were subsumed within their parent bodies. There were several conservative and socialist parties. Interest groups were re-forming and their relationships with political parties were in a process of redefinition. Economically, much of Japan was still suffering, since most of its pre-war industrial establishments had been dismantled.

Meanwhile, momentous developments at the international level were impinging on Japan's political landscape. Former colonies in Asia and Africa were winning their independence after centuries of colonial rule. Closer to home, China was overtaken by a Communist regime and Korea raged with the war that would divide the nation ideologically. Of great significance to Japan was the intensifying Cold War between the Soviet Union, Japan's closest neighbour geographically, and the United States, Japan's closest ally strategically. This was a period of international instability, as the power relations that would determine the international order for the following three decades took form. Japan's political parties, divided as they then were along ideological lines, inevitably responded to this international scenario.

Two characteristics of Japan's political landscape in the first post-war decade have special significance for understanding current party politics in Japan. First, in this period Japan experienced a number of short-lived coalition governments. Although ideologically opposed to each other, the conservatives and socialists joined forces to form these coalitions (see Table 2.1). Second, policy preferences of some elements of the conservative parties were often closer to those of

Table 2.1 Coalition governments, 1946–49

Date	Prime Minister	Parties
6/1946	Yoshida Shigeru	Liberal/Progressive
4/1947	Katayama Tetsu	JSP/Democratic Party/ People's Co-operative Party
3/1948	Ashida Hitoshi	Ditto
1/1949	Yoshida Shigeru (third cabinet)	Democratic Liberal Party/ Democratic Party

the socialists than to those of their own party colleagues. In other words, there was some degree of overlap in policy preferences between the conservative and socialist parties.

Coalition formation

Japan's first post-war election was held in April 1946. No party obtained a majority in the lower house. In view of this, the leader of the Liberal Party (*Jiyūtō*), Hatoyama Ichirō, began negotiating with the Japan Socialist Party for a possible coalition government.[2] These plans has to be abandoned, however, as Occupation authorities purged Hatoyama from his party leadership. Yoshida Shigeru took over the Liberal leadership and, in June 1946, formed a coalition government with another conservative party — the Progressive Party (*Shimpotō*). This government continued until the next election, held in April 1947 under revised electoral rules.[3] In this election again, none of the three large political parties — the Liberal Party, the Japan Socialist Party and the Democratic Party (*Minshutō* — the Progressive Party after a name change) — was able to obtain a majority of seats in the lower house. After intense negotiations, a new coalition government was formed consisting of the JSP, the Democratic Party and the small conservative People's Co-operative Party (*Kokumin Kyōdōtō*). Socialist Katayama Tetsu took the reins as Prime Minister.

A third coalition government was formed eleven months later, in March 1948, after Prime Minister Katayama stepped down as a result of his inability to hold together the competing interests of his own party and those of his coalition partners. The result was effectively just a change at the top. To replace the socialist leader, the leader of the Democratic Party, Ashida Hitoshi, formed a coalition government with the same political parties.

The Ashida cabinet, however, did not last long, not least because of the involvement of a Cabinet minister in a well-publicised scandal, and the breakaway of a renegade group of Democrats, who joined Yoshida's party, which had become the Democratic Liberal Party (*Minshu Jiyūtō*). The Second Yoshida Cabinet, formed upon the fall of the Ashida government in October 1948, held a very brief and tenuous grip, with only 150 seats in a 466-member lower house. This government collapsed even faster than its predecessors, and a fresh election was held in January 1949.

In this election, Yoshida's DLP registered a stunning victory. The party increased its pre-election strength to 269 seats in the lower house. Just as stunning in the extent of its loss was the JSP, which had its seats drop from 144 to 48; many of its high-ranking politicians were defeated. The other conservative party, the Democratic Party, also performed poorly.

Although Yoshida could easily have formed government on the basis of his party's own strength, he invited the Democratic Party to join his Cabinet. Opinion on this issue within the Democratic Party was divided. In the end, Yoshida offered several Cabinet positions to Democratic Party members, making the third Yoshida Cabinet another loose coalition, this time of two conservative parties. Thus, in three-and-a-half years in the early post-war period, three general elections were held and four coalition governments held office. By any standard, this can be regarded as an unstable political environment.

Policy convergence

The second characteristic of the early post-war scene which is resonant in the mid-1990s is the overlap and disjunction in policy orientation between and within political groups of the Left and the Right (see Figure 2.1). The locus here was national security. One important issue concerned the new constitution, which Prime Minister Yoshida and his followers in the conservative party defended strongly. The socialists, also great supporters of the constitution, were closer to Yoshida on this issue than were his ideological partners in the other conservative group who were Gaullist-revisionists in favour of revising the constitution.[4] And unlike the Gaullist group, both the JSP and the Yoshida group opposed national rearmament and defence build-up. Another issue, the Japan-United States Security

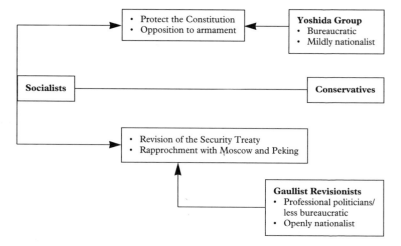

Figure 2.1   Party orientation
Source: Adapted from Kataoka Tetsuya, *Creating Single Party Democracy*, p. 7

Treaty, inspired a different set of cleavages. While Yoshida was in favour of the Security Treaty, both the JSP and the Gaullist revisionists favoured its revision. These two groups also favoured rapprochement with Moscow and Peking, which the Yoshida group disavowed.

The two characteristics considered above, that is, formation of coalition governments, and schism within the conservative camp, alongside the crossover of policy between the JSP and various elements of the conservatives, can be seen again post-1993. With the 1955 system in place, division within the conservatives had not altogether disappeared, even though the conservative parties had united under a single party. It is true to say, however, that party leaders tried to keep their disagreements within the party room and out of public view as far as possible.

The 1955–89 period

The pre-1955 phenomenon of frequent changes in both party alliances and government coalitions changed dramatically with the establishment in 1955 of two unified parties, the JSP and the LDP, the beginning of the so-called 1955 system. Between 1955 and 1989 the LDP dominated both houses of the national parliament almost exclusively. At times the party registered decline in its electoral fortunes, though it was never likely to lose its ruling position. In the 1976 and 1979 elections the LDP lost its lower house majority, but was quick to secure support from independent conservatives, enabling it to form government with relative ease. After the 1983 general election, in which the LDP lost its parliamentary majority, it was forced into a coalition government for a short period with another conservative party, the New Liberal Club (NLC), established in 1976 as a breakaway group of the LDP.[5] There were no policy divisions or policy influence by the NLC in this coalition. Thus formation of coalition governments was inconsequential when compared with the pre-1955 coalition manoeuvrings. After the party unifications in 1955, the battle lines between the conservative and socialist parties were clearly drawn.

Unlike the pre-1955 period, in this period conditions prevailed which sustained the LDP's parliamentary dominance. Here it is neither possible nor necessary to cover in detail the complex circumstances that enabled the LDP to rule Japan continuously for thirty-eight years.[6] However, as a backdrop to understand party machinations from 1993, some key elements should be pointed out.

First is the extent of support for the party. A number of highly influential interest groups strongly supported the LDP. Big business was one of the party's most outstanding supporters. This was not surprising since the business community had been instrumental in uniting various conservative elements into a single party. The powerful agricultural sector was another loyal supporter. Furthermore, since the nation's rapid economic growth and rising affluence were achieved under the LDP regime, the party attracted a sizeable majority of urban and semi-urban middle class voters. In this way, the LDP drew support from a wide range of interest groups and voters. Some observers have characterised the LDP as a 'department-store' type of party which has something attractive on offer to a wide range of customers. According to Okimoto, the LDP has been truly a 'grand coalition', especially in terms of the spectrum of interests it represented.[7] The party also managed to develop an unusually cosy working relationship with the bureaucracy, so cosy that a number of retiring bureaucrats staked out their political careers with the LDP.

The second element has been the capacity of the party to judiciously manage and largely avert internal disaffection. Although presenting as a unified conservative party, strong disagreements between party members on a range of policy issues continued in a way very similar to that of the early post-war period. As in the earlier period, the constitution, security and defence, and the nature of Japan's relationship with the People's Republic of China, were among key issues that inspired intense debate and division among the conservatives. Despite these internal divisions, however, LDP politicians publicly displayed a strong sense of unity, driven by their shared concern to keep a firm grip on the reins of government and therefore prevent the socialists from mounting a serious challenge. In order to satisfy influential faction leaders and their cohorts, the LDP followed a convention that allowed most elements within the party to share positions in government and in the party organisations as equitably as possible. This 'karaoke democracy'[8] has served as one means of keeping internal divisions within the party in check.

The third element has been the ineffectiveness of the opposition parties. The LDP organised itself in such an effective way and managed the economy so well that it maintained its long-term rule so that even the largest of the opposition parties, the JSP, was never able to mount a serious challenge. While the socialists criticised 'monopoly capitalism' and occasionally fought for better wages for workers, the JSP never provided an economic blueprint for the nation. As a 'progressive' party it also failed to articulate policy on such important issues as pollution, consumer prices, and liberalisation of the distribution system and agriculture. It did little to call for better social welfare programs nationally, or fight for better status for women and minority groups. As Pempel puts it,[9] 'Basically it was a party with one arrow in its policy quiver — preventing the return of fascism or authoritarianism'. On the top of these shortcomings the party was internally riven. This continued even after its Right wing broke away to establish the DSP five years after the party was united, in 1955.

Other opposition parties were similarly poorly organised. Thus the relative weakness of the opposition helped prolong the rule of the LDP.

A fourth and crucial factor was the then-prevailing influence of international, particularly Cold War, politics. The Cold War had produced an ideologically-driven hostility between the US-Western liberal capitalist camp and the Soviet-led socialist camp. The United States found in Japan an invaluable strategic ally; Japan found the United States a valuable protector. The two nations forged strong security and economic links, reflected in a bilateral security treaty and growing trade, commercial and other ties. The United States provided a nuclear umbrella for Japan and Japan, in turn, served as an important military base for the US Army, used for keeping in check actual and potential Soviet influence in East Asia. With a pro-US LDP and a pro-Soviet JSP, American interest in keeping the LDP in power was enormous. So strong was it that the CIA was reported to have pumped huge amounts into LDP coffers to sustain the party's hold on power.[10]

Party politics between 1989 and 1993

1989 was a landmark year on Japan's party landscape. It was marked by political overflow from major events originating both domestically and externally. Domestically, in early January the death of Emperor Hirohito ended the long Shōwa era, and the reign of the man in whose name Japan had pursued its Pacific War atrocities. Later, the LDP lost its upper house majority for the first time since the party was established in 1955. Japan's tenuous 'bubble economy' also began to show signs of strain around this time: there were recession, economic hardship and uncertainty. Internationally, the Berlin Wall was demolished, symbolising the beginning of the end of East-West ideological tension. With this came the weakening of Moscow's stronghold over the Soviet states. As in the early postwar period, a new international order was emerging.

The strong personal appeal of Doi Takako as leader of the Democratic Socialist Party, voters' disappointment at the sexual improprieties and obviously ineffectual stance of Prime Minister Uno, their anger at the government for introducing a consumption tax, and rural voters' rage over further liberalising imports of farm products, all promoted the rise of the SDPJ and the sudden decline of the LDP in the upper house election. One could, however, argue strongly that voters punished the LDP in the safe knowledge that its loss of majority in the upper house would be nowhere near as damaging to Japan's overall interests as it could have been had Cold War hostilities prevailed, or had they vented their grievances in a lower house election that would have ousted the LDP.

The results of the upper house election did not set a trend, and the LDP again performed strongly in the next national election following its 1989 upper house débâcle. Neither was the performance of the JSP in that election a trend-setter. In the 1990 lower house and the 1992 upper house elections, the socialists more than lost ground. The LDP was able to recover lost ground in these elections, though events since 1992 made the LDP's electoral position increasingly vulnerable, leading to the party's eventual defeat in the 1993 general elections.[11]

In 1988, the LDP suffered a tremendous setback after the Recruit scandal shocked the public so much that it eventually forced Prime Minister Takeshita to resign. Bandaid solutions, like the appointment of 'Mr Clean' (Kaifu Toshiki) as party President and Prime Minister, did put a temporary brake on the party's decline. There was, however, discontent within. In May 1992, a former LDP politician and Governor (1983–91) of Kumamoto Prefecture formed the conservative Japan New Party (*Nihon Shintō*). This move clearly signalled the dissatisfaction of some conservative politicians with the LDP's organisation and management of government. Within the LDP, the Takeshita faction, hitherto the most powerful, weakened under a series of challenges wrought by an ever-intensifying internal conflict of interests. By the time Kanemaru Shin, an influential member of the Takeshita faction and renowned as LDP 'kingmaker', resigned from the Diet in November 1992 (forced to admit he had received 500 million yen in illegal political contributions), the Takeshita faction was in tatters.

The Miyazawa government (1991–93) proved incapable of holding together the competing interests and factions within the party. Miyazawa's administration was unable to address the burning issue of political reform in any satisfactory manner. In June 1993 a vote of 'no confidence' was passed, in which a number of LDP parliamentarians crossed the floor in the Diet to vote with the opposition against the Miyazawa government. The Ozawa-Hata group, which had previously established the Reform Forum 21 within the LDP, established a new conservative party, the *Shinseitō* (Renewal Party), and a small group of first and second-term LDP parliamentarians, who had previously organised the Utopia Club, also bolted from the LDP to form a new independent party, the *Shintō Sakigake* (New Harbinger Party), led by Takemura Masayoshi.[12]

On the international front too, conditions that had kept the various elements of the LDP together in post-1955 were changing fast. China, although still Communist in its political structure, had for some years been moving rapidly towards a market-oriented economy. With the end of the Cold War, Japanese voters and interest groups felt freer to take risks with their votes and their political strategies, and experiment with change. The LDP's long-term internal divides and factional politics, which had until then been kept behind closed doors, began to be drawn into public forums. Partly this was because some elements of the conservative party were no longer worried about their former ideological opponent, the Social Democratic Party. With the dissolution of the Soviet Union and greater independence in its former satellite states, the LDP's perceived threat of a Soviet invasion weakened substantially, and with it the LDP's intense fear of a Left-wing political party winning government in Japan.

With a so-called 'end of ideology' in the post-Cold War years, the socialists have officially abandoned the party's rigid stance on Article IX of the Japanese constitution, the peace clause. After decades of staunch opposition, the party has recognised Japan's Self Defence Forces and the US-Japan Security Treaty, two of the key issues that had clearly distinguished the socialist party from the LDP. With this, the ideological distinction between the conservatives and socialists has blurred, and differences between the former opponents have become less to do with party platforms and ideology and more with the personal policy preferences of key leaders. Under these circumstances, in the post-Cold War era the former largest opposition party seemed to have lost its role to function as opposition to Japan's ruling party.

When we look at political events just before and in the aftermath of the July 1993 general election, several important characteristics of this period demand our attention. Some of them suggest a return to something like political conditions of the pre-1955 period. First, instead of a united conservative party, there now exists a number of conservative parties, with different views on a range of policy issues. The Social Democratic Party, formerly the largest opposition party, is also on the brink of splitting, rent with internal policy differences. Second, and facilitated by the relative absence of clear ideological and policy differences as well as the will to govern, in 1994 the SDPJ and the LDP formed a coalition to take government. This move constituted a political marriage unthinkable under the 1955 system, but one which is clearly similar to the parties' posturing during the early post-war years.

In these actions we see how the interaction of domestic and international political developments have induced the breakdown of the 1955 system, and the beginning of a new political era in the 1990s.

The new election system

While a potent mix of political events contributed to the breakdown of the 1955 system, one particular ingredient begs our attention at this point, before we consider future prospects. This is the new electoral system, adopted in 1994. This will have significant implications for party politics. A lower house election under the new system is not legally due until the middle of 1997, but most political analysts agree that this will be held before that (see Chapter 13).

Since the new electoral system combines two types of electoral districts — single-member districts (SMD) and electorates for proportional representation (PR) — we need to take into account both these types when considering the future shape of the party system. The SMD requires a winning candidate to obtain a clear majority, i.e. more than 50 per cent of the district's votes, except in cases where there are multiple candidates. Precedents overseas indicate that such districts generally produce a competitive party system in which two major political parties compete, and the rest remain on the periphery. The smaller parties are naturally displeased at this prospect. The introduction of this system is a major departure from the medium-sized district system which encouraged some parties to run multiple candidates, since it was possible for candidates to be elected with as little as between 15 and 25 per cent of the vote.

In the PR districts, the story is slightly different. The PR system encourages smaller parties to run their candidates since there is always the possibility they might win a few seats, as is the case with the upper house of the Diet. However, unlike the upper house PR system, the lower house system is based on the bloc system under which Japan is divided into eleven blocs.[13] Smaller parties stand a far better chance of winning seats in a nation-wide PR system than they do in a bloc PR system, though it is virtually certain that some smaller parties will secure some seats in the lower house via the bloc PR system.

It is possible, indeed probable, that the new electoral rules will allow only a limited number of political parties to run successfully in the SMD.[14] Yet this may not necessarily produce a two-party system. Unlike Britain, Japan does not have a class-based society, where voters identify themselves strongly with parties rather than candidates. Given that class is less of an issue to Japanese voters in a society where the overwhelming majority hazily identify themselves as 'middle class', it would appear that a sizeable number of these voters will readily change their party and candidate preferences from election to election on the basis of policy appeal. Such a process will produce a large pool of floating voters who are not ideologically bound to one of two specific parties. Another reason why a typical two-party system is unlikely to result is because of the PR system, which permits smaller parties to win a few seats.

Proliferation of new parties

Because changes to the electoral system remain to be tested, parties are naturally positioning themselves so as to win the maximum number of seats. The LDP remains a unified party, though its strength has diminished as some members — some of them extremely influential — have bolted to establish new parties themselves, or joined one of them. In addition to the Shinseitō and Shin-Sakigake, both formed in 1993, the following parties have also been established with the breakup of the 1955 system.

The Liberal Party (Jiyūtō) was formed in April 1994 by seven LDP Diet members, including the late Watanabe Michio. The Jiyūtō was led by Kakizawa Kōji, who became Foreign Minister in the two-month Hata administration. With its fall in June 1994, some Jiyūtō members returned to the LDP fold, while others joined Ozawa's Shinseitō. Also in April 1994, The New Vision Party (*Shintō Mirai*) was established by five more LDP renegades, led by Kanō Michihiko. It did not join the Hata Cabinet, but gave its support to the Hata coalition from the sidelines. *Kōshikai*, another conservative party, was formed after the collapse of the Hata government. Kōshikai was led by Noda Takeshi. Supported by the Hata-Ozawa group, it nominated its key member, Kaifu Toshiki, to run as a candidate for prime ministership against the LDP-SDPJ-Sakigake candidate, Murayama Tomiichi. These three parties and another party, *Kaikaku no Kai*, later organised themselves into a group called *Jiyū Kaikaku Rengō*, which is led by Kaifu Toshiki.

An umbrella party consisting of renegades from the LDP and some former opposition political parties that had also participated in the Hosokawa and Hata coalition governments was launched in December 1994. It is called the New Frontier Party (NFP or *Shinshintō*), and is led by Ozawa Ichirō. The party's launch brought together more than 200 Diet members at Minato Mirai in Yokohama, and there was much fanfare.

Most of the opposition parties have positioned themselves as a unified group under the NFP in preparation for elections under the new election system. The question of how long they will stay together as an umbrella party is nevertheless anyone's guess. Moreover, the NFP does not have upfront a star politician with broad appeal to ordinary people, like Kōno Yōhei, who led the New Liberal Club in the late 1970s, Doi Takako (SDPJ) and Hosokawa Morihiro (JNP).[15] The same old faces no longer hold public appeal. Moreover, Ozawa's style of politics is abrasive and the relationship he has forged with the Kōmeitō is resented by many within the umbrella party.[16]

The ruling LDP-SDPJ-Sakigake coalition is also saddled with contradictions. The SDPJ is in a very vulnerable position. It pulled out of the Ozawa-backed Hata government in April-May 1994, and very soon joined a new coalition government with the LDP. The idea of this LDP-SDPJ coalition government had been triggered by a scheme of Ozawa's. He planned to back Watanabe Michio. Ozawa aimed to create a coalition government of conservative and centrist parties, to connect coalition remnants with the Watanabe-led new party, and cut from the twenty or so SDPJ Left-wingers whose opinions on policy issues such as Japan's international contributions and tax reform differed from the SDPJ line. Meanwhile, while in coalition with the LDP, the socialist party has lost its identity to such an extent that it is unlikely it will continue in its present form. Its poor performance at the 1995 upper house election is one indication of this.[17] Because of the strong possibility of breakup, some elements within the party want to create a new democratic league (*Shin Minshū Rengō*). Since there is the possibility that eventually two major conservative political parties might emerge from party realignments, socialist leaders like Kubo and Yamahana have been in favour of creating what they call a 'third force', together with a section of the DSP, the JNP and the New Harbinger party.

The LDP is also undergoing transformation. Mention should be made of the current generational conflict between young LDP members and older ones. Young LDP members are in favour of strengthening their political base by forging ties with members of the SDPJ and Sakigake — the two parties that have formed coalitions with the LDP. Young LDP politicians like Katō Kōichi, Yamasaki Taku and Koizumi Junichirō have allowed members of the SDPJ and Sakigake to join their study groups. On the other hand, older LDP politicians such as former LDP Prime Minister Nakasone advocate an alliance of conservative forces between the LDP and Shinshintō.

It is likely that in the fluid political climate politicians will move from one party to another, as each major party tries to entice those candidates who have the strongest chance of winning in a single-member constituency. Such cases have been reported in Hokkaido and Tohoku and are surely in train in other parts of the country.[18] It is also likely that new parties and new alignments of parties will continue to reshape Japan's party line-up over the next few years.

Interest groups and political parties

Interest groups are no longer as tightly tied to a particular party as they were during the 1955–89 period. The Keidanren (Federation of Economic Organisations), Japan's largest and most influential economic association, announced in 1994 that it would no longer act as a conduit for the flow of funds from business sources to politicians. The changing relationship between political parties and the corporate sector is echoed in a comment made by a senior official of Keidanren, who claimed: 'We used to know when an election would be called because politicians would ask us for campaign funds about six months ahead of time. Now we haven't got a clue.'[19] Farmers, who have hitherto been staunch supporters of the LDP, are rethinking their strategy and at one stage expressed interest in forming their own party to protect their specific agricultural interests.[20] Some elements within the Shinshintō have strong support bases in rural communities which will influence, and be influenced by, any collective decision by the agricultural lobby.

It is also extremely difficult to assess the role of labour unions and the parties they will support. Such LDP executives as former Secretary General Mori Yoshirō and Policy Board Chairman Katō Kōichi have been strengthening their outreach to labour unions. The LDP has been holding frequent meetings with labour unions centring primarily on *Jichirō* (National Prefectural and Municipal Workers Union), a stronghold of Murayama, who headed the three-party coalition from mid-1994 to early 1996. Senior LDP officials have also held meetings with other unions such as *Jidōsha Sōren* (Confederation of Japan Automobile Workers Unions) and *Zentei* (Japan Postal Workers Union). The LDP has adopted a severe stance towards such anti-Murayama organisations as *Zendentsū* (Japan Telecommunications Workers Union), which appears to have forged links with Shinshintō.

Politicians (read the LDP) and bureaucrats in Japan have in the recent past generally been regarded as partners (although not equal) in progress, two major legs of what many called 'Japan Inc.'. However, their interests are nowadays sliding out of alignment. Bureaucrats naturally do not want to lose their power in the political process, but today's politicians are leaving less room for them in the decision making process and are now more prepared to chart policy options which bureaucrats are reluctant to endorse. It is well known that Finance Minister Takemura in the Murayama administration, for example, has had problems in dealing with some of the Ministry of Finance officials.[21]

Ideology vs policy

One of the aims of the new election system is to draw voters' attention to policy issues and away from candidate-based pork barrel politics. Ideology is now no longer the defining principle of Japan's political parties. Yet neither are these political parties organised on the basis of policy positions. For example, it is difficult neatly to place Japan's political parties along the lines of policy divisions as classified in Figure 2.2. Constitutionalists and revisionists are found in both the LDP as well as the 'new superparty', the Shinshintō. Members of the LDP and socialists are divided in their views on whether to support large government or to embrace the concept of small government. In the latter half of 1996 it is not clear as to who stands for what, since political parties are in the throes of establishing distinctive identities. It is clear from Ozawa's book[22] that he has grand aims for a 'big Japan'. The Kōmeitō, one of Ozawa's key allies, on the other hand, opposes removal of the freeze on participation in United Nations peacekeeping operations. Thus, amid political realignment, players are working out their strategies with an eye to the power struggle between the Ozawa Ichirō-Ichikawa Yūichi group and the anti-Ozawa-Ichikawa group. Foremost is each Diet member's calculations for their own political survival. Recently politicians have joined or abandoned particular parties on the basis of narrow personal interests, such as party or government postings. Some high-ranking politicians such as Kakizawa Kōji left the LDP just before the formation of the Hata Cabinet in May 1994, to serve on the front bench of the Coalition. Once the Hata Cabinet collapsed two months later, however, Kakizawa returned to the LDP.

Conclusion

The above discussion has shed light on how Japan's party politics is undergoing fundamental restructuring. The process which began around the late 1980s was boosted in 1993 with the breaking away of Ozawa, Hata and Takemura from the LDP and the LDP's fall from government. The new electoral rules passed in 1994 have

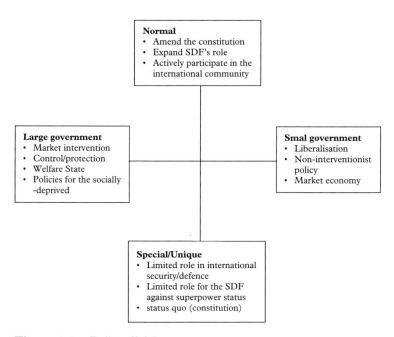

Figure 2.2   Policy divisions
Source: Adapted from Okino Yasuharu, (1995) *Gendai Nihon no seiji*, p. 124

proven another catalyst for large-scale political restructuring in Japan. With the end of the Cold War, Japan is more comfortable than in earlier years with political instability, at least for a short while. Given the way in which politicians and parties are positioning themselves,[23] it seems likely that in the short-to-medium-term, two major parties and a number of smaller ones will set the course of party politics in Japan. In the long term it is possible that a two-party system — both conservative like the Republicans and Democrats in the United States — may emerge, but as 40 per cent of the membership in the lower house will come from PR districts, smaller parties will still secure places in the lower house through this system. These smaller parties will have a crucial balancing role to play, especially at times when neither of the two major parties is able to gain a majority in the lower house. The Japan Communist Party appears likely to retain its present form, though with fewer seats in parliament under the new electoral system.

The current shape of party politics in Japan is extremely confusing to Japanese voters and indeed to some extent even to the nation's political luminaries. This is one reason why the turnout rate at the polls has become lower and lower.[24] The number of voters with no party preference is increasing. A *Mainichi Shinbun* public opinion survey taken in December 1994 showed that those not supporting any political party was 44 per cent, an increase of 3 per cent over the last survey. A *Yomiuri Shinbun* survey showed that more than 50 per cent of respondents said there was no party they wanted to support.[25] Voters' apathy results from their distrust of politicians. Although powerful politicians are dominating the course of party politics as we move into the second half of the 1990s, it appears that eventually domestic and international policy issues, more than anything else, will become the defining characteristic of party politics in Japan.

Notes

1. There seems to be a consensus among most scholars that the 1955 system owes its origin to the merger of the two wings of the socialists to form the Japan Socialist Party, and the formation of the Liberal Democratic Party from the union of the conservative Liberal and Democratic parties; see Masumi Junnosuke, '1955-nen no seiji taisei' (The political system of 1955), *Shiso* (Thoughts), June 1964. This standard interpretation of the 1955 system has, however, been challenged by a number of scholars: see Kataoka Tetsuya (ed.) (1992) *Creating Single-Party Democracy: Japan's Postwar Political System*, Hoover Institution Press, especially his Introduction.

2. This section draws heavily on Ishikawa Masumi, (1994) *Sengo seijishi* (A history of post-war politics), Tokyo: Iwanami Shinsho and J.A.A. Stockwin (1982) *Japan: Divided Politics in a Growth Economy*, London: Weidenfeld and Nicolson.

3. After experimenting in 1946 with a large-sized district system in which two to fourteen members were elected from each district, in the 1947 election Japan reverted to the medium-sized district system which had been in operation since 1928.

4. Kataoka, *Creating Single-Party Democracy*, p. 7.

5. Kōno Yōhei, president of the LDP from mid-1993 to mid-1995 and Foreign Minister in the Murayama government (June 1994 to January 1995), was one of the principal politicians to form the NLC in 1976. The NLC merged with the LDP in 1986.

6. There are many scholarly English language works on this subject. See, for example, Nathaniel Thayer (1969) *How the Conservatives Rule Japan*, Princeton University Press. For a more recent analysis, see Gerald Curtis (1988) *The Japanese Way of Politics*, Columbia University Press. In Japanese, see Satō Seizaburō and Matsuzaki Tetsuhisa (1986) *Jimintō seiken* (The Liberal Democratic Party in office), Chūō Kōronsha.

7. Daniel Okimoto (1988) 'The Liberal-Democratic Party's Grand Coalition', in Daniel Okimoto and Thomas Rohlen (eds) *Inside the Japanese System*, Stanford University Press.
8. Inoguchi Takashi, *Daily Yomiuri*, 5 July 1994.
9. T.J. Pempel, in his comment on this paper, 21 May 1996.
10. *Sydney Morning Herald*, 10 October 1994.
11. See Purnendra Jain (1993) 'Is the "Mountain" Back in its Place? Interpreting Japan's House of Councillors Election of 1992', *Pacific Review* 6 (1) and Purnendra Jain (1993) 'A New Political Era in Japan: The 1993 Election', *Asian Survey*, November.
12. As T.J. Pempel has suggested in his comment on this chapter, it would be relevant to examine the motivation behind establishing the various splinters from the LDP. Personalities and ambitions were important, but other differences such as policy and generational gaps could also be motivating factors. On policy matters, see Ozawa's (1993) *Nihon kaizō keikaku* (A plan to remodel Japan), Kōdansha, and Takemura's (1994) *Chiisakutomo kirarito hikaru kuni Nihon* (Japan — a small country but shining completely), Kobunsha.
13. For details on the new electoral system, see Purnendra Jain (1995) 'Electoral Reform in Japan: Its Process and Implications for Party Politics', *Journal of East Asian Affairs* (Seoul), Summer/Fall, pp. 402–27.
14. It is not surprising, then, that some politicians, especially from the Social Democratic Party, are in favour of revisiting the newly-introduced electoral system. See *Asahi Shinbun*, 16 February 1996.
15. See Steven Reed's chapter in this volume.
16. In the July 1995 House of Councillors election, *Shinshintō* fared much better than was expected by many analysts, which may have given the party a push as its leaders realise the benefits of standing together.
17. In a bid to improve its image, the SDPJ in early 1996 changed its Japanese name from *Shakaitō* to *Shamintō* (Social Democratic Party) and has made changes in the design of its official flag. See *Asahi Shinbun*, 16 February 1996.
18. *Yomiuri Shinbun*, 22 November 1994.
19. *Far Eastern Economic Review*, 24 August 1995. Also see Kubota's chapter in this volume.
20. See Iwai's chapter in this volume.
21. See, for instance, a series of articles on *sei to kan* in *Bungei Shunjū*, November 1994; in particular, see Kishi Nobuhito, *Ōkurashō vs Takemura zeisei 300-nichi sensō*, pp. 112–19.
22. Ozawa Ichirō, *Nihon kaizō keikaku*.
23. Some politicians have been exploring the idea of merging the Socialist Party with Sakigake. See Sachiko Sakamaki, 'A Question of Survival: Leftist Parties Flirt with Merger', *Far Eastern Economic Review*, 24 August 1995.
24. The turnout rate at the 1993 election was the lowest (67.26 per cent) in post-war history. See Okino Yasuharu (1995) *Gendai Nihon no seiji*, Tokyo: Ashishobō, p. 147. Also see Ishikawa's chapter in this volume.
25. *Mainichi Shinbun*, 7 December 1994; editorial of *Yomiuri Shinbun*, 7 February 1995.

3
New heights, louder message: abstentions in Japan's national elections, 1993–95

Masumi Ishikawa

Voting has never been compulsory in Japan, and there have always been those who are eligible to vote who have not exercised that right, for whatever reason. Yet when the number of eligible voters who do *not* vote has come to exceed the number who *do* vote in Japan's national elections, we have cause to look critically at the reasons for this rising level of abstention. Is it simply a sign of the people's lack of interest in national politics? Or is some of this default deliberate, explicitly to express disdain for the nation's politicians? Are there systemic explanations as well? Whatever else, such a decline in voter turnout surely casts doubt on the faith of the electorate in the representative capacity of both electoral candidates and the political parties to which they belong.

Japan's national elections in the 1990s have yielded ever-lower voter turnout rates. By the July 1995 upper house election, for the first time in Japan's post-war election history, abstentions out-numbered actual votes. This trend has surprised some political pundits who had expected that with prospects for a change in the ruling party stronger than at any time since 1945, voters might be inclined to return to the polls to use their voice. After all, 1990s' party politics in Japan has been marked by uncharacteristic change — in composition, structure and allegiances/coalitions.[1] The winds of change did not, however, entice more voters to the ballot boxes; indeed, there were proportionally less than ever before in Japan's post-war history. The trend signals clearly that irrespective of the changes in faces and parties at the nation's political helm, growing numbers of Japanese perceive their vote to be useless.

In this chapter I focus on abstentions in two national elections, the July 1993 lower house election and the July 1995 upper house election. Both set new heights in the rate of voter abstentions. A growing sense of alienation has prompted former voters to abandon the old parties and reject the new. Voters seem to doubt the effectiveness of elections in bringing the voice of the electorate to government. More of them than ever are choosing to 'vote' with abstinence while there are no political parties or politicians with whom they can identify. This trend inevitably has implications for political life in Japan, since the competition between parties to secure support and maximise votes continually intensifies.

The eligible voting population and relative voting shares

Japanese citizens do not need to register in order to vote. When they reach twenty years of age, they automatically begin to receive notices of local and national elections, a kind of ticket for the polls. The notice is issued by local government offices based upon residence records, and indicates date and designated polling place. All Japanese citizens residing in an electoral district for at least three months receive the election notice. The eligible voting population is therefore all Japanese citizens aged twenty or above, and all receive their polling ticket automatically when an election is due.[2]

Before looking at the rate of voter turnout within the eligible voting population, I shall clarify my analysis technique. Rather than looking at relative shares of votes I will look at absolute shares. A relative voting share is calculated as a proportion of the total of those who actually voted. An absolute voting share adds in the number of non-voters with the number of voters, so that we can calculate the number of votes cast as a proportion of the whole eligible voting population. Using absolute voting share data allows us to analyse changes in the share of votes for each party in relation to the share of abstentions, and to assess the significance of abstentions *vis-à-vis* overall votes cast. This enables us to see abstentions, in a sense, as another political party.

The 1993 lower house election

This election was held on July 18. It was a sunny Sunday when equivocating voters could easily be enticed into participating in social activities rather than heading to the polling stations. In the lead-up to this election, television programs had focused on the possibility of a non-LDP government to the extent that they were criticised for displaying bias.[3] The new parties (Japan New Party, and the LDP splinter parties, Shinseitō and Sakigake) were gaining popularity. These apparently ripe-for-change conditions inevitably enhanced expectations of an increased voter turnout. But the actual result on election day indicated that the electorate's feelings of alienation from the political system were perhaps as strong as the expectations aroused by the prospect of a change in power.

A graph comparing the 1993 election performance with earlier lower house election performances appears in Figure 3.1. The absolute share of votes for all the smaller parties decreased slightly. The real losers, however, and the parties whose performance accounts most for the increased abstentions, were obviously the largest two parties. Their sharp downturn is striking. The LDP scored by far its worst ever showing, with a 25.9 per cent absolute share. Even if we added on the shares for the LDP breakaway parties (Shinseitō's 7.1 per cent, and Sakigake's 1.86 per cent), the LDP's loss of support was substantial. The socialists, too, fared close to their worst ever, falling to a miserable 10.9 per cent absolute share. Shares for Komeitō, the DSP and the JCP changed little from the previous general election in 1990. The JNP drew a 5.3 per cent share in its first lower house poll.

In Figure 3.2 we see the breakup of absolute shares of votes in this election. The clear 'winner' was abstentions, the highest proportion ever then recorded in any Japanese general election. Accounting for precisely one-third, abstentions took up the largest share of eligible voters. We shall see that the nature of the electoral system helps to skew abstentions upward in a twelve-year cycle for upper house elections, but this explanation does not apply in this case. So why did one-third of those eligible to vote not exercise their voting right at all? Since it was the two largest parties that failed to draw their supporters to the polls, what had turned off their former supporters?

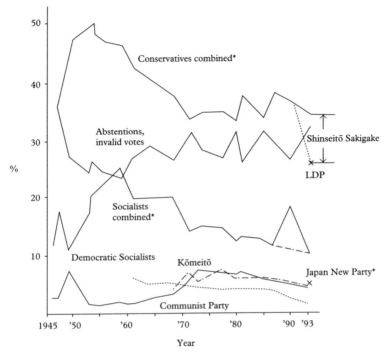

Note
* Conservatives combined
  Up to 1990 includes all conservatives and conservative independents. In 1993 includes LDP, Shinseitō, Sakigake and related independents and other conservative independents but excludes JNP

* Socialists combined
  Includes Left and Right wings, Rōnō group, Shaminren, and socialist independents

* JNP includes JNP-affiliated independents

Other parties also include their related independents

Figure 3.1   Absolute share of votes by party in Japan's general elections

Reasons for abstention, 1993

The 1993 election was made necessary only because renegade LDP members crossed the parliamentary floor in a vote of no confidence against the LDP government. Personal and party re-alignments had already begun fundamentally to transform the

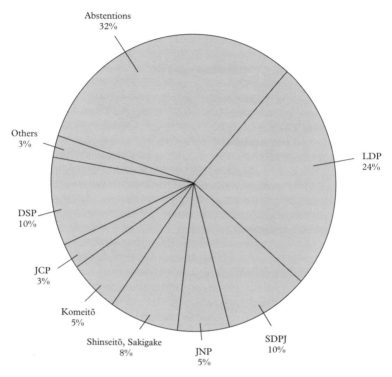

Figure 3.2   Absolute share of votes by party in Japan's 1993 general election

shape of Japan's party lineup, but the election forced by the successful no-confidence motion provided the catalyst for even faster politicking. Support for the LDP (the Miyazawa Kiichi Cabinet in particular) had reached new lows,[4] and the depth of the split with the breakaway parties was finally revealed. As personal ambition over-rode the façade of party unity, many traditional LDP supporters were clearly left in the lurch. Neither the other long-standing parties nor the new parties formed from the LDP breakaways presented attractive alternatives for their vote. Many traditional socialist supporters, too, felt abandoned, as the SDPJ floundered in political limbo. Shackled by its views of itself as an 'opposition' party, the SDPJ made only feeble attempts to offer what voters were looking for and establish a new identity for itself. As a consequence the party not only failed to catch disillusioned LDP supporters, it also failed to retain many of its own supporters.[5]

That the LDP still retained its grip on the largest number of seats held by any one party, even while losing its majority, suggests that voters had not truly expected a change of power — rather, a government with the LDP continuing to play a central, if somewhat less powerful, role. No one could have expected such a relatively unknown and unlikely local level player as Hosokawa Morihiro to vault from the political backblocks to become Prime Minister, even in the event of a non-LDP coalition government. There was little reason, then, for voters to believe this election would bring effective change to an obviously corrupt and entrenched parliamentary system, whatever contrary messages the mass media conveyed. Abstentions absorbed this slack of disillusioned voters.

The intervening two years, July 1993 to July 1995

Even with the change of government that this election brought, indeed, with *three* changes of government inside two years, the electorate remained disaffected. We might consider that this outcome is to some extent not *despite* these changes at the top, but *because* of them, for the string of coalition governments that subsequently came to power made it patently clear to the electorate that partisan politics would rule, with apparent disregard for voters. Voters had at first welcomed the prospect of the first non-LDP government in almost 40 years, commending the Hosokawa Cabinet with an approval rating of 71 per cent.[6] To many in the electorate, Hosokawa was a refreshingly different Prime Minister, almost an amateur in national politics and apparently aloof from the bribery and other political conniving among his peers. But even the Hosokawa Cabinet fell after eighteen months, when Hosokawa himself resigned because of allegations of corruption. The successor administration under LDP defector Hata Tsutomu lacked real commitment to the task of governing and made no mark in its evanescent two months in office.

The ensuing grab to govern, the bargaining, blocking and brokering between power-hungry politicians, delivered government to a coalition of apparent ideological opposites, the LDP, the socialists and Shin-Sakigake in June 1994. It was a blatantly opportunistic political bunfight between all parties, with obvious disregard for the will of the people who had voted these politicians into parliament to represent voters' interests. The new coalition under socialist Prime Minister Murayama Tomiichi left voters just as discouraged at the parties and politicians who represent them as had the two non-LDP coalitions.

From the outset, the disapproval rating of the Murayama Cabinet exceeded its approval rating.[7] The Socialist Party had not simply formed an 'illicit' union with its long-standing nemesis. The party had in fact made a mockery of the nation's electoral politics since after decades in opposition it had finally come to government only after it had fared close to its worst ever electorally, losing more seats than any other party in the previous 1993 election. Voter distrust in the Socialist Party was running particularly high. In July 1995 as the nation faced its next national election for the upper house, the electoral mood was flat. The new opposition Shinshintō (NFP or New Frontier Party) — an agglomeration of most opposition parties that united Shinseitō, Kōmeitō, the JNP, the DSP, and a number of LDP deserters, in December 1994 — was also attracting little support. Voters were unconvinced by the flimsy new garb that parties had donned hoping to win the voters' trust, or at least their vote.[8]

The 1995 upper house election

This election was held on 23 July, and was another abstention record-setter. This time there were more of the eligible voting population who did not vote than these who did vote. The results of this election did virtually nothing to change the overall balance of power between the ruling and opposition parties.

At this point let us review briefly the election system for the upper house so that the implications of voting behaviour will be clear. Every three years, one-half of the upper house's 252 seats (126 seats) are up for election for six-year terms. Voters cast two ballots, one for their preferred party under the nationwide proportional representational (PR) system and one for an individual candidate in either single-seat or multiple-seat local constituencies.[9] The proportion of votes that a party wins in the nationwide contest determines its allotment of the fifty seats filled under this system.

Results of this election, alongside the previous upper house election, appear in Table 3.1. The ruling three-party coalition, then led by Socialist Prime Minister Murayama gained a total of 68 seats, giving it five more than half of the 126 contested seats. However, as individual parties, both the LDP and the SDPJ suffered their

Table 3.1   Results of the 1992 and 1995 House of Councillors elections

	1992				1995		
	PR	Local	Total		PR	Local	Total
LDP	19	51	70		15	35	50 (seats)
	33.3	45.2			27.4	28.6	(shares)
Kōmeitō	8	6	14				
	14.3	7.8					
DSP	3	2	5	NFP	18	24	42
	5.0	4.2			30.7	27.7	
JNP	4	0	4				
	8.1						
SDPJ	10	14	24		9	14.3	17
	17.8	15.8			17.0		
JCP	4	2	6		5	10.4	8
	7.9	10.6			9.6		
Others	2	2	4		3	6	9
	13.6	16.4			15.3	19.0	
Total	50	77	127		50	76	126

Key
PR   Proportional Representations
Local   Local Districts
LDP   Liberal Democratic Party
DSP   Democratic Socialist Party
JNP   Japan New Party
SDPJ   Social Democratic Party of Japan
JCP   Japan Communist Party
NFP   New Frontier Party

worst-ever results, particularly the SDPJ, which could not lay blame on breakaways. The party's pre-election strength, itself the result of severe losses in the 1992 upper house election, dropped by a further seven seats (almost one-third) to only 17 seats. A devastated Murayama offered to resign, though the heads of the LDP and Sakigake persuaded him to stay in office, recognising that his departure from the Prime Minister's position would effectively pull the rug out from under the coalition's hold on office.

Both the major opposition parties, the NFP and the JCP, made substantive gains in the election. The NFP, with 18 seats, bettered the LDP, with 15 seats, in the nationwide (PR) constituency. In the overall count, however, the LDP, with 49 seats, bettered NFP, with 42 seats. What the seat numbers do not tell us is the number of voters who produced these results. The seat numbers conceal the significant political reality that of the 96,759,025 people who were eligible to vote in this election, only 44.5 per cent actually did. This may not have changed the political landscape in Nagatacho — the hub of Japan's political life located in central Tokyo. It was by no means expected to. But the all-time-high abstention rate that surprised even well-informed election-watchers induced shock and self-examination in all parties.

Reasons for abstention, 1995

Why did more than 55 per cent of the population of eligible voters stay away from the polls in the 1995 election? We are right to suspect that the record-low turnout was largely the product of dissatisfaction within the electorate. But there are other systemic factors that helped to produce this result and we shall turn to those here.

Leisure ahead of voting

A major factor was that 23 July was a Sunday, the day of the week when Japanese elections are normally held. In part this is because of the availability of voting facilities. The school gymnasiums that are commonly used as polling stations are usually unavailable on other days of the week. More importantly it is because of the availability of voters. Since most members of the paid workforce are not required to work on Sunday they do not need to seek special time off to vote. But this particular Sunday in 1995 was the first day that many families were free to go on outings together, since public elementary and junior high schools had just broken up for the summer vacation. For most parts of the country, the bright sunny day came after the long weeks of the rainy season. Many people headed off on outings, leaving too early and returning too late to make it to the polls.

The 'boar phenomenon'

A second factor was that 1995 was the Year of the Boar which, for reasons associated with the electoral system rather than the zodiac system, helped ensure a lower voter turnout than usual. As it happens, the forces at work within the Japanese electoral system that provide least incentive for voters to go to the polls (a function of unified local and national elections) operate on a twelve-year cycle[10], the low point begun in 1947, a year of the boar, producing the 'boar phenomenon' in subsequent national elections.

The graph in Figure 3.3 plots the rate of abstention *vis-à-vis* individual party performances for all upper house elections from 1947 to 1992. The rate exceeds 30 per cent for all occasions, though it jumps well above 40 per cent each twelve years (with the exception of the 1992 peak, which I explain below). What makes this twelve-year cycle is a coincidence of the three-year upper house elections with the four-year local government elections, so that the two elections are held in the same year. The cycle began in 1947, the year when Japan adopted its post-war constitution, and elections were held that year for all local and national assemblies.

Why should the turnout for upper house elections be so low when local assembly elections take place in the same year? The answer lies in election campaigning and political opportunism. The people who campaign for upper house candidates are mainly local assembly politicians or those who plan to run for the next local assembly election. These people ask voters to cast ballots for the national candidates who the campaigners themselves support. But they are not stumping only for these Diet candidates. They know that the campaign also serves as a good public relations exercise for their own cause as they seek election to the local assembly.[11]

In each Year of the Boar, local government elections are held in April, three months before the upper house election. The newly elected members of local assemblies are settling down to four-year terms just as upper house electioneering takes off, so are not enthusiastic about campaigning for these candidates when the next election for their own office is so far away, and their personal benefit is therefore minimal. Voters are apathetic, as well. A significant proportion of eligible voters hold the view that voting for the upper house is something you do when someone influential asks you to vote for a particular candidate.[12] In the Year of the Boar, many of these potential voters were not approached actively by local politicians since campaigning had been low key, and they saw no reason to go to the polls.

Figure 3.3 Abstention rates and party performances in upper house elections, 1947–95

The 1992 upper house election as trend setter

The 1992 upper house election was the exception to the Boar phenomenon, since it created a new abstention peak in a non-Boar year. Several factors came into play in that year that were to be repeated three years later. The 1992 upper house election was also held on the first Sunday of the summer vacation. And, as in 1995, it was not just the fine weather and the holiday that encouraged people to shun the polls. In the 1992 election, voter confidence in parliamentary politics was extremely low. In the previous upper house election in 1989, voters had come eagerly to the polls for two main reasons: to punish the conservatives in the wake of the Recruit stock-for-favours scandal that implicated many LDP leaders, and to support the efforts of the SDPJ to repeal the much-reviled consumption tax.[13]

For all voters' efforts in 1989, the consumption tax was not repealed, even though the electorate had given the opposition parties a majority in the upper house. Furthermore, the revelations of political corruption continued apace. In the 1992 upper house election, disillusioned voters did not give the SDPJ a second chance. Neither did they return their full support to the LDP which had eagerly anticipated restoring its pre-1989 strength in the upper house. A small share of voters pinned their hopes on Hosokawa Morihiro's two-months-old Japan New Party, giving it four seats in the House. But almost half of the eligible voters did not use their vote at all. For many of these, the abstention *was* their effective vote. The abstention trend was well underway.

Abstentions as a message to politicians

We cannot know what proportion of those who did not vote took this action deliberately to signal their disapproval or disgust. Nor can we know the specific intentions and grievances of these deliberate abstainers. We *can* know that it was an unambiguously negative comment on the nation's politicians and the electoral system that brings them to office; it was far from applause or encouragement. We also know that more and more of the electorate have sent this negative message throughout the 1990s. We know that this rising abstention level signals an ever-deeper political malaise, and that this has increased as politicians have taken bold self-serving steps that serve effectively to insult the electorate. Voters recognise that their vote cannot register their voice.

Growing numbers of Japanese voters feel at a loss. Many still want Diet members who are elected from their local constituencies to play the role of promoting local interests by negotiating for subsidies from the central government. The 1990s have proven that Diet members cannot be expected to do much more than that. It seems clear that they can do nothing to really change national politics so that it fairly represents the people. Institutional arrangements continue to stifle even the most committed political reformers and to reward with electoral success those candidates who are tarnished publicly with corruption and misdemeanour.

The malaise and the abstentions have not been confined to the national level of government. The trend towards growing abstention has occurred in sub-national elections as well. The term of office for all governors and mayors of local governments and members of local assemblies is four years. The polling rate of 60.5 per cent in the unified local elections in 1991 was the lowest ever recorded. In addition, unified local elections for prefectural assemblies in April 1995 drew to the polls 56.2 per cent of the eligible population, to again set a new record low. Furthermore, those who came to the polls in April 1995 shunned the candidates supported by traditional parties. Non-party-affiliated entertainers-turned-politicians, Aoshima Yukio and Yokoyama Nokku, were elected as governors of Tokyo and Osaka respectively, in an obvious expression of the public's disillusion with the established parties. As in national elections it is not that would-be voters have taken their voting responsibilities lightly. On the contrary, it is because they *are* deeply concerned at the state of political play, because there has been no party candidate who they believe to be worthy of their vote, that they have chosen to abstain.

Conclusion

In the 1990s, growing numbers of Japanese voters have turned to new means to express their disillusion with the nation's institutional politics. In their droves, they have deliberately shunned the polls. Record-setting abstention levels in the 1992 and 1995 national elections did not just reflect the electorate's discontent with specific administrations or particular parties. Abstainers intended to signal their frustration, to send a message to their parliamentary representatives to polish their act.

Voters have become ever more conscious of the politicking between party players and the corruption that has driven party politics. Media coverage has brought this to their attention. Continuing scandals have fed into voters' feelings of alienation from the political system and their distrust of their elected representatives. Voters have watched with anger in the 1990s as successive governments have fallen while they pushed, or claimed to push, for political reform. In the never-ending tussle for power between individual politicians, parties and coalitions, the constituency appears to have been sidelined. The response of many in the constituency has been to withdraw their vote.

Their actions have consequences for the democratic process. The freedom not to vote has allowed the creation of an amorphous bloc of would-be voters who have no-one and no party to which they can confidently give their vote. Deliberate abstentions have begun to function almost as a surrogate political party or at least as an attractive voting option. Abstentions in the 1992 and 1995 national elections have thus sent a louder message through the corridors of power in Nagatacho. The challenge ahead for the nation's politicians is to respond to this silent but powerful voice, to bring abstainers back to the ballot boxes, and to show through their behaviour as true representatives of the people that they deserve the votes that the Japanese electorate has been enfranchised to cast.

Notes

1. See P. Jain's Chapter 2 in this collection.
2. In spite of this of course, eligible voters are not legally obliged to vote.
3. In October 1993 it was revealed, just after the lower house election, that the press section manager of a television station had ordered his subordinates during the election campaign to, 'report with the intention of the realization of the birth of a non-LDP government'. The matter understandably became politicised.
4. According to an *Asahi Shinbun* survey in December 1992, support for the Miyazawa Cabinet was 20 per cent, and disapproval ran at 63 per cent. In September 1993, support for the LDP was 32 per cent.
5. According to an *Asahi Shinbun* survey, while support for the SDPJ was still 17 per cent in April 1993 before the election, support for the party fell to just 12 per cent in September, post-election.
6. Based on the *Asahi Shinbun* survey of public support for this Cabinet.
7. In July 1994, just after the Murayama Cabinet came to office, support for the Cabinet was 35 per cent, with a 43 per cent disapproval rating, according to an *Asahi Shinbun* survey.
8. In an *Asahi Shinbun* pre-upper house election survey in July 1995, 56.7 per cent of respondents answered that they did not have a favourite political party.
9. There are 47 constituencies equivalent to 47 prefectures — the largest administrative divisions of Japan. Among them, 24 are single-seat, 18 are 2-seat, 4 are 3-seat and one is a 4-seat constituency.
10. The twelve animals, in their order, are as follows: rat, ox, tiger, rabbit, dragon, snake, horse, sheep, monkey, rooster, dog and boar.

11. Although Japanese law prohibits door-to-door visits as part of election campaigns, members of local assemblies and their campaigners do in fact carry out campaigns including methods that are similar to door-to-door visits.
12. It is generally believed that such votes can result in profits for the locality, such as subsidies from the central government.
13. On the issue of financial corruption in relation to the 1989 and 1992 House of Councillor's elections, see, for example, Purnendra Jain, 'Is the "Mountain" Back in its Place? — Interpreting Japan's House of Councillor's Election of 1992', *The Pacific Review* 6 (1), 1993, pp. 77–84.

4
The changing legislative process in the transitional period

Minoru Nakano

The Liberal Democratic Party's fall from grace and government in July 1993 was a sign of mood for change in Japan's political system. The shift in government to a seven-party coalition heralded a wave of changes to the system's institutional workings. One domain where such changes have had significant consequences is the legislative process, where power relations, as well as decision-making structures, have begun their transformation.

In this chapter I explore two years of change in the Japanese legislative system, change triggered by the political upheaval of the Japanese summer of 1993. I begin with an overview of these upheavals, since they set the pace for this period of transition and the three coalition governments that followed. I then consider consequential changes, first in the formal decision-making structures of the legislative system, and then in the informal power relations that have shaped, and been shaped by this system. To illustrate these findings I present two case studies of legislation that failed in its passage through the parliament. I conclude this analysis with my perspective on the prospects for an equitable and efficient legislative system as Japanese party politics continues its transition into the twenty-first century.[1]

Overview of changes in government, July 1993 – July 1995

The birth of the Hosokawa Cabinet in August 1993 ousted the Liberal Democratic Party from a 38-year hold on the reins of Japan's national government. Such a dramatic shift in power, coupled with the showy performance of the new, relatively young Prime Minister Hosokawa Morihiro, inspired almost romantic expectations of the fresh political life that would follow. One indication of this sentiment was the 80 per cent support rate that the new cabinet attracted in those early heady days after its formation.

The birth of the Hosokawa Cabinet had only been made possible by a fracturing of the LDP's factional line-up. This saw the formation of the breakaway group, *Keiseikai*, and with it, a departure from the LDP of enough of its elected representatives to deny the party a majority in the election that the breakaway members would soon help to force. The breakaway of Keiseikai weakened the organisational energy that the party's pluralistic factional politics had generated over almost four decades.[2] Keiseikai members were then instrumental in bringing together the seven dissimilar parties that *en bloc* could push the LDP from government. Hosokawa surfaced as leader of the coalition because the party that he had formed the year before, *Nihon Shintō* (Japan New Party or JNP), was able to secure the casting vote to forge the coalition.

From the outset, Hosokawa was expected to operate as a 'one point getter'. Thus it surprised virtually no-one that his administration had little success with passage of legislation through the Diet. Two exceptions were the celebrated Bills for electoral redistribution and for regulating political donations, the legislative feat that became Hosokawa's last bow. It may be unsurprising that Hosokawa proved to be a lame duck Prime Minister so soon into his term of office since he possessed scant leadership skills and little political savvy. Further, with his Cabinet sustained by a flimsy coalition of seven parties and one Diet faction, its unwieldy nature seemed destined to split the coalition. With Hosokawa's retreat from the post nine months after securing it, the end came sooner rather than later.

A new government, headed by Hata Tsutomu, continued with the same coalition of parties, though a few further months of office proved the arrangement completely unworkable, and tore that coalition into its constituent parties. The new coalition that took office united the most unlikely political bedfellows, and excluded the real political force behind the previous coalition, the redoubtable Ozawa Ichirō. Ozawa, the former LDP strategist who had led the breakaway Keiseikai and induced the LDP's downfall, had become the nemesis not just of the LDP but also of the Socialist Party (Shakaitō or SDPJ), which had pulled out of the earlier coalition largely because of his overbearing style. The LDP, the SDPJ and the new small party, *Shintō Sakigake* (New Harbingers) had reason to unite as an anti-Ozawa bulwark despite their obvious differences in political philosophy. The three formed an unlikely coalition government under socialist Prime Minister Murayama Tomiichi in June 1994.

The Murayama administration survived its first rocky year of office, appearing set to hold the reins of power until a national election due to be held by June 1997. But Murayama's leadership had clearly been precarious and he was unable successfully to manage even his own party. The Murayama administration was a rare and obviously temporary coalition whose days in government were numbered.[3] While the tenuous three-party coalition continued to govern the country, personal and party realignments proceeded apace, both within the coalition's borders and beyond. They included the formation of Shinshintō (New Frontier Party or NFP) as the umbrella party for most of the opposition parties.

We can recognise some noteworthy changes in the style of policy-making and general decision-making by politicians throughout the period July 1993 to July 1995. These have inevitably influenced legislative procedure. If we consider these in terms of the governability of political and administrative elites, Japan's legislative process has generally fallen into what we might describe as a plural stagnation, rather like the confusion of the unstable Weimar Republic of the 1920s.

In this fluid political situation there has been no decisive political leadership. Decision-making on critical issues has been virtually postponed by all three coalition governments. The issue of the style of policy-making necessary to generate a fresh and stable legislative process is surely an important one for those who are interested in Japan's political landscape. We will need, however, to observe several national elections under the electoral rules passed into law in November 1994 before some indicative patterns emerge.

Changes in the formal structure of the legislative system

To identify and explain change we must first establish what was already in operation in 1993 when the first coalition took government.

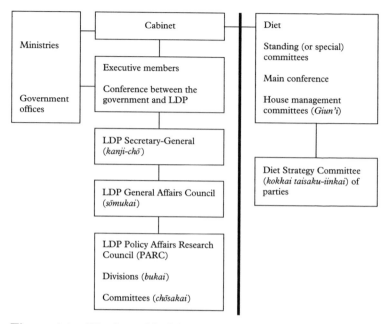

Figure 4.1 The formal legislative system under LDP governments

During the years of the LDP regime, key policy initiatives generally came from two sources — bureaucrats and PARC, the LDP's Policy Affairs Research Council. PARC itself has consisted of several divisions, research commitees, sub-committees and groups of *zoku* or 'tribe' Diet members who were concerned with specific 'hot' policy issues. The main formal organisation in the legislative process was the standing committee, though for controversial legislation and budget decisions the Diet strategy commitee exerted strongest influence. Figure 4.1 provides a detailed representation of this structure.

The legislative process is almost always more complicated and difficult for a coalition government than it is for a one-party government. This is because a coalition government requires negotiation among its member parties, as well as with opposition parties. Partly for this reason, coalition governments since 1993 have tried to reform the formal policy-making structure to help overcome the problems that inhere in intra- as well as extra-government negotiations. Figures 4.2 and 4.3 indicate the configuration of the formal legislative structures under the Hosokawa and Hata and Murayama administrations respectively.

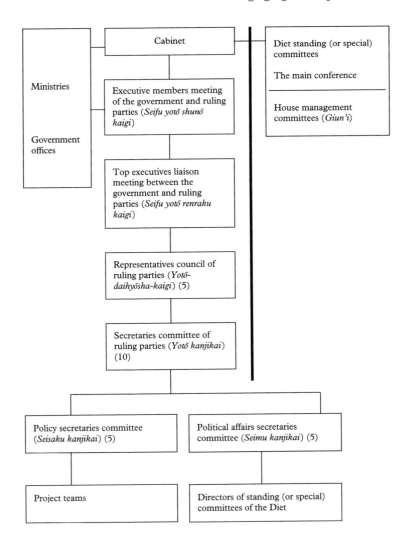

( ) = number of members

Figure 4.2 The formal legislative system under the Hosokawa and the Hata governments

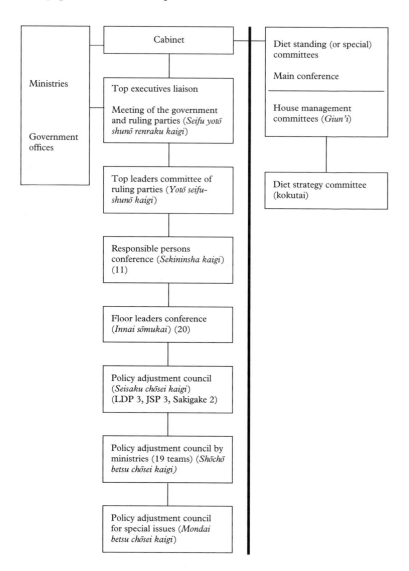

Figure 4.3 The formal legislative system under the Hosokawa and the Hata governments

Source: Murukawa Ichirō and Isogami Yasukuni (1994) *Nihon no seitō*, Tokyo, Maruzen

It is not simply to mollify the negotiation process that these procedural changes have been introduced. The procedural changes are also the product of efforts to fashion a more open legislative system rather than continuing the *misshitsu seiji* or 'politics behind closed doors' which had been the way of the LDP governments. Despite their efforts, however, coalition leaders have been unable successfully to implement organisational reforms. Let us consider the main measures that coalition leaders have taken in their attempts to achieve greater transparency in the legislative process.

The Hosokawa regime established the Chief Executives Meeting of the Government and Ruling parties (*Seifu yotō shunō kaigi*) to discuss the management of government. This committee was always, however, a 'half' organisation, neither a formal government body, nor a formal body of the ruling parties.[4] The Council of Representatives of the Ruling Parties (*Yotō daihyosha kaigi*), comprised of five secretary-chiefs, was the final decision-making group, with a *de facto* responsibility for Diet strategy politics.

The Murayama administration re-formed the Council of representatives into the Council of responsible persons (*Yotō sekininsha kaigi*). This administration also established a new and independent body, the Floor leaders conference (*Innai sōmukai*), in a further attempt to foster openness and democratic rule in parliament. The eleven-member Council of responsible persons includes representatives of both the Floor leaders conference and the House of Councillors (*Sangiin*).[5]

Policy-making and decision-making among the coalition parties has usually been committed to the Policy secretaries council (*Seisaku kanjikai*), which has had several project teams. This council has been the equivalent of the LDP's Policy affairs research council. In order to escape Diet strategy politics (*kokutai seiji*), coalition leaders tried to move the primary arena for negotiation with opposition parties to the house management committees. Consequently, 'in principle' politics (*tatemae seiji*), involving confrontation with opposition parties, continued during the Hosokawa and Hata administrations.

Generally, the coalition parties in these administrations aimed at regularising policy-making and decision-making procedures so that no one body in particular would stand out.[6] Nonetheless, while the Hosokawa government in particular was concerned to set up a new system, in practice this did not operate as expected. Informally, much of the old-style politicking continued.

The eagerness of the Hosokawa administration to reform the decision-making process was obvious. Yet so too was the gap that quickly formed between the appearance of new organisational structures and the reality of personal influence beyond these seemingly formal structures. As one example, the coterie led by Ozawa Ichirō and Ichikawa Yūichi (of *Kōmeitō*), the so-called *Ichi-Ichi* line, easily managed to operate beyond the formal organisational framework for decision-making. Ozawa's persuasive (though to many abrasive) personal manner and his distinctive style had obviously been successful under the 'double power structure' (Prime Minister and influential others) of the LDP regime, and could not easily be diluted by the new structures.

In the case of deliberations over reform of the Japanese Self Defence Forces (SDF), under the formal decision-making structure, responsibility should have remained with the Policy secretaries committee. In reality it was the Representatives council of ruling parties that dealt ultimately with this issue. Similarly, in the process of choosing a Prime Minister to succeed the outgoing Hosokawa, conflict arose between the Government and ruling parties' executive members meeting and the Council of Representatives of the ruling parties before settling on Ozawa's frontman, Hata.[7] Under all three coalition governments there are cases like this that highlight how far, and how often, political reality has been removed from the officially set-down decision-making procedures.

After a year in office, co-operation between the LDP and the SDPJ as coalition partners resulted in the passage of some legislation. There was, for example, revision to the act supporting victims of atomic bombs, and the passage of further legislation to settle claims of the victims of Minamata disease, who had earlier been denied compensation. Both cases involved clear concessions by the LDP to the SDPJ. Nonetheless, when it came to who called the most important shots within the top echelons of government, it was not Murayama. He continued to appear as a puppet Prime Minister of the LDP, just as Hosokawa was a puppet Prime Minister of Ozawa's powerful Shinseitō.

The factors we have just considered reach far into the legislative structure. They clearly indicate that in order to understand the actual conditions of the legislative process during the two years of coalition governments, we need to look beyond the formal, officially set-down procedures. To grasp the changes (and the continuities) after the downfall of the LDP in 1993, we also need to consider the informal structures and the personal power relations that underscored them.

Changes in the informal structures of the legislative system

Under LDP dominance to June 1993, the formal and informal legislative structures, and the power relations between key players, had been shaped by the powerful forces of the '1955 regime'. In 1955 the Liberal Party had united with the Democratic Party to form a firm political flank, and during the latter half of the 1950s and through the 1960s this regime exercised hegemonic control over the Diet. Yet for all its muscle, LDP dominance produced relative stability within the legislative system and relative consistency in the relationships between its main actors — Diet members, parties, bureaucrats, interest groups and so forth. I have classified the patterns of this system in earlier studies.[8]

How has the legislative process changed since coalition governments came to power in July 1993? I have developed a new typology that is useful for understanding the formal and informal structures that have held sway since then. In this new typology I have classified patterns in power relations as influence systems, in the light of what actually happens in the legislative process. This typology identified the politics of three inextricably linked domains: the executive, Nagatachō, and the Diet.

Executive politics of the government and ruling parties (*Seifu yotō kanbu seiji*)[9]

Although the LDP left government in July 1993, we could still observe its effects on the moves of the new governments' top leaders, as well as upon their critical decisions. Largely this was due to former-LDP strongman Ozawa and his *Shinseitō* party which served as the main vehicle for carrying LDP influence into the Hosokawa and Hata coalitions. Nonetheless, since the fall of the last LDP government under Miyazawa Kiichi, the top leadership and final decision-makers in the coalition governments have been sustained by two things. One has been the Prime Minister in charge of Cabinet, and the other the influential policy-making organisation, party, or dominant individuals within the coalition, depending upon the issue. A comparison of the three different systems under the Miyazawa, Hosokawa and Murayama governments appears in Table 4.1.

Table 4.1　Executive politics of the government and the ruling party (*Seifu-yotō kanbu-seiji*)

Sub-system	Last years of the LDP government	Hosokawa coalition government	Murayama coalition government
(1) Cabinet politics (*Kantei seiji*)	• Double power structure since the Miyazawa Cabinet (Prime Minister and dominant key persons: *Jitsuryokusha Keiseikai*) • Prime Minister became a puppet of *Keisekai*	• Double power structure (Prime Minister and dominant key persons: Ozawa-Ichikawa) • Prime Minister proved a puppet of Ozawa, although Hosokawa tried to reinforce the Cabinet's function	• Double power structure (Prime Minister and executives of LDP) • Prime Minister seemed a pseudo-puppet of LDP (the opposition *Shinshintō* had the Shadow Cabinet)
Examples of legislation	• Political reform bills collapsed — *Keiseikai* splits the LDP	• Political reform acts only. • National welfare tax legislation collapsed	• Bill acknowledging 50 years since the end of World War II • Education policy (Murayama succeeded in obtaining LDP's concession)

(2) Executive politics of the ruling party and Finance Ministry (*Yotō Ōkura kanbu-seiji*)	• Executive of PARC and Finance Ministry-co-operative	• *Shinseitō* Secretary General Ozawa and Deputy Finance Minister Saitō • Executive members of *Shinseitō*	• LDP wins back some control over Finance Ministry
Examples of legislation	• Fundamental Budget formula decision • Political negotiations at budget time • Medium/ small-scale tax reform	• Stratagem of National welfare tax legislation	• Deputy Finance Minister reshuffled
(3) Bureaucrats as leaders of politics (*Kanryō shudō seiji*)	• LDP's control of bureaucrats effective • Bureaucrats-led areas decreasing	• Revival of bureaucrats' dominance in policy-making (PARC, *zoku* influence declining rapidly)	• LDP's control of bureaucrats surviving, but declining
Examples of legislation	• Labour politics, pension politics	• Budget/ diplomacy/ tax reform/ trade and industry	• Settlement of special governmental corporations: bureaucrats' resistance was successful

In some ways this bipolar power structure has served the Diet well. It has meant that the Prime Minister, as merely head of a majority among Diet factions (*kaiha*) or coalition parties, has not held the reins of power alone. This has avoided the risks of over-concentration of power within the parliamentary system, which would occur if the Prime Minister were the exclusive final arbiter. This bipolar structure should be reworked to help maintain a more open system with the administrative capacity for coping with critical situations.

Another beneficial feature of the new legislative structures has been their ability to maintain a reasonable distance between the dominating influences of both the LDP and the Finance Ministry (*Ōkurashō*) on the one hand, and the legislative process on the other. Broadly speaking, the relationship between political parties and bureaucrats has shifted away from a system of mutual consultation and watch-keeping towards greater independence between players. As Prime Minister, Hosokawa sought to remove prerogative over decisions on the Budget from the Finance Ministry to the Cabinet.

Ozawa meanwhile tried to consolidate his influence within the new legislative structures by making best use of his connections with bureaucrats, including those from the Finance Ministry. This was an interesting move in the light of a rising swell of public opinion in support of down-scaling the mighty Finance Ministry,[10] making attempts to fall back on connections with it rather a risky political strategy.

Nagatachō politics[11]

Nagatachō is the geographic heart of Japanese political life, the district in central Tokyo that is home to the National Diet building, the headquarters of the main political parties and the streams of political life that flow between these. It is here that the legislative process is lived out. Nagatachō has throbbed with the politics of three underlying forces: *habatsu* (factions), *zoku giin* (tribes of Diet members) and *jitsuryokusha* (cliques of the most adroit Diet members), all of which have shaped the legislative process.

Habatsu (faction) politics

Table 4.2 provides comparative detail. Strictly speaking, the direct influence of LDP factional politics upon the legislative process declined during the 1980s, though it continued in an indirect manner through the specific policy expertise of Diet members from each faction. In the latter half of the 1980s, faction politics itself became more oligarchic, losing the energy derived from earlier, more pluralistic and competitive factional in-fighting.

Table 4.2   Nagatachō politics

Sub-system	Last years of the LDP government	Hosokawa coalition government	Murayama coalition government
(1) Faction politics	• 1980s: policy decision-making function declined; plural to oligarchical. • 1990s (last years of '1955 regime') oligarchy to hegemony of factional veto power: Keiseikai predominant. • 1993: Keiseikai split: LDP-predominant system finished	• Vestiges of Keiseikai through Ozawa and Shinseitō: their influence on decisions quite strong • Five coalition parties (new: Shinseitō, Nihon Shintō, Sakigake; old: Kōmeitō, Minshatō) became as factions (five faction politics): oligarchical	• An early integrated party/three coalition parties: co-operative • LDP: old influential faction system dividing into two groups: *Shukyū-ha* and new *kaikaku-ha*. • SDPJ: Left and Right factions sharply divided and confrontational

(2) *Zoku* politics	• PARC: quite influential in making budget and tax reform. • *Zoku* and *zoku* Diet members influential on respective interest politics. (LDPs *zoku* politics reached the peak of its influence on policy decision-making)	• *Seisaku kanjikai* (Policy secretaries council) and its divisions (project teams) established anew. • Policy-making rule: bottom-up, except for tax issues (project team work restricted within scope of policy framework that bureaucrats made in advance) • *Zoku* Diet members of Shinseitō retained their influence (LDP's PARC tried to reconstruct; work quality improved)	• *Seisaku-Chōseikaigi* (Policy adjustment council: PAC) (A)┌──┴──┐(B) *schōchō-betsu* *mondai-betsu* (committees (committees by ministries) by issues) (Neither (A) nor (B) has decisive power; members report to their party only on the matter discussed) • LDP *Zoku*'s influence weaker than ever (interest groups and bureaucrats keep double stance)
(3) Dominant key persons politics	• Executives of Keiseikai faction: Takeshita, Gotōda, Kanemaru, Nikaidō (exercised	• Ozawa tried to retain supreme influence in coalition government (decision-making style:	• *Insei* declining • Murayama government criticised top-down styled decision-making

hidden	top-down)
supreme	• Ozawa's
influence	supporters:
insei)	pro-
• Ozawa	bureaucrats
responds to	and interest
political	groups
corruption	(bureaucrat
with	supporters
Keiseikai	are *not* the
break away	leading
	current
	among
	ministries)

The forceful sway of the Keiseikai group over LDP factional politics through its predominant power of veto, reached a critical point in June 1993 when Keiseikai members broke ranks with the LDP, and destroyed the party's hold on government. The LDP's factional politics lost not only its competitive energy, but its hold on the legislative process, although Shinseitō (the party that Ozawa's breakaway LDP faction set up) did take part in the new government. But because of this, it became impossible for the Hosokawa coalition to sweep away the influence of factional politics, however much he and many in his coalition sought to do so. On the contrary, because one of the seven coalition parties was Ozawa's Shinseitō, faction politics were carried into the new government and continued to influence the legislative process.

Furthermore, of the seven parties and one Diet faction of the House of Councillors that formed the coalition government, five of the parties functioned in the new government virtually as factions. These parties formed an 'oligarchic faction system', bringing the influence of their 'factional' confrontations and differences into the legislative process. This outcome lends weight to the proposition that a coalition of a relatively large number of parties provides a ready breeding ground for factional politics between and within its party members, further intensifying its fragility. Consistent with this notion, the Murayama coalition government of just three parties has managed to present a more integrated front than the two previous coalitions. It is clear, however, that despite the need to at least appear unified, the Murayama coalition, too, has been deeply riven with the factional politics of the LDP and fallout with many socialists.

Zoku (tribe) politics

As we saw in Table 4.2, independence in policy-making and decision-making was formally ordained in the systems introduced by the Hosokawa administration. Informally, however, two significant restrictions remained to work against achieving independence. One was that bureaucrats framed their policy proposals in advance of the Bills' introduction to the Diet.[12] The other was that the most influential coalition member, Ozawa's Shinseitō party, made important decisions in a top-down, dictatorial manner.

The Murayama administration introduced PAC (the Policy adjustment council or *Seisaku chōsei kaigi*) and its two sets of discussion committees (one in line with the ministries, the other in line with the nature of the issue) to rid the system of these unwanted influences. These new policy-making bodies have been conducive to a more open and democratic style of operation. They are not, however, the final arbiters. The real decision-making power has returned to the LDP's PARC. This is largely because PARC is a mature rather than a fledgling policy-making body and thus has long and varied experience. As the Chair of PARC, Katō Kōichi has gained superior power in the policy-making domain.

In this environment the *zoku* (tribe) Diet members who in the previous decade clustered around a specific policy issue, in a style known as zoku politics, have lost ground in the power game. The official restructuring has denied them easy access to the decision-making process. *Zoku* could operate as they did only because *zoku* Diet members, interest groups and bureaucrats formed a trinity, acting as one in a specific policy area. *Zoku* politics thus formed closed and essentially non-competitive policy zones.

By contrast, coalition governments have generally tried to promote a more open and competitive system in which more interests and voices contest. Interest groups and bureaucrats have been forced to study all parties' positions to determine where their best prospects for alliance lie. The interest groups themselves are no longer monolithic, and now form into bands of leaders and interested others. For example, in the case of the Japan Medical Association, leaders support the LDP as before, though other members of the Association direct their support as they like, in a manner that they perceive best serves their individual interests.[13] In this way, conditions under coalition governments have made it more difficult for *zoku* to unite around a policy issue since there is greater freedom for interested parties to express their interest through alliances outside the earlier triad arrangement. Nonetheless, the new arrangements still give rise to policy-expert Diet members.

While we are considering policy expertise, we should consider what had become of PARC during the LDP's term out of office. In sum, the body became more diligent. The tasks of its members were expanded. PARC's chair, Hashimoto Ryūtarō, asked each division to carry out its own research on measures for easing government regulations (*kisei kanwa*) and on more solid policy counter-measures against the lingering economic recession. Each division was instructed to try to make Diet member's legislation (*giin rippō*) and Diet members were instructed to listen to the claims of interest groups themselves.[14] This has proven to be a prudent approach to preparing PARC for retaking decision-making ground should the LDP return to one party rule.

Jitsuryokusha (adroit clique) politics

Alongside the decline of *zoku* politics has come the decline of jitsuryokusha politics. Here it was the most politically adroit people (jitsuryokusha) in the Diet who held sway, dominating decision-making while remaining hidden from view (also known as *insei* or 'seclusion politics'). The decline of jitsuryokusha clout within the legislative system is primarily a function of three factors also contributing to the *zoku* decline. First, the decision-making routes have been multiplied. Second, public criticism of the double power structure has intensified, making its existence more tenuous. Third, individuals who are capable of controlling both the parties and the bureaucrats are fading from the scene. In July 1996, at the end of two years of coalition government, conditions are ripe for the further retreat of jitsuryokusha from the legislative process.

Diet politics[15]

As part of the long-winded trend towards reforming Nagatachō politics, we can recognise that the most strident efforts to reform the politics of the Diet have been made since the birth of the coalition governments. I compare styles of Diet politics under the differing governments in the 1990s (the last years of the LDP regime, the Hosokawa coalition and the Murayama coalition) in Table 4.3. Here we can observe in detail the shifts in the relationship between politicians and bureaucrats. The politicians have taken a number of steps to reduce the involvement of bureaucrats in Diet politics. One clear indication of the declining bureaucratic input is the drop in frequency of bureaucrats responding to Diet members' questions during the National Budget committee meetings in both houses of parliament (see Table 4.4).

Table 4.3   Diet politics (*Kokkai seiji*)

Sub-system	Last years of the LDP government	Hosokawa coalition government	Murayama coalition government
(1) Principles politics (*tatemae seiji*)	• Farcical exchange between LDP and opposition parties (opposition's questions and government's answers in Diet committees were all controlled by bureaucrats) • Substantial answers by government committed chiefly to bureaucrats (*seifu iin*). • House management committees (*Giun'i*) as the stage for approval.	• Coalition parties tried to reform Diet politics. a. to restrain bureaucrat members speaking at Diet committees; b. to rearrange House management committees as the place for essential talking and negotiation between ruling parties and opposition.	• Reform-oriented as was the Hosokawa government. (Shinshintō in opposition, proposed to government that Diet should be the stage for debate among politicians rather than bureaucrats).

| (2) Diet strategy politics (*kokutai seiji*) | • Political bargaining oriented — conciliatory negotiation between LDP and opposition (forced voting on confrontational bills often carried out with prior consent between ruling party and the opposition)
• A skilled chairman of the party *kokutaii* became qualified to be a party executive member or a leader | • Denial of *kokutai-seiji*
• House management committees as basis for negotiation between ruling parties and opposition: confrontational
• Among ruling parties: Political affairs secretaries committee (virtually a a party representatives conference: *Kakutō daihyōsha kaigi* conducted *kokutai-seiji*) | • Floor leaders conference established in order to keep democratic appearance
• Negotiation between the ruling parties and opposition parties: based on House management committees: confrontational |

Table 4.4 Answering frequency of government committee members (*Seifu iin*) in Budget committees of both houses

Diet session number	Government administration	House	Deliberation term	Days	Frequency of answers by bureaucrats	Frequency per day (average)
120	Second Kaifu administration	LH	1991 Feb.–Mar.	8	318 times	40 times
		UH	Apr.	6	362	60
123	Miyazawa	LH	1992 Feb.–Mar.	7	265	38
		UH	Mar.	7	452	65
126	Miyazawa	LH	1993 Jan.–Feb.	7	289	41
		UH	Mar.	7	474	68
129	Hata	LH	1994 May–June	9	177	20
		UH	June	7	186	27
132	Murayama	LH	1995 Jan.–Feb.	6	133	22
		UH	Mar.	7	222	32

LH = Lower House
UH = Upper House
Source: Yomiuri Shinbun, 8 May 1995

It is not simply the relationship between politicians and bureaucrats that has changed Diet politics. Another dimension of the changing undertow in the Diet is the relationship between the politicians themselves as party members: those in government *vis-à-vis* those outside. Coalition governments have tried to reform the unspoken rules and implicit conventions of politicians' behaviour in the Diet. The result has been two major shifts in Diet politics. One has been the move away from reliance on bureaucratic input towards a forum for more active debate between politicians on the Diet floor. The other has been away from the run of conciliatory bargaining among parties in which money could buy favour and influence, to more open negotiation between the government and the opposition parties. This suggests a shift in style away from *tatemae seiji* (principle-based politics) to *honne seiji* (politics with substance, or conciliatory politics).

These new trends under the coalition governments may signal some degree of reform. Yet the coalitions have also introduced a new set of difficulties. The most serious are not those arising between the ruling coalition parties and the opposition parties, but between the ruling parties themselves (and sometimes inside the parties, too). The ruling parties have had to bear considerable costs in attempting to create even the appearance of consensus among themselves. For example, individual members of the Diet's standing committees cannot speak out decisively, independent of their parties' support. The members simply transmit to their party colleagues what was discussed at committee meetings and wait for the party's judgement to relay back to the committee. This has been described as *hongoku ni sodan suru* (consulting with the mother country) in Nagatachō.[16]

Case studies of collapsed legislation

To illustrate the consequences of reform and the shifting patterns of influence under the coalition governments it is useful to observe what has actually happened in the legislative process under these conditions. For this reason I discuss two specific cases where Bills failed in their passage through the Diet. One is the Hosokawa government's Bill to introduce a new welfare tax, and the other is the Murayama government's Bill for reconstructing special semi-governmental corporations (*tokushu hōjin*).

The Hosokawa government's tax bill

Legislation put forward by the Hosokawa government to introduce a welfare tax was in fact the initiative of Ozawa Ichirō (the principal string-puller of this coalition) and Deputy Finance Minister Saitō. The Bill was originally justified to the public on the grounds that a welfare tax was necessary in the light of Japan's rapidly ageing society. This questionable piece of legislation sought to raise the level of consumption tax from the present 3 per cent to 7 per cent, within three years. But the tax was clearly not for the purposes of welfare, whatever its name suggested.

A quick review of the process of the proposed Bill from drafting to eventual pigeon-holing reveals secrecy, deception and departure from the official legislative procedure. A small handful of ministerial secretaries from the Finance Ministry began to draft the Bill in secrecy in autumn 1993. Nonetheless, in his 1994 New Year interview giving 'My Vision for the 21st Century', Prime Minister Hosokawa made no mention of the intended tax increase, even though the Bill had already been prepared. Just one month later, however, Hosokawa made a curt public announcement of the proposed legislation.

There was mixed reaction from the coalition parties, and within the parties themselves. When Secretary General of the SDPJ, Kubo Wataru, reported the Bill to his party, opinion within the SDPJ was split. One group rejected the Bill absolutely while another supported it if revision to the tax law was possible. Sakigake likewise rejected the Bill, though for different reasons. Then-Chief Cabinet Secretary and leader of Sakigake, Takemura Masayoshi, had not been informed in advance about the issue. Sakigake rejected the Bill, largely because of the procedural improprieties that were involved.

Coalition members remained intransigent. The government established a consultative committee consisting of representatives of the coalition parties in a last ditch effort to resolve the issue. But Cabinet could not reach a final uniform decision. In the end the government had no choice but to pigeonhole the Bill.

There is much that we can learn from this travesty. The case highlights the absence from the legislative scene of both a true promoter of welfare policy and a plan for legislation to address the issue of Japan's ageing society and its wide-reaching consequences. The case is also resonant with the opportunism and careerism that continue to drive the legislative process in Japan under coalition governments, irrespective of particular coalitions' aspirations for reform of the legislative system and their attempts to achieve an open and fairly representative system.

First, we can observe the canny style of bureaucrats in the Finance Ministry. The Bill itself was designed by the Ministry's bureaucrats to secure a tax increase, i.e., *inter alia*, a greater financial harvest for the Finance Ministry. The Ministry tucked away the Bill, waiting until the time was ripe to present it. When the Ministry did expose the Bill it was in the guise of a welfare issue which, in the Ministry's misjudgement, the government ultimately opposed. This strategy exposes the arrogance and deceptive tactics of Finance Ministry bureaucrats, especially since they were well aware that there was no unified government control over them. It was 'When the cat's away, the mice will play'. They did, but without success.

Second, we can see the hawkish style of the coalition's real power centre. Ozawa Ichirō colluded with the Finance Ministry bureaucrats to initiate the Bill. Ozawa's forceful, top-down style of administration was abrasive, resented and rejected within the coalition. Ozawa could not control the damage that resulted from this débâcle because of his unconcealed rancour towards two essential coalition players — the SDPJ, as one of the biggest parties in the coalition; and then-Chief Cabinet Secretary Takemura, who formally had direct responsibility for the issue but whom Ozawa had defiantly side-stepped. Plainly, to observe formal procedure, Ozawa, with Prime Minister Hosokawa and Deputy Finance Minister Saitō in tow, should all have acted upon their official accountability to cabinet members.

Third, we see the ineffectual style of Hosokawa as Prime Minister. Hosokawa's actions throughout this legislative drama made it clear that he had been drawn into a policy trap without carefully considering the consequences. Word around political circles suggested Hosokawa was short on political savvy. One pressman has told how, in a media interview, Hosokawa bumbled his way through questions about the welfare tax with bursts of laughter. The welfare tax Bill symbolised Hosokawa's maladministration, one in which 'the sovereign reigns but does not rule'.

Fourth, we see the renegade style of Ichikawa Yūichi, Secretary General of the Kōmeitō another of the main parties in the Hosokawa coalition. Kōmeitō has from its outset functioned as the political arm of Sōka Gakkai, the influential religious body that feeds the party with people and finance. The large majority of Sōka Gakkai members disagreed with raising the consumption tax, in large part attributable to members' occupations. Yet Kōmeitō's Ichikawa became one of the most active supporters of the tax. Ichikawa has always been recognised as a virtual heretic within the party and his political philosophy has strayed further and further from the party's original disposition. With Ichikawa as its Secretary General, Kōmeitō has increasingly lost the strong backing of Sōka Gakkai.

For all the divisiveness that this tax Bill created, it was also fuel for some unlikely alliances. The socialists and Sakigake took advantage of the various cleavages to forge a relatively strong partnership. Their accord continued beyond the life of the first coalition and ultimately into a coalition with the LDP. The SDPJ itself, however, did not remain a monolith. The party's stance on the tax Bill polarised its members between Left and Right, deepening the rifts that had already begun to sunder the Socialist Party and now appear likely to force its complete demise.

Legislation for reconstructing special semi-governmental bodies

Unlike the case of the welfare tax, this issue has not unfolded with the blessings of the bureaucrats but in the face of their stubborn resistance. Several earlier radical attempts to dismantle semi-government offices (*tokushu hōjin*) have been repelled. Resistance has come not just from the bureaucrats, whose interest in preserving the status quo is strong and obvious. Another source of resistance has been certain Diet members who themselves receive pay-back benefit from supporting the interests and privileges that the existing institutional structure provides. Labour unions have also joined the resistance forces.

We can see how this mix of competing interests is played out in the move by the Murayama government to partition NTT, Japan's telecommunications corporation. In this case *Zendentsū*, the National Telecommunications Workers' Union, is positioned to resist vehemently any moves towards a partition. The union may have gone along with moderate political negotiation had it been mediated by Rengō (the Japanese Trade Union Confederation). However, Zendentsū can no longer turn to Rengō for mediation since it has become virtually a non-political body under the presidency of Ashida Jinnosuke.

In the face of this array of forces competing over semi-governmental restructuring, the Management and Coordination Agency (*Sōmucho*) within the Prime Minister's office established a reading room for inspecting information concerning semi-governmental bodies. The agency appeared to have facilitated freer access to information about government and quasi-government bodies. In effect, though, the move side-stepped the central issue of institutional restructuring. This issue remains unresolved, marked by bureaucratic recalcitrance, and it needs commanding political leadership if it is to be resolved.[17]

Perspective on change in Japan's legislative system

On the basis of two years' performance we can say that the task of effectively managing a fledgling coalition government along the legislation road is complex and hugely difficult. At first, problems were compounded by the unwieldy nature of a seven party line-up. Yet even the smaller three party coalition has been fragile — a product, surely, of bringing together disparate, former-opponent parties. At this point I shall summarise my perspective on the central features of the changing legislative landscape as they have surfaced in my analysis here.

Real channels of power — changes and continuities

Both the Hosokawa and Murayama governments took steps to break the secrecy that had marked the legislative process under the LDP. Both sought to reform its organisational structures. But if we focus upon the real channels of power and influence within this process, we find that policy-making, and decision-making generally, have not fundamentally changed. We see that some of the patterns which took shape under LDP rule have remained entrenched, despite attempts at corrective renovation. For this reason I hold that the typologies I developed for explaining the legislative process under LDP rule to June 1993 retain much of their explanatory power for developments in the subsequent two years — and beyond.

It is useful for this overall analysis to consider if and how legislative procedure has changed across different types of policies since the coalition governments came to power. I shall use the following typology to distinguish policy types:

- interest allocating: policies providing public services or benefits, and allocating individual interests and values;
- compensatory: policies to reform social and public institutions;
- regulative: policies that control or attach conditions to social action;
- redistributive: policies that distribute and redistribute public services, benefits or other value among social groups.

Legislative procedure for interest-allocating policies has changed from a reasonably predictable process under LDP rule to an obscure and disorderly process under the coalitions. Nevertheless, bureaucrats, big business and other interest groups, including those that operate at the local level, have managed to forego the support of political parties and have developed strategies to operate in a political environment that lacks strong leadership.

As regards compensatory policies, only the basics of political reform were achieved under the Hosokawa administration. The more concrete measures and administrative restructuring that are necessary for true reform have not yet been applied. In May 1995, a Bill to promote government decentralisation passed the Diet under the Murayama administration. This legislation sets out only a basic legal framework, though discussion of a firmer working plan was well in hand by July 1995. One of the most important issues concerning compensatory policies that is likely to surface on the legislative agenda is the issue of 'crisis administration', especially in the light of central government floundering in the wake of the Kobe earthquake disaster in January 1995.

Regulative policy had long been the bureaucrats' favourite. This type of policy enabled them to support and protect Japanese industries through the nation's period of high-speed economic growth in the 1960s and 70s. At this time these policy measures were naturally welcomed by business interests. Not surprisingly, big business has rallied against the current trend towards easing these regulations, one of the key reasons why progress with deregulation has been infamously slow. A proverb is pertinent here. For the bureaucrats it is a clear case of 'warming a snake in their bosom'.

With redistributive policies, those concerning social welfare in the form of social security, public pensions, medical care and so forth embody the most critical challenges facing Japan's rapidly ageing society. These policies are also the most politically contentious and difficult to legislate. They inevitably require increased government expenditure, which translates as tax reform, something which never fails to escalate political tension. The broader issue will not be essentially ideological in the way that constitutional revision, national defence or the use of energy resources are. Rather, it is a problem of policy vision — more precisely the *absence* of policy vision — and measures to realise this vision, as Japan approaches the twenty-first century with a comparatively much 'older' society than in times past.

This crucial issue could, indeed should, drive the structure of Japan's political parties towards a more efficient and responsible system of government. One of the most portentous questions looming on Japan's political landscape is whether the nation should move towards large government (as in the Swedish style of welfare state) or small government (along the lines of the American style of welfare society). For the time being, a series of well-publicised critical issues, including reforms to government and public administration, diplomatic and trade tensions, industrial restructuring and so foth have remained unresolved and have sidelined this broader question. Furthermore these issues are likely to persist in a political climate marked by frustration and weak, dishevelled, sometimes non-existent leadership.

Principal legislative actors

Some of the changes and continuities in the real power channels within the legislative system are borne by the responsibilities assigned to, or assumed by the principal actors on the scene. These include the Prime Minister, Cabinet and Diet members, political parties and bureaucrats. With the transition to a different configuration of roles and responsibilities among these principal actors, we can observe all of them jostling to retain, regain, or create positions of influence within the new system. The legislative process will be shaped fundamentally by both the allocation of roles and responsibilities to political positions, and the personal styles of those who occupy these positions.

The position of the Prime Minister is crucial. Since coalition governments have come to power, we have seen some politicians attempt to move final decision-making to the Prime Minister, and to reinforce *Kantei seiji* (politics around the Prime Minister's residence). The YKK group (Yamasaki Taku, Katō Kōichi and Koizumi Junichirō, leaders of the younger generation of the LDP) advocates a system of government in which the Prime Minister is chosen by plebiscite, discretion of Cabinet colleagues is extended beyond present limits, and party politics is more independent of other political forces than it is at present. With two years of coalition government rule, the propriety of the Prime Minister retaining single-handed control over government offices without requiring the consent of Cabinet remains a divisive issue. It is a particularly sharp point of contention between the legislative bureau of the Cabinet and the legislative bureau of the lower house.

The Cabinet bureau holds that the Prime Minister is incapable of dispassionately carrying out such an enormous responsibility. The lower house body argues that the Prime Minister *is* capable, and the project team of the ruling parties affirms the lower house view. The project team also favours establishing a system of Prime Minister's advisers.[18] Ozawa Ichirō advocates that two existing posts, Vice Minister (*fuku daijin*) and Policy-making Councillor (*seisaku shingikan*), be filled by Diet members in order to draw them more directly into the policy-making arena. Both visions aim to establish a strong core of leadership at the top, while maintaining distance from volatile and inefficient coalition party politics, as well as from the leverage of bureaucrats. Any moves in this direction are for the time being hamstrung, since there are no people generally recognised as having these qualities equipping them for such a powerful leadership position.

The position of political parties is also pertinent. In recent years and especially since the LDP's loss of government in 1993, all political parties in Japan have eagerly faced the prospect of a new party system. Several scenarios are likely. One involves a three-party formation around the established conservatives, the new conservatives and the liberal social democrats. Another sees a two party system forming around the old conservatives and the new conservatives. In any case, reformation of the parties will continue, since in the present line-up, the parties themselves as well as the coalitions they have formed, are riven with multi-layered conflicts, and some appear to be in self-destruct mode.

The LDP has its divide between old and new conservatives and both Shinshintō and the SDPJ contain remnants of the '1955 regime' within a flank of members who reject that system. Kōmeitō has been rent by endless internal conflicts. Its leaders have a kaleidoscope of tactics for alternative combinations of parties. Some say that Kōmeitō may be excluded from any conservative grouping, since the conservatives in general have voiced their doubts about the behaviour of the Kōmeitō leaders. On the other hand, some of the unestablished political groups, too, are pursuing a new type of party, such as a network-type civic party or a local party.[19]

The position of bureaucrats, especially those from the Finance Ministry, who have wielded such heavy clout in the legislative process, is also important. Under the multi-party governments, bureaucrats have managed to perform their tasks well overall, within a legislative system whose lines of power are complex and oblique. Bureaucrats are expected to soon re-stake their political position. Above all, in the interests of preventing collusive practices between Diet members, bureaucrats and other vested interests, much freer access to government information will need to be built into the legislative process. Public airing of the Budget-making processes of the Finance Ministry is both long overdue and imperative.

Conclusion

The first two years of Japan's 1990s' coalition governments, from July 1993 to 1995, have inevitably seen changes in the ways the legislative process is played out, both inside and outside the Diet. The nature of the change has not been inevitable, since it has been driven by unofficial as well as official procedures. Ideology has faded from the scene, personal, factional and party divides have set the agenda, and the party system itself remains in transition.

Japan's legislative seas have been choppy, while Diet members have been involved in the legislative process in various capacities. Diet members have played out their roles as members of factions, parties, coalitions and oppositions, of committees and other formal institutional groupings, as representatives of their constituencies, and as individuals. The non-elected players on the legislative scene — bureaucrats and interest groups — have had to recast their nets into these shifting seas in search of new alliances. The future structure of Japan's party politics remains unpredictable, at least until a few elections under the 1994 electoral rules give some indication of how things will develop. Whatever direction it takes, the key players on the legislative scene will continue to look for chances to influence the legislative process. In the volatile political environment of the mid-1990s, this is one of the few features of the legislative landscape that is not likely to change.

Notes

1. In researching this chapter I conducted personal interviews and hearings with two Diet members, one each from the LDP and *Shinshintō*, one research member of PARC, and one pressman from *Tōkyō Shinbun*. In the interviews and hearings, I used both universal and subject-specific questions. These people and institutions also supplied relevant materials.
2. Nakano Minoru (1992) *Gendai Nihon no seisaku katei* (The policy-making process in contemporary Japan), Tokyo: University of Tokyo Press. The English version of this book was published by Macmillan in 1997.
3. While this chapter was being prepared for publication, Murayama resigned as Prime Minister and was replaced by the LDP's Hashimoto Ryūtarō, who had been widely tipped for the post.
4. Murakawa Ichirō and Isogami Yasukuni (1994) *Nihon no seitō* (Japanese political parties), Tokyo: Maruzen.
5. Kida Masatoshi (1994) *Renritsu seiken jidai no seisaku keisei* (Policy-making in an age of coalition government), in Horie Fukashi and

Colloquium for Political Reform (eds), *Renritsu seiken jidai no seijigaku* (Political science in an age of coalition governments), PHP Kenkyūsho.

6. Murakawa and Isogami *Nihon no seitō*.
7. Kida, *Renritsu seiken.*
8. Nakano Minoru (1993) *Nihon no seiji rikigaku* (The Political Dynamics of Japan), Tokyo: NHK Press; Nakano, *Gendai Nihon no seisaku katei.*
9. Nakano, *Nihon no seiji rikigaku*, Chapter 1.
10. See special report, *Sengo gojūnen Nihonjin no sentaku* (The Choice of the Japanese People Fifty Years after World War II), Part 4, *Mainichi Shinbun*, 6–9 June 1995.
11. See Nakano, *Nihon no seiji rikigaku*, Chapter 2.
12. Kida, *Renritsu seiken.*
13. Author's personal interview with Nukaga Fukushirō, member of the lower house and Deputy Chairman of the commerce and industry division of PARC, 15 May 1995.
14. Author's personal interview with Nukaga, 15 May 1995, and with Takahashi Toshiko, Research Member of PARC, 31 May 1995.
15. See Nakano, *Nihon no seiji rikigaku*, Chapter 3.
16. Personal interview with Nukaga, 15 May 1995.
17. For the details provided in these case studies of collapsed legislation I am indebted to a personal hearing with Mr Obata Kōichi, Deputy Director of the Political Division of Tokyo Shinbunsha, 28 May 1995.
18. *Asahi Shinbun*, 26 June 1995.
19. Personal hearing with Mr Obata, 28 May 1995 and interview with Ito Tatsuya of *Shinshintō*, a member of the lower house and a board member of the Budgetary Committee of the House, 17 May 1995. Also see *Tokyo Shinbun*, 3–9 February 1994.

5
Reforming Japanese politics: highway of change or road to nowhere?

J.A.A. Stockwin

> Japan's most pressing need is a change in the consciousness of our people. Let us begin by removing the fences and educating the people to their own responsibility for themselves.[1]

There is no doubt that the reform program put forward by Ozawa Ichirō, Japan's most articulate and persuasive champion of political reform, is fundamental and all-encompassing. Ozawa would have Japan change some of the most basic principles of its politics, embedded since the 1950s. Rather than politics by consensus, he would move towards politics by strong leadership and individual choice. Rather than government by unelected elitist bureaucrats, he would shift the balance in favour of government by elected politicians, responsible to those who elected them. Rather than political dominance by a single political party, he would change to truly competitive party politics, preferably two large parties genuinely competing. Rather than over-regulation of the economy, and over-control of many other aspects of people's lives by government, he would deregulate so far as possible, thus 'removing the fences'[2] that confine people and suppress their individualism. Instead of government from the centre, he would increase the effective autonomy of local regions and authorities. Instead of an election system encouraging factions, money politics and personality voting, he would move to one encouraging competition between parties over matters of policy. And whereas Japan in its foreign policies was unable adequately to defend its national interest, he would convert it into a 'normal state', able to defend itself like any other.[3]

Ozawa, moreover, was not merely theorising. Though a central member of the central faction of the Liberal Democratic Party (LDP), he was prepared to split both faction and party in pursuit of these reformist aims. When, as a direct result of his group's defection from the LDP in June 1993, the ruling party was defeated at the general elections for the House of Representatives, on 18 July, he worked with subtlety and flair to ensure that a truly reformist government should replace the LDP. Although Ozawa was not the only architect of the eight-party Hosokawa government that followed, he can legitimately claim to be its principal midwife. This was a government that attained amazing popularity.[4]

Two-and-a-half years after these heroic events, one could be pardoned for wondering what has happened to reform. The Hosokawa government, which broke so dramatically with the past by excluding the LDP, was succeeded, after the nine-week interlude of the minority Hata Cabinet, by a government in which the LDP was once more included, albeit as part of a coalition of three parties, and without securing the prime ministership. That position went to Murayama Tomiichi, Chairman of the Social Democratic Party of Japan (SDPJ, formerly JSP), who soon after his elevation acted to drop several of his party's long-standing and cherished policies. These were to do with the constitutionality of the Self Defence Forces, opposition to the Japan-US Security Treaty, and attitudes to the national flag and national anthem in schools.[5] Even though in practice the influence of the Socialists within the Murayama Cabinet was not wholly subordinate to the will and attitudes of the numerically superior LDP, one veteran LDP operator assessed the assimilation of the SDPJ in a graphic fashion:

> We have swallowed the Socialists and we have them in our stomach. All that remains is for the gastric juices to digest them.[6]

In January 1996, the LDP finally, after a gap of two-and-a-half years, regained the prime ministership, as Murayama resigned, and the recently elected President of the LDP, Hashimoto Ryūtarō, took over.

The first argument which we wish to advance in this chapter is that, during the period from the fall of the Hosokawa government in April 1994 until the latter half of 1996, the reform program was in a kind of limbo. This did not mean, however, that it was dead. The key to understanding what was happening to aspirations for reform lay in the fact that all members of the House of Representatives in 1995 and 1996 had been elected under the old system of election. If they were to be re-elected, they would have to contest elections whose date was yet to be announced, according to a completely different and unfamiliar set of rules.[7]

This has led to a long period of political uncertainty about where the balance of political advantage really lies: an atmosphere unconducive to bold and comprehensive political reform. There is a related problem, namely that in such uncertain political conditions, the kind of leadership necessary to promote reform is slow to emerge. Paradoxically, however, without reform, such leadership seems unlikely to emerge except in a particularly fortunate combination of circumstances.

In the first half of 1996, the Hashimoto government was working to consolidate its position against the challenge from the principal party of opposition, the *Shinshintō* or New Frontier Party, now led by Ozawa. It seemed to be in its interests to postpone elections as long as possible (they were ultimately conducted in October 1996), no doubt with the ultimate aim of returning the LDP to the situation where it would have a parliamentary majority in its own right. Prospects for the renamed *Shakai Minshutō* (Social Democratic Party),[8] still in coalition with the LDP and Sakigake party in early 1996, appeared to be poor.

The second argument to put forward, however, is that once elections are held under the new system, the way will be more open for developments favouring reform. If we look back over the history of attempts to reform the political system going back as far as the 1950s, we find that radical reform of the lower house electoral system has repeatedly been targeted as a *sine qua non* of fundamental system reform.[9] It is arguable that the greatest achievement of the reformist Hosokawa government was to pilot through both houses of the National Diet, against fierce internal and external opposition which undoubtedly contributed to its own collapse in April 1994, a series of Bills radically altering the way the Japanese electorate will choose its representatives. Moreover, it was a significant accomplishment of the Murayama government that it oversaw the consolidation of the reform, including the drawing of new constituency boundaries. When we consider that the two prime ministers immediately preceding Hosokawa, the Liberal Democrats Kaifu and Miyazawa, were both forced out of office essentially because of botched attempts at reforming the electoral system, we can well appreciate the magnitude of the achievement accomplished by Hosokawa and consolidated by Murayama. It is, moreover, a reasonable presumption that this would never have been achieved without Ozawa. For it was largely on his initiative that forty renegades split from the LDP in June 1993, precipitating the removal from office of the ruling party which had seemed to rule forever.

The third principal concern of this chapter relates to the long-term ideological implications of a changed electoral system, and more broadly, of the process of political reform in general. A common view, particularly on the Left and centre Left of the political spectrum, is that an electoral reform creating predominant first-past-the-post, single-member constituencies, is likely to privilege the Right wing, both by favouring large, rich parties and by opening up the political system to the possibility of strong personal leadership from the top, leadership capable of overriding many of the checks and balances entrenched in the existing system. Conversely, and for essentially the same set of reasons, such changes tend to be favoured among many (though not all) sections of the political Right. While there is much evidence to suggest that the reforms may favour Right wing over Left wing politics, nevertheless the proposition needs to be subjected to rigorous investigation. In particular, two considerations need to be borne in mind: first, that 'Right wing' and 'Left wing' as categories of political analysis may be seriously inadequate in the political conditions of the 1990s; and second, that if political parties, groups or movements that we might designate as 'Left wing' were to play their cards intelligently, the new electoral system might well prove to hold advantages for them, as well as disadvantages.

Politics under the 'old' system

In order better to understand the dilemmas presented by attempts to reform Japan's system of politics and government in the 1990s, we must first describe the '1955 political system', so designated because 1955 was the year in which the LDP came into being, dominating all subsequent governments until its fall from power in 1993. We shall first list what we believe to have been the basic features of that system, and then identify features that have been subject to change over time.

The basic characteristics of the system were the following:

1. Relations between the executive and the legislature were based upon the 'Westminster model'. Here the electorate, in electing a parliament, directly elected a government, comprising a cabinet formed from selected members of the majority party or parties. Members of Cabinet were in most cases the political heads of particular ministries, meaning, in effect, that there was a substantial fusion of power between the executive and legislative branches of government. In this sense, the system differed, conceptually and in practice, from the American system of government. Indeed, one of the intriguing features of the Occupation was that the mostly American occupiers should not have seriously attempted to introduce into Japan American-style separation between Congress and the presidency.

   In the Japanese case, there has been further consolidation of the 'fusion-of-powers' model by virtue of strong and self-confident government ministries and the ability of the LDP to secure its re-election at successive general elections over nearly four decades. We might even call this aspect of the Japanese system 'Westminster plus'.

2. If the first characteristic of the system suggests centralisation of power, the second suggests its dispersal. Political leadership has been characterised by a collegial, consensus-based style. The power of the Prime Minister has ranged between weak and only moderately effective, with a very few conspicuous exceptions. Many issues have been settled elsewhere than in Cabinet, which has often given the impression of being the decision-maker of last resort.

3. Not only have the government ministries exercised extensive political influence in their own right, but were able to 'colonise' the ruling party, and to a lesser extent, the corporate sector. In the case of the LDP, as many as one-quarter of lower house Diet members have been former officials of ministries, while substantial numbers of government officials join the boards of companies after retirement from their ministries. It is a reasonable supposition that this 'colonisation' has been used extensively for consolidating bureaucratic power within the governmental machine as a whole, though against this must be set the intense inter-ministerial rivalries that result in acute jurisdictional and policy rivalry.

4. During the period of single-party dominance, a particularly conspicuous formation within the LDP was the *habatsu* (faction). *Habatsu* were intra-party organisations, usually revolving round a single leader who would be a prominent politician within the party, and serving certain functions for their members.

These included strategic bargaining over the distribution of posts within Cabinet, party, party committees etc. and, second, the channelling of funds from business firms and other donors to faction members, to finance electoral and other political activities.

Selection of the party president (guaranteed to become Prime Minister as long as the LDP maintained its parliamentary majority) was always a matter of factional competition and manoeuvre. Although the constant rivalry between long-lasting and well-organised *habatsu* obviously divided the party and on occasion created serious ructions within it, at the same time, paradoxically, the existence of *habatsu* served as a binding force. There were two reasons for this. First, power contests were kept at one remove from policy contests (with which *habatsu* were not primarily concerned) and the impact of potential divisions over policy was reduced. Second, the practice developed of a consensual distribution of power between factions, rather than winner-take-all.

5. The nexus between politicians and electors rested rather heavily on a rural-based, personality-appeal style of electioneering, emphasising parish-pump pork-barrelling rather than national policy choices. One reason for this was the serious electoral malapportionment which had arisen as the result of chronic failure to compensate adequately for movements of population from the rural areas to the big cities. This meant that by the 1980s, the value of a single vote in the most over-represented rural constituency was worth between three and four times the value of a vote in the most under-represented urban one. The second factor contributing to an emphasis in campaigning on personality, rather than party or policy, was the fact that constituencies elected multiple members, while each elector had only one vote. In many parts of the country the LDP was so dominant that it could prudently endorse several candidates for the same constituency, in the realistic expectation that all or most of them would be elected. This led to a situation where each LDP candidate set up and became heavily reliant on a *kōenkai* (personal support machine) to enable him or her to maximise votes won. There were even cases where an aspirant LDP candidate, refused endorsement by the LDP because otherwise too many LDP candidates would be competing against each other in the same constituency, was nevertheless elected as an unaffiliated candidate as a result of the effectiveness of his *kōenkai*. A much-noted characteristic of *kōenkai* was their localised and personalised nature; generally speaking, issues

of national policy figured rather little in their deliberations.[10]
The result was a series of political inputs in which local
constituency interests and pork-barrel figured prominently,
but politicians felt themselves less pressured by the electorate
on policy matters of national importance.

6. Opposition parties throughout the period of single-party
dominance were relatively weak (though for a while in the
1970s and again in 1989–90 they appeared to constitute an
electoral threat to the LDP). As a result, the electorate was
not presented a realistic electoral choice, as when there is a
genuine prospect, based on past experience, that a vote against
the government of the day might result in its demise. From the
late 1950s onwards, the weak link in the ranks of opposition
parties was arguably its largest element, the JSP (SDPJ), which
often gave the impression that it did not really want to take
office, and would not know what to do with government should
the electors choose it to govern the country.[11] Even so, the
opposition parties between them were able to exercise an
important veto power, and their policy proposals were at times
appropriated by an LDP government. The most obvious
example of veto power was the opposition's ability to block
constitutional revision, where a two-thirds majority of each
house of the National Diet was required (as well as a simple
majority in a national referendum) for constitutional revision
to occur.[12] For much of the period of single-party dominance,
a dialectic could be observed between opposition parties as
'boots-and-all' resisters of government, and opposition parties
as 'clients' of a government acting as 'patron'. On the other hand,
the tradition of opposition parties as proponents of an alternative
set of policies translatable into government policies by victory
at the next election was in the Japanese case remarkably weak.

7. The system was affected by a widespread phenomenon of
'money politics' and by political practices which elsewhere
would be regarded as corrupt, and were widely regarded as such
in Japan itself. The reasons for this were both structural and
legal. They were structural in the sense that in order to be
elected and to survive financially as a politician, a far greater
income than that provided by the state was essential. They
were legal in the sense that the laws on corruption were full of
loopholes, and could be easily evaded. This was undoubtedly
a factor in the LDP splits which took place in 1993, and forced
it out of office.

8. The international dimension to the '1955 political system' is
also important. This system coincided in time with the Cold

War between the United States and the Soviet Union. When the Cold War ended, so did the single-party dominance at the core of Japan's '1955 political system'. This was hardly a matter of chance. The issues involved are too complex to go into here, but a fundamental point to be made is that the Cold War and the Japan-US security relationship that was a consequence of it, in the early post-war years gave Japan a certain international stability, while arguably also allowing its governments to avoid confronting difficult international choices. While not accepting in their entirety the 'free rider' arguments levelled by Americans at Japan over a long period, we would nevertheless argue that Japanese governments were given the chance to make foreign policy within broadly safe and predictable parameters. A further related point is that while the Cold War continued, the JSP (SDPJ) was regarded by both political conservatives and American government officials as more or less an 'anti-system' party, acceptable neither as a coalition partner nor a member of an alternative government. This, too, ended with the Cold War, and the SDPJ duly found itself as a member of three of the four coalition governments that followed the collapse of the '1955 political system'.[13]

If the eight elements identified above represent with reasonable accuracy the essentials of the 1955 political system, it should not be assumed that it did not change over the thirty-eight years it was in existence. The following may be identified as aspects of it that changed or evolved over the period. The system in 1993 differed in important respects from that in 1955:

1. The long period of LDP dominance enabled the party to develop its own expertise and sources of information across a range of policy areas, so that government officials' jealously guarded monopoly of specialist knowledge gradually became less important. The emergence in the 1970s of groups of Diet members holding in common an interest in a specific area of policy, and known as *zoku* (tribes), was a symptom of the breaking of the bureaucratic knowledge monopoly. The *zoku* turned into something akin to American 'iron triangles' in the sense that they linked up with groups in ministries, and with interest groups having similar policy concerns. At times, accusations of corruption were levelled at some of the *zoku*, not least those concerned with the construction industry.[14]

2. It was also possible to detect a gradual reduction in the degree of bureaucratic dominance over the corporate sector. This declined with the removal of many bureaucratic controls, and

with the enormously increased wealth of corporations, which consequently no longer had to be concerned with government-controlled sources of capital through the banking system.

3. A gradual lessening in the policy and ideological differences between the LDP and the opposition parties was evident by the late 1980s though signs of merging could be detected much earlier. From at least the early 1970s some LDP political leaders (most famously Tanaka Kakuei) sought to develop links with some of the parties of opposition, and these were indeed established, mostly on a person-to-person basis.[15]

4. The long period of LDP rule coincided with a gradual trend towards interest group pluralism, and away from the uniform corporate dominance of the early post-war years. Interests which commanded large numbers of votes in key constituencies, particularly agriculture, but also small and medium industrial enterprises, were able to exert effective pressure on government from an early stage. This extended eventually into the phenomenon described by Inoguchi as 'mass-inclusionary pluralism'.[16] The process, most noticeable in the 1970s, of governments facing crisis as the result of external pressure, and acting to 'buy off' interests, is described by Calder in his book *Crisis and Compensation* (1988).[17] The pattern is, however, complicated by the fact that in the 1980s, facing a different sort of crisis, that of overspending resulting from these same compensatory policies, the government was able to implement measures of economic retrenchment even in the face of interest group pressure.

5. A further political change that has become crucial in its implications is the shift from relatively predictable patterns of electoral behaviour from the 1950s to the 1970s, to a much less predictable pattern from the late 1970s onwards. Thus, the twenty years from 1955 to 1975 saw a steady fall in the number of those voting for the LDP and JSP (SDPJ), with a corresponding rise of votes for smaller parties of the centre and far Left (their votes, however, were concentrated in the cities). During the 1970s, with the drastic slowing of economic growth which followed from the first oil crisis of 1973–74, electoral support for the LDP paradoxically began to bottom out, and then revive. In the 1980s, electoral behaviour becomes notably more unpredictable, with the LDP performing well in some elections (1980, 1986, 1990), and badly in others (1979, 1983, 1989 [upper house] and 1993).[18]

  Instability appeared to be linked with rising political apathy, measured by declining voting turnout rates.

6. Corruption is an issue that has rarely been out of the headlines in Japan from the 1940s onwards (and, indeed, there were important pre-war precedents). But from the scandal involving the Recruit Co., which first broke in 1988, questions of corruption dominated the newspaper headlines almost continuously, and this seemed to match an increase in concern among the articulate public.

7. Within the LDP itself, younger members of parliament were by the 1990s manifesting substantial dissatisfaction with the rigid system of seniority promotion that had developed over the past two decades or so.[19] This 'generation gap' was important in bringing about the splits in the party that occurred in 1993.

8. The collapse of the Soviet Union and ending of the Cold War in 1989–91 to some extent removed the external pressure on Japan by the United States. This had always favoured stable, conservative government and had regarded the Left wing opposition parties as essentially unacceptable participants in government. The most spectacular fruit of the removal of this pressure was the entry of the SDPJ (JSP) into the Hosokawa government and the appointment of a Socialist Prime Minister in June 1994.

Grasping the parameters of the new political system

Let us here recapitulate our main argument, which is in three parts: first, that there is little prospect of a serious reform process resuming or gaining momentum until after elections for the House of Representatives have been held; second, that the current period, deeply disillusioning though it may seem to proponents of reform, ought not to be seen as a good indicator of trends and prospects once elections have taken place; and third, that the ideological implications of what happens after the elections need to be examined with great care and without too much reliance on ideological alliances and cleavages that have existed in the past.

The reform program of the Hosokawa government was crucial in setting the agenda for reform of the political system. Ultimately it had neither the political will, nor the luck, nor enough time, to realise much of its program. The Hosokawa government did, however, devise a credible and potentially realisable agenda of reform in a coherent and comprehensible fashion. This ensured that things could never again be entirely the same. Many of the components of this agenda had in fact been part of political discourse of years. But the right circumstances for reforms to be put into practice as a program did not exist as long as the LDP dominated. Weak leadership, which the reformers regarded as the central problem of the old system, itself had the effect of making reform next to impossible under it. The successive travails of prime ministers Kaifu and Miyazawa illustrate this graphically.

Even though the result was a compromise, there seems little doubt that reforming the system of election for the House of Representatives will make a difference to the way the overall system works. In this sense it may be seen as a solid achievement by the Hosokawa government. Part of the disillusionment with the government, and thus with the reform process as a whole, has stemmed from the fact that it is difficult to explain to the electorate that reforming the election system is important for the success of the broader reform program. Most voters have been understandably more concerned with economic issues attendant upon the era of slow economic growth and rising unemployment that has followed the collapse of the economic 'bubble' early in the 1990s.

Nevertheless, reforming the electoral system is important. The old system of multi-member districts, with no voter preferences able to be expressed beyond the first, was tailor-made for pork-barrel parochial politics and immobilist checks and balances between multifarious interests. In so far as the electoral system immobilised the politicians, the bureaucrats were accorded power without adequate control. Admittedly, this situation was complicated by the fact that by the 1980s, LDP politicians were involved in 'iron triangles' with powerful government officials and interest group representatives. Arguably, however, this was more a case of politicians becoming involved in a bureaucratic process played largely by bureaucratic rules, than of politicians forcing government officials to conform to a centrally determined political agenda.[20] The process as a whole was widely dispersed among different agencies and committees, and programmatic political leadership was difficult to assert.

What, then, of the new electoral system? First, it is a compromise between two kinds of electoral system, whose prononents had radically different aims in mind. Those wishing to favour competition between large political parties capable of aggregating diverse interests into a coherent political program wished for all or most seats in the House of Representatives to be elected in British-type single-member districts. The supporters of this approach tended to be politically conservative and could be accused of wishing to eliminate, or greatly reduce the representation of parties of the Left.

Those, on the other hand, who were in favour of proportional representation, were for the most part from smaller and more vulnerable parties, proposing as far as possible an accurate representation of opinion as it existed in the electorate. Broadly speaking, though not entirely, these were people on the Left of the political spectrum. The debate over which system to adopt during the period of the Hosokawa government had the effect of shifting the emphasis towards the first school and away from the second. Whereas the initial proposal was for equality of seats (250–250) between the two types of constituency, and for the 250 proportional representation seats to be elected from a single national constituency,[21] the final result was 300 single-member seats plus 200 proportional representation seats in 11 regional blocs. An important concession to those favouring proportional representation was that each elector is to have two votes, one for each constituency. This means that the 200 proportional representation districts will not simply mirror party vote distribution in the single-member districts (as would have been the case had the elector been given only one vote), but will enable voters to express a quite different party preference (say, for a minor party) in the proportional representation districts.

Quite apart from the theoretical merits or disadvantages of this system, what is likely to be its effect on politics and political decision-making? In order to answer this question, we need to make a number of assumptions about electoral results.

Our first assumption is that the 300 single-member seats will be overwhelmingly the preserve of large parties. As of February 1996, this meant the LDP and the Shinshintō, but there were indications of possible party realignments preceding elections, particularly if these were long postponed.[22] In general, the LDP appeared to be performing more strongly than the Shinshintō, the former's effectiveness boosted by the advantage of being back in office.

This leads on to our second assumption, less certain than the first, but with considerable circumstantial evidence to back it up. It is that the renewed advantages of incumbency were likely to serve the LDP well in the approaching elections, providing it did not once again split. The possibility of splits could not be ruled out, but their likelihood appeared even greater in the case of the Shinshintō than in that of the LDP.

Third, so far as the 200 seats to be contested by proportional representation were concerned, there was also likely to be a heavy representation from the large parties, many of whose candidates were contemplating standing for election in both types of constituency, as they were permitted to do under the new law. Such representation as the smaller parties (including the SDPJ) were able to achieve was likely to be in the proportional representation districts. In practical terms, their best chance for exercising political influence after the elections lay in the scenario of an even balance between the two large parties, whereupon they might be able to enter into a coalition arrangement with one or other of the large parties.

Our fourth expectation is a long-term weakening of factions within parties, in particular within the LDP. Indeed, LDP factions already appear to have lost influence by comparison with their importance up to 1993. This does not mean the elimination of factionalism as such, but rather a structural shift away from factions as the principal channels for funding and as bodies brokering distribution of office.

The reasons for believing this lie in the elimination of single non-transferable vote multi-seat electorates, and the tightening of laws on corruption (even though this is clearly unlikely to be eliminated altogether). Both together should create a more centrally directed and at the same time flexibly structured political environment within parties.

Following on from this, as a counterpart to the weakening of factions, we should expect to see a strengthening of party organisation in the large parties, particularly in the LDP. How far this strengthening will go is difficult to predict, but it could result in a more flexible, less stereotyped system for promotion and task allocation within the party.

Assuming that, in the course of putting the new electoral system into operation, something similar to this outline emerges, it can be reasonably assumed that politics will be somewhat more fluid than it was under the long period of LDP ascendancy. This will be the case even if the LDP should emerge once again with an absolute majority of seats. With a looser and less rigidly structured internal party organisation, there is more scope for bold and assertive political leadership to emerge. The LDP was shaken out of its complacency by being thrust into opposition in 1993, and then having to cohabit with its erstwhile enemy, the SDPJ, on return to office. This, coupled with the weakening of the factional structure which had been at the core of its informal organisation, suggests a different kind of emerging politics.

Our third and final argument relates to ideology and policy cleavage. One widespread assumption about the political trends of the 1990s is that a salient feature of the '1955 system' has been extinguished or is close to extinction — namely the Left-Right polarisation of politics between conservatives and socialists. The ending of the Cold War combined with the fall from office of the LDP in 1993 dealt a severe blow to the concept of socialism in Japan, and even to that of social democracy, with which it was often confused. If socialism was no longer a serious contender for the minds of the electorate, it was argued, that meant there was no real ideological alternative to the kind of capitalist system that prevailed in the Japanese economy. Our argument is that a number of crucial choices for Japan remain to be made, and are likely to be the stuff of political debate for years to come. Principal among these are the following:

1. Small government versus big government, or to put it in a different form, a free market system resulting from wholesale deregulation and involving minimal government controls, versus a politico-economic system which, though capitalist, involves a wide range of controls by government, is a live debate. A number of associated issues are attached to the 'small government versus large government' dichotomy, notably a questioning, in the Japanese cultural context, of a philosophy of capitalism glorifying the individual and individual interests, as against the interests of groups and the common interest. A related question is whether the kind of rampant litigiousness prevalent in the United States is appropriate in Japanese conditions. Although in the difficult economic circumstances of the 1990s arguments have strengthened for government roles to be greatly reduced, the view that the market alone cannot be trusted to optimise the common interest remains powerful.

2. The 'pacifism' versus 'normal state' argument still divides Japan's political class as it does the population at large. It is difficult to envisage a rapid resolution of this controversy, even if one assumes a conservative dominance of politics after the next elections. We may rather expect that new developments in the international relations of East and Southeast Asia, as well as in Japan itself, may serve to keep the controversy very much alive.

3. The nature of the state in its relations with the electorate is likely to continue to create divisive controversy. Even though we have argued that the new electoral system may well tip the scales in favour of stronger political leadership, there are certain to be diverse pressures leading in the opposite direction. The question of whether or not to revise the Constitution will remain a live issue, not only in relation to Article 9 (the 'peace' clause), but also to the structure of relations between the executive, the legislature, the judiciary and the electorate. We may expect some furious political debate on these questions in years to come. Associated with this also are questions which involve interpretation of the Constitution, such as decentralisation of

government and the role of the bureaucracy in policy-making. The theme of open government is also likely to command increasing attention as the decade advances.

Conclusion

We have argued for cautious optimism regarding the prospects for political reform in Japan. We have stressed that up to the general elections for the House of Representatives held under the new and radically changed arrangements, the pursuit of reform has been much inhibited by political factors. After the elections, however, we may expect a new political environment, from which new directions, and new leadership, may arise. There is a real sense in which the old system has outlived its usefulness and new ideas are needed.

At the same time, there is likely to be considerable continuity between the old system and the new. Blueprints for a new system such as that put forward by Ozawa have done much to propel Japan in the direction of reform. The Ozawa vision, however, despite its great impact, has met determined opposition from various sectors of political opinion. Various different approaches to reform have also appeared, and indeed the Hosokawa Cabinet divided in a rather spectacular fashion over the nuances of the reform program. Even though there have been many complaints since 1993 about political instability and stagnation, perhaps the healthiest sign for the future of Japanese politics is precisely the diversity of views which we have sought to elucidate. General uniformity of political outlook and prescription casts doubt on the openness of a political system, suggesting that official coercion and obfuscation are at work. The fact that debate between philosophically different approaches to the complex business of governing a modern state is able to flourish without too much let or hindrance, warrants a reasonably positive assessment of the future.

Notes

1. Ichiro Ozawa, *Blueprint for a New Japan*, Tokyo, New York and London: Kodansha International, p. 12.
2. At the very beginning of his book (p. 9), Ozawa recounts a visit he made to the Grand Canyon National Park, where he was amazed to

see no fences, no 'no entry' signs and no park attendants telling people to be careful or warning them away.

3. Ozawa, *Blueprint for a New Japan,*. pp. 93–150.

4. See public opinion polls giving the Hosokawa Cabinet an unprecedented 71 per cent approval rating, *Asahi Shinbun*, 8 September 1993. The rating was still 70 per cent in November, but fell to 60 per cent in December, still an indicator of almost unbeaten prime ministerial popularity (*Asahi Shinbun*, 22 December 1993).

5. The formal position of the SDPJ had long been to regard the Self Defence Forces as unconstitutional, oppose the Security Treaty as problematic for Japan's security and to frown on the obligatory use of the flag and anthem in schools.

6. Takeshita Noboru, quoted in *Tokyo Insideline*, 30 July 1994, p. 1.

7. The new lower house electoral system became law in November 1994. Out of a total of 500 seats, 300 are to be elected according to the 'British' principle of first past the post in single-member constituencies, and the remaining 200 by proportional representation in eleven separate regions. The voter will have two votes, one for each type of constituency, and, strangely, candidates may stand for both constituencies. Unlike the old system, where the voter had to write in the name of his or her preferred candidate, he or she will now mark a name printed on the ballot paper.

8. From the time of its foundation in 1945 the party was always known in Japanese as *Nihon Shakaitō* (Japan Socialist Party), but for some years in the immediate post-war period, and then again from 1991, it was known *in English* as Social Democratic Party of Japan. The decision of the party congress in January 1996 to change at last the *Japanese* name to *Shakai Minshutō* (Social Democratic Party) was an important psychological break with the past, though the *shakai* (social, socialist) element in the official title remained, despite the preference of some on the Right of the party to remove it in deference to the sentiment that everything related to 'socialism' was discredited.

9. Prime Ministers Hatoyama, in the mid-1950s, and Tanaka, in the early 1970s, both attempted to bring in a system based essentially on first-past-the-post voting in single-member districts. Most reform packages discussed from the early 1980s onwards also included reforming the electoral system as an essential condition for further systemic reform.

10. For a classic account in English of *kōenkai*, see Gerald L. Curtis (1971) *Election Campaigning Japanese Style*, New York and London: Columbia University Press.

11. In lower house elections from the 1950s to the 1990s, the JSP always ran fewer candidates than would have been required to form a majority in the House. This was because many sitting JSP Diet members would have felt threatened by extra JSP candidates splitting the JSP vote in their (multi-member) constituencies. Deciding how many candidates to run was always a tricky business for large parties under the old system.

12. Constitution, Article 96.
13. The SDPJ was a member of the Hosokawa, Murayama and Hashimoto governments, but refused to participate in the Hata government after Ozawa had devised a grouping of government parties that would have excluded it.
14. On *zoku*, see Inoguchi Takashi and Iwai Tomoaki (1987) *Zoku giin no kenkyū* (A study of legislative tribes), Nihon keizai shinbunsha.
15. A recent example is the close co-operation in the early 1990s between Kanemaru Shin of the LDP and Tanabe Makoto of the SDPJ over contacts with the Democratic People's Republic of Korea (North Korea).
16. Inoguchi Takashi (1983) *Gendai Nihon seiji keizai no kōzu* (The composition of the contemporary Japanese political economy), Tokyo: Tōyō Keizai Shinpōsha.
17. Kent E. Calder (1988) *Crisis and Compensation: Public Policy and Political Stability in Japan, 1949–1986*, Princeton: Princeton University Press.
18. The 1993 result is, however, problematic in this regard. The LDP lost this election and found itself out of power for the first time in most voters' memories, yet the result was caused more by the fact that it split than by a swing against it. Seats won by candidates representing the LDP, Shinseitō and Sakigake, all of whom had been LDP members up to a month before the election, constituted a comfortable majority of total seats.
19. See J.A.A. Stockwin, 'Parties, Politicians and the Political System', in J.A.A. Stockwin, Alan Rix, Aurelia George, James Horne, Daiichi Itō and Martin Collick (1988) *Dynamic and Immobilist Politics in Japan*, Basingstoke and London: Macmillan, pp 22–53, especially Table 2.3 on p. 41.
20. A contrary view, namely that in essence Japanese government officials dance to tunes imposed on them by politicians, according to the theory of principals and agents, seems to this writer both to oversimplify and to distort reality (J. Mark Ramseyer and Frances McCall Rosenbluth (1993) *Japan's Political Marketplace*, Cambridge, Mass. and London: Harvard University Press). More pertinent is the following comment: 'Politicians' expertise in policy-making does not necessarily increase their independence from bureaucrats, especially when politicians rely on the bureaucracy for policy staff, and when a highly specialized subject, such as tax policy, tends to create a small circle of specialists (Junko Kato (1994) *The Problem of Bureaucratic Rationality: Tax Politics in Japan*, Princeton: Princeton University Press).
21. For details, see *Asahi Shinbun*, 28 August 1993.
22. A few months before the October 1996 general elections, a new party called *Minshutō* (Democratic Party) was formed, largely from politicians who had belonged to the SDPJ, Shinseitō and Sakigake.

6
Japanese bureaucracy: coping with new challenges

Takashi Inoguchi

In 1995–96 the Japanese bureaucratic system faced a number of extraordinary dilemmas.[1] These ranged from scandals surrounding the government's bail-out of home finance institutions (*jūsen*), and its largesse to pharmaceutical firms that had allowed HIV-contaminated blood to be used in transfusions even though known to be infected, to the *Monju* nuclear reactor accident, and public outrage at local and national bureaucratic business entertaining (*kankan settai*). This chapter takes up the task of making sense of these challenges to the bureaucracy. After summarising the major issues and their key features, we will explore the collective symptoms of a national bureaucracy grappling with global forces impacting on what has for centuries been a domestic political domain.[2]

How these four failures took place

The *jūsen* bailout

Whether or not central government should use taxpayers' money to bail out the bankrupt jūsen loan companies that had made bad housing loans became a major issue of 1995–96. Japan's *jūsen* loan companies had extolled the virtues of home ownership and became the driving force behind dreams of owning one's own home. They were strengthened by a national policy grounded in the logic that citizens (potential voters) would promote political stability by owning their own homes. For the last two decades or so it had been common for financial institutions to make long-term low-interest loans to families who did not yet own their own homes. It was also common practice for the *jūsen* loan companies, as for general loan companies, to use real estate as collateral for these loans.

In the latter half of the 1980s, however, economic circumstances changed substantially. Guided by policies aimed at exchange market liberalisation and expansion of domestic demand, with checks on inflation, the so-called 'bubble economy' blew out rapidly. Much of this was the consequence of reactions to the 1985 Plaza Accord that had forced up the value of the yen, and the *Maekawa Report*, outlining measures for market liberalisation and expansion which were implemented as national government policies. A plan to liberalise the exchange market within the financial services market was promoted. This enabled banks to move into the housing loan market that had until then been the province of the *jūsen* companies. Consequently, as banks occupied more of the market held by the *jūsen* institutions, the latter had no choice but to seek new lending roles. They started to diversify, favouring real estate companies rather than the salaried workers with dreams of owning their own homes, their traditional clients.

The home finance institutions differed from banks in that they did not have their own capital resources. They started drawing money from asset-rich financial institutions that had originally developed out of agricultural co-operatives. Although these had large investment assets, they were often ignorant of practical methods for best using their funds. They followed a trial-and-error method of investment management, without consulting specialist advisers. When the economy overheated at the end of the 1980s, the Ministry of Finance attempted to impose overall regulations on lending institutions, but for some reason, the home finance institutions were exempt from these regulations.

As business conditions further overheated, it became impossible for the government to continue supporting a financial system that was throwing the economy into chaos. In the early 1990s, the bubble burst. The market plunged into recession. Because of the sharp drop in the value of real estate, much of the land that had been used as security for home loans also suddenly fell in value. Like dominoes, the home ownership financial institutions, the agricultural finance institutions, and eventually even the banks themselves faced ruin. Despite their awareness of the imminent threat of large-scale bankruptcy, during the first half of the 1990s all these financial institutions remained impassive. Why, then, did the Ministry of Finance wait until 1995 before it started to address this calamitous situation? One of the Ministry's proposed remedies was to use fiscal 1996 taxpayers' revenues to bail out the bankrupt institutions, a measure that was only passed by the Diet in April 1996.

This fiasco has given rise to many questions. If the financial institutions themselves were aware that their activities would culminate in bankruptcies, why did the government feel responsible for bailing them out? Furthermore, how did the government assess that not only the home finance institutions, but also the local banks and agricultural financial institutions, bear a heavy share of responsibility for the situation? And why is the burden that the government has levied on agricultural financial institutions relatively light, in comparison to the relatively heavy responsibility attributed to the banks? Furthermore, what were the real driving forces behind liberalising the financial market in the wake of the *Maekawa Report*, and why were exceptions later applied to favour jusen related financial institutions? The Ministry of Finance and the Ministry of Agriculture, Forestry and Fisheries are directly involved in the jusen problem.

Let us examine the behaviour of the bureaucracy in the *jūsen* scandal. First, the bureaucracy has taken into account the interests of members of Japanese society who are socially weak and vulnerable. Addressing their concerns has been a pivotal issue for the bureaucracy. The home ownership incentive plan itself is testimony to that. The home finance institutions were regarded as special cases, exempt from general regulations, because they had virtually taken over the roles of banks in providing home buyers with finance. This was in comparison with the relatively light burden imposed on the agricultural financial institutions. The bureaucrats' desire to continue to support a system that encouraged home ownership is obvious. They initiated the move by the government to use taxpayer revenues to prevent the financial institutions from going bankrupt. These were bankruptcies that sent a negative message through the marketplace. The financial system was severely shaken, affecting the entire Japanese economy, which was especially vulnerable while in slow recovery from recession. There were serious repercussions in an electorate which had prided itself on its high savings rate.

Second, relative to the strength of the marketplace, industrial sectors provided a focus for the government's industrial policies for regulation of industry and 'administrative guidance'. When regulatory and other market mechanisms were applied, they did not fit with then-current global liberalisation. Permission was granted both for banks to enter the *jūsen* sphere (*jūsen* had almost taken over the role of the banks in providing home loans) and for large-scale investment by the agricultural financial institutions in the *jūsen* financial system. Even when the sharp fall in the value of mortgages continued, no real action was taken on the mortgages that the agricultural financial institutions had used as security by way of an agreement between the Ministry of Finance and the Ministry of Agriculture, Forestry and Fisheries. The Ministries' inaction is revealing.

So is their action. By defending the financial institutions the Ministry of Finance and the Ministry of Agriculture, Forestry and Fisheries both sent clear signs of their preferential treatment of workplaces that figure prominently as destinations for bureaucratic *amakudari* (literally, descent from heaven).[3] The Ministry of Finance especially had targeted the home finance institutions as eventual workplaces for its retiring bureaucrats. Today, however, amakudari works against labour market trends in an age of global market liberalisation, since it usually functions as a delayed remuneration for poorly-paid bureaucrats, compensation for their strong performance during long years of active service. Bureaucrats must retire at a relatively early age (from their mid-40s to the beginning of their 50s), and if they cannot be guaranteed a second or third career destination, clearly their morale will fall.

In this context it is important to note that bureaucratic salaries are comparatively less than those for workers in large private sector enterprises. For middle-to-upper-echelon bureaucrats, their salary is less than half that for comparable positions in the private sector. If bureaucrats perceive that they will not be rewarded with amakudari, they are likely to leave the bureaucracy and join the private sector much earlier in their careers. If the Japanese bureaucratic system inherited the samurai spirit, upholding the ideals of strength and endurance in the context of a simple, economical lifestyle, this tenacity is not everlasting. Even though bureaucrats enjoy certain benefits such as the shield of official authority and a great deal of political power and social prestige, the prospect of losing their opportunity for amakudari is becoming a matter of increasing concern for them.

Ten years ago, one *amakudari* destination was sufficient, but in the mid-1990s, if a bureaucrat does not have a number of temporary amakudari destinations arranged for post-retirement employment, his remuneration will not be enough to support him and his family. If one does not wear many hats, it is virtually impossible to survive financially.

The HIV contamination

The Ministry of Health and Welfare has a fixed procedure under law for dealing with treated blood products to guarantee their safety in blood transfusions. Despite this procedural requirement, the Pharmaceutical Affairs Bureau in the Ministry of Health and Welfare acted to protect huge profits of the pharmaceutical and medical industries by failing to apply the legislation to ban the sale and use of infected treated blood products. The Ministry of Health and Welfare knew that the blood was tainted with the HIV-AIDS virus, and therefore could be responsible for the transmission of AIDS across the country. Nonetheless the Ministry continued to conceal this information for over ten years.

Hashimoto Ryūtarō, who was the Health and Welfare Minister at the time, expedited a complete policy reversal when he became Prime Minister in 1996, appointing Kan Naoto as Welfare Minister. Kan, a former active participant in citizens' movements, continued to criticise the actions of the Health and Welfare Ministry even after becoming a Diet member. Immediately after assuming his Cabinet appointment, Kan learned that the Ministry of Health and Welfare had permitted the sale and use of AIDS-infected blood, He issued a full-scale public apology and promised to guarantee compensation to infected patients. The bureaucracy, however, had not wanted even to admit its impropriety, let alone promise compensation.

What are the points to be noted in this situation? The first concerns the increasing power of the politicians *vis-à-vis* the bureaucrats. Minister Kan was a new appointee. Because he had not risen through the Ministry of Health and Welfare, he was free of ties to the bureaucratic power structure. This is significant, since in Japan it has been the bureaucracy, rather than politicians, who emanated an aura of superiority and efficiency; independent actions by politicians are relatively rare. In recent years they have been more frequent than many realise. In the first half of the 1990s, Koizumi Junichirō, as the Post and Telecommunications Minister, and Nishioka Takeo, as the Education Minister, undertook radical policy and personnel changes to reverse bureaucratic decisions. In the future we may see similar decisive behaviour from politicians, especially as the importance of the public sector *vis-à-vis* the private sector declines.

The increase in private sector activity under conditions of global market liberalisation has marked a major turning point in bureaucratic involvement. These conditions have meant that by comparison with the public sector, which remained tightly constrained by national borders and taxes, the self-confident private sector's strength has naturally increased. Since politicians largely represent the interests of the private sector, their power is also increasing with a more powerful private sector.[4]

The second point to be noted is the disproportionate clout of 'generalists' over 'specialists'. In the Japanese bureaucracy, emphasis is placed on 'impartial and neutral' judgments based on a lofty overview of society. Attention should be paid to this emphasis, for, in a system charged with having a hierarchical structure, narrow viewpoint and pro-government bias, how these affect the bureaucracy's capacity for impartiality must be considered. Within the bureaucracy, generalists are lauded while specialists are targets of scorn. Specialists are considered to be 'subject-specific fools' who insist on following their narrow viewpoints and interests and find it difficult to be representative of the system as a whole. For this reason, technical officers with specialised knowledge are often ranked at a much lower level than generalists. Often, generalists, who tend to come from law schools, have high levels of responsibility, and can intimidate technical officers.

Miyamoto Masao's experiences are one particularly well-known example. After becoming a medical doctor and working in an American hospital, Miyamoto became a quarantine officer in the Ministry of Health and Welfare. He then wrote a book that criticised the Japanese bureaucratic system, and was subsequently in effect forced to resign.[5]

Like Miyamoto, technical officers in the Ministry of Health and Welfare's Pharmaceutical Affairs Bureau have also been intimidated. They, too, have turned against the system and have taken defiant stances on contentious issues. In order to do so, they have developed a strategy of nurturing close relationships with industry. In the Pharmaceutical Affairs Bureau, people regarded as generalists have often not received an appropriate level of education in pharmaceutical affairs. Rather, as high-level employees who are proud of their loyalty, personal ethics and sense of responsibility, they rely for their credibility on the widely accepted idea that they are capable of comparatively balanced judgments. In Japan, possessing a doctorate is considered a barrier to promotion within the bureaucracy. So generalists who hold high positions in the Ministry of Health and Welfare often have to take on trust reports prepared by specialist groups. They are also influenced by reports presented by non-governmental committees and research groups (the 'academic group'), consisting of doctors and pharmacists.

Dr Abe Takeshi, a medical doctor and former leader of the Ministry of Health and Welfare's AIDS research group, stated in a scholarly journal that untreated blood products should not be used because they carried the risk of AIDS contamination.

Nevertheless, while he was head of the research group, the ministry took completely the opposite action.[6]

A third point to be noted is the close relationship between the bureaucracy and industry. Through the Tokugawa and Meiji eras, up to the present, these relationships have been distinctive. The official stance of the bureaucracy — that it represents justice, neutrality, and the common good of the people — has been extremely difficult to maintain. The heart of the problem lies in the huge disparity between the official stance and reality. As the private sector consolidated its strength, the bureaucracy became quasi-representative of the gains of the private sector, because of 'lobbyist' pressure. Bureaucracy has assumed the character of a special branch office of industry with its own interests and boundaries. There is increasing pressure on the bureaucracy to disclose such information, a problem remaining to be tackled head-on in the future.

The Monju nuclear power plant accident

At the Monju nuclear power plant in Fukui prefecture, plutonium is combined with uranium in a nuclear reactor. The plant functions as an extremely efficient energy source. Damage to any one part of the reactor causes the entire system to be shut down. In 1995, an accident at the reactor allowed liquid sodium to escape, producing a volatile situation where a major explosion was highly possible. The nature of the accident was only disclosed publicly on videotape some time afterwards. Public outrage about the incident led the plant's information officer to suicide.

There are a number of important features to be noticed about this. First, there is the difficult political problem surrounding the potential linkage between nuclear energy and nuclear weapons. Because of a delay in disclosing information about the Monju incident to the public, formation of a consensual resolution to the problem was also delayed. A key consideration was that Japan is a resource-poor country (especially in fossil fuels) and so needs to import a high percentage of petroleum from overseas. Fears that global petroleum reserves will run out in some thirty to fifty years, have focused attention on the use of nuclear energy as an alternative energy resource. Nuclear energy is, however, rather easily capable of conversion to nuclear weapons, making the nuclear debate highly sensitive. Grassroots opposition in Japan to the very existence of nuclear power plants has been extremely strong. Clearly, a high degree of prudence is necessary when dealing with matters concerning nuclear power generation. While some in the bureaucracy were aware of the inherent dangers of the accident at the Monju reactor and were devising strategies for its management, they did not make special plans to inform the public about the potential gravity of the situation. Instead, the bureaucrats remained obstinate in their silence, not even seriously considering providing a detailed explanation to the public.

Generalists, not specialists, are those within the bureaucracy who have the right to make public announcements. Yet they have an unfortunate tendency of conforming strictly to national policy. Scientists and other specialists who are affiliated with deliberative committees and research groups follow suit. One could go so far as to say that because there is so little public discussion of issues, there is a tendency not to pay adequate attention to relevant information. This is especially the case with new scientific opinions.

Kankan settai

Kankan settai is the practice of the officers of local municipalities providing business entertainment for their counterparts at the same level in the national bureaucracy. Basically, this involves using public funds to draw favourable treatment from the federal authorities, with officials of local municipalities entertaining federal officials either while they visit the locality on inspection tours or at the municipalities' offices in Tokyo. Funds spent in this way are referred to as *shokuryōhi* (expenditure on food and entertainment).

In 1993, Nagasaki prefecture spent 117 million yen on kankan settai, 70 per cent of which was spent by the prefecture's Tokyo office. The local municipalities argue that if they do not adhere to this tradition, they will not receive appropriate levels of funding from the central government. According to Governor Tanaka of Nagasaki Prefecture:

> When the bureaucrats go out drinking, it is not thought of as entertainment — completely the opposite, in fact. Rather, for the sake of the welfare of the local area, the bureaucrats offer their time until the middle of the night. We feel business entertaining makes working so late more enjoyable. As other prefectural governors are desperately competing for large projects for their areas, we cannot help but follow this fixed practice. Because of the entertainment, working late is definitely effective.

Even though the power of the federal government has weakened while authority has decentralised, this has not led to the disappearance of *kankan settai*. There has been no change in the division of responsibility for projects. Both urban and rural prefectures still carry out small projects, with larger projects coming under the jurisdiction of the federal government.

A significant feature of *kankan settai* is that it is similar to the earlier links between the central government and local municipalities, where authorities from the capital city set out on inspection tours of localities and were entertained in high style so that they did not receive a negative report. In recent times, although the principal purpose has changed (to become acquisition of funds), and business entertainment in Tokyo has become important, the principle of currying favour has not altered. Local municipalities are entrusted with various duties which can be divided into two main types: they act as agents for the federal government, and have responsibility for carrying out local affairs.

In past times the power held by the local municipalities ranged over a wide variety of areas, within the boundaries set by central government. Local municipalities were responsible for construction, transportation, education, and welfare, and basically kept the federal government's policy changes on track. Central government was responsible for areas like national security and the economy, and developed courses of action for the municipal authorities to carry out. As with current arrangements, the municipalities were limited in their courses of action. Where they failed accurately to determine the mood of central government authorities, and to be granted as much freedom in their decisions as possible, it became common for municipalities to use entertainment as a strategy. For the central government authorities, the agenda was judgment of the capacity of their local agents and assessing the mood of the times, including ensuring proper implementation out of national policies. It was from this tradition that drinking with and becoming acquainted with colleagues arose.

With the lengthy period of recession in the 1990s, the '3Ks' *kōsaihi* (social/entertainment expenses) *kōtsūhi* (travel expenses), and *kōkokuhi* (advertising expenses), were cut back. Japanese citizens have come to expect bureaucrats to show some self-discipline. Despite the recession the municipal level has been slow to respond to needs for economy, leading to public opposition.[7]

Let us now turn to the role of the bureaucracy as pivotal in Japanese history. Then we will consider the specific features of the four failures in the context of Japanese politics. Pursuing this can provide us with insight not only into why the bureaucracy behaved as it did, but also into what it should do to cope with situations like these in future.

The pivotal role of the bureaucracy in Japan

The bureaucratic system formed around the central government in Japan can be understood in several ways: in terms of ancient or traditional statutes; by laws introduced during the Meiji era; or by focusing on the bureaucracy in the post-war era. The bureaucracy is especially powerful in modern Japan. Its origins are in the Tokugawa era. Consideration of this history is crucial, in order to deepen understanding of the ethos and behaviour of the bureaucracy in its present form.[8]

The first conspicuous feature of the Japanese bureaucratic system is that in its early days, it did not follow European lines. In Japan, the political system did not emerge from medieval absolutism. The foundations of its political structure were laid in the early years of the reign of Tokugawa Ieyasu (17th century). The disarmed *samurai* occupied positions in the bureaucracy which was the core of the Japanese political system, so that such values as organisational loyalty, ethics, and high educational attainment permeated the system.

Except for the Edo shogunate, the bureaucracy of each clan was extremely small, and the numbers of *samurai* who lived on land near the castles were in the tens or hundreds. Instead of their assuming roles as leaders of town and village administration, merchants and farmers formed the administrative network. Today, the 'smallness' of government is a major feature of the Japanese bureaucracy. As this small-scale bureaucratic system continued to grow, the upper classes of the samurai groups residing in the towns near the castles did not always hold title to their lands. In the period after the Middle Ages, through continuous modifications in land-holding, there were few samurai in the upper classes who held assets other than land.

Characteristics of 'smallness' and 'consensus majority' were reinforced in the modern age. At the beginning of the twentieth century, a majority of the bureaucracy came from the former samurai class (even in the 1920s, 50 per cent of bureaucrats came from samurai class families). The bureaucracy inherited the practice of using university graduation as the main factor in determining its hierarchical system. There was no change in the trademarks of organisational loyalty and ethics.

The concept of consensus majority was further strengthened after the Meiji Restoration mobilised national sentiment centring around the Emperor, and expanded political participation from local to national levels. The bureaucratic system represented and emphasised the acquisition of public good and gains for the whole nation, in turn strengthening its own claims to legitimacy. Concurrently, by introducing a national parliamentary system, the bureaucracy promoted a positive image of neutrality and fairness.

After World War II, despite the reforms carried out by the Occupation forces, the structure of the bureaucratic system remained essentially intact; in fact, over the course of the following half-century, these traditional aspects became even stronger. One reason may be that the influence of the main competitors of the bureaucracy during the first half of the twentieth century was considerably weakened. Another reason could be that because the public sector played such an important role in Japan's post-war reconstruction and growth, the bureaucracy's pre-war power base became even stronger. One can argue that in the few years directly after the War (the Reconstruction Era), the Economic Stabilisation Board was the power centre of government; that in the intermediate post-war period (the period of high-speed growth), it was the Ministry of International Trade and Industry; and that in the later post-war period (from the first oil shock of the early 1970s), it was the Ministry of Finance. 'Small' government prospered during these periods, making the best use of quasi-governmental auxiliary organisations and sub-contracting enterprises. National consensus on economic priorities was further consolidated under the guidance of the LDP. A clear division of labour developed between the bureaucracy in Tokyo in charge of policy and the members of the political parties, especially the LDP, who were in charge of the electorates in voting districts.

In order to explain the relatively steady decline in the influence of the public sector and the bureaucratic system, it is necessary to consider the role played by global trends. Since the mid-1980s, the Plaza Accord and its consequences, the globalisation of economic activities and the further liberalisation of markets have played major roles in terms of reducing the relative importance of the post-war bureaucratic system. It is evident that these international trends have had a significant impact. Indeed, they have come as major shocks to the bureaucracy, especially as market liberalisation has encroached on its former domain. It has not been easy for the bureaucracy to withstand these powerful tides of globalisation and liberalisation because it has maintained its assumptions about the self-contained nature and permanence of Japan's bureaucratic framework within its national borders, one that has endured for many centuries. Through its important duties of monitoring projects and providing guidance and caution to project workers the bureaucracy has not simply survived, but has effectively governed the nation.

The nature of the challenge facing Japan's bureaucratic structure has changed in every period of the country's history. Concerns about religious influence and colonisation from abroad led to Japan's isolation in the early modern period of its history (the Tokugawa period, seventeenth to mid-nineteenth centuries). These challenges, which mainly centred on military unification and political stability, were domestic in nature. During this period, the bureaucracy succeeded in defining its own character.

Moving into the modern period (Meiji-Taishō-Shōwa periods, mid-nineteenth to late twentieth centuries) the challenges facing Japan became international in nature and scope, and, in rising to them, the slogan of 'rich nation, strong army' was born in the early Meiji years. Japan's way of meeting these external challenges was to confront them together. It has continued this approach. Thus, even after World War II, when the nature of international competition changed from military to economic, there were no fundamental changes. Japan resolved not to lose its foreign competitiveness, and the bureaucracy followed suit, returning to its earlier character.

The inevitable forces of economic liberalisation and market globalisation started to permeate the bureaucratic system from around the time of the Plaza Accord of 1985. Hitherto the challenges facing the so-called modern Japanese bureaucracy had allowed it to continue operating according to the notion of Japan as a single entity. This notion became unsustainable as the country was drawn into a global economy, and distinctions based on national borders became ambiguous or irrelevant as the effects of mutual interdependence among nations have intensified.

This gives rise to a series of big questions that will help explain how these challenges will be taken up. How will liberalisation and globalisation impinge? How will these global forces develop? How can these concepts be uniformly applied all over the world? The major concern should be recognising the point at which the economy, government, society, and culture should be maintained within fixed boundaries. The major challenge directly confronting the Japanese bureaucratic system, especially given its historical character, is how domestic security and stability can be maintained.[9]

Many have given careful thought to how effective the semi-hallowed tradition of the Japanese bureaucratic system remains. The succession of scandals involving the bureaucracy, including those dealt with here, have created public disaffection. Let us consider the bureaucracy's response.

How the bureaucracy manages scandal

The *Jūsen* bailout

The *jūsen* was a forced breakthrough for the Ministry of Finance. Although various methods for handling the situation were suggested from both within and outside government offices, the status quo has prevailed. The *jūsen* problem has not been completely resolved by the use of public expenditures. The bureaucracy has reaffirmed its role as the organ responsible for protecting the socially disadvantaged, so the agricultural financial institutions and trust companies could be legitimately bailed out. Skirting criticism of the use of public funds, the Ministry of Finance has requested those financial institutions involved in the bailout, especially city banks, to raise funds to reimburse public monies used to bail out the financial institutions. It must also be noted that rather than liberating financial markets, Japan continues to exercise caution in this area. Difficulties in the progress of securities market negotiations between Japan and the United States are a manifestation of this caution. Since 1994 a notion has been gaining currency that by attempting to wrestle concurrently with market liberalisation and expanding domestic demand, the Ministry of Finance invited both the creation of the bubble economy and then its collapse. The extent of the role played by the United States is well recognised in this perception. With global trends, there are fears that excessive and hasty market liberalisation domestically could rupture the nation's cultural identity.

The *jūsen* episode confirms the Japanese bureaucracy's tenacity in carrying out its role while bending to public criticism, and its continuing concern for weak sectors of Japanese society.

The HIV contamination

The Minister of Health and Welfare, Kan Naoto, made a highly political and courageous decision in handling this case. On learning of the problem, the Minister forced the responsible officials to be redeployed, and to own up to their direct involvement in the infected blood affair. This caused the bureaucracy itself to be charged with responsibility for clarifying what had happened. It was not unusual for Kan to have acted as he did; those in the most responsible positions have often responded to inherent weaknesses within the bureaucratic system. It was to be expected that intervention by politicians levelling criticism at an intermittently lax bureaucratic system would lead to some improvements. In June 1996, the Tokyo Prosecutor's Office started its investigation of the key officials and doctors involved for allegedly 'causing death while on duty'. It appears as if key people like Professor Abe who worked for the Ministry's research group might be indicted, while other prominent actors like key bureaucrats might be indicted for minor offences. This outcome is basically consistent with the Japanese bureaucracy's time-honoured ways of handling failures and mistakes.

The Monju nuclear accident

The Japanese government's treatment of the Monju reactor accident, coupled with the methods used for handling plutonium in nuclear power generation (which is related to the larger problem of the nation's expanding demand for energy), also ties in with concerns for the country's long-term survival. International opinion (including that of the United States government) is sceptical of Japan's continuously independent stance on methods of using plutonium. Against this, the government argued that Japan was forced to adhere to its policy so as not to retard the nation's technological development. Assuming that popular opinion was crucial in supporting this stance, high level councils, executive deliberative committees, and study groups were organised to influence public opinion.

The Monju episode has many of the features of the Japanese bureaucracy's response to very serious issues. The officer in charge committed suicide, taking responsibility himself. There was clearly general ignorance of the science involved on the part of bureaucratic generalists. There was general secrecy about what was a highly sensitive matter, and the bureaucracy mounted an aggressive campaign to put its views to the public.

Kankan settai

The *kankan settai* issue was handled by gradually reducing the amounts spent on by local government entertaining central government officials. Central government has recentralised its power in areas such as national security and national emergencies where it should not have delegated such power to local governments. It has also begun to delegate power to local governments in those areas where these governments should handle their own affairs within the larger national framework. Within the central government, provision has been made for dealing with the competitive nature of relations between different divisions. Using decentralisation of authority as a slogan, the Ministry of Home Affairs has preferred to put responsibility for such arrangements under its own jurisdiction. Big business and the Office of the Prime Minister have, however, insisted on a two-pronged policy direction: that the central government maintain an iron grip on certain essential areas such as guaranteeing national security, while working towards a complete transfer of power in most other areas. The latest legislation for a rise in the consumption tax from 3 per cent to 5 per cent provides a financial basis for such policy initiatives to take root, since one-half of the consumption tax increase will go directly to local government, without going via central government. In other words, local government officials will not feel the need for *kankan settai* to central government officials since they will have their own tax revenue available in abundance. This response represents the pragmatic and largely effective style of the Japanese bureaucracy in handling its mistakes.

In examining the above scandals, we can observe that the pivotal nature of the bureaucracy within the Japanese government appears to be gradually changing. Historically, the bureaucratic system was the sole authority around which society was constructed, but even with the recent scandals, this situation has not changed. Comparisons with the United States and France are instructive. In the United States, the President, Congress, the judiciary, and the state governments that make up the system either overrule or overwhelm the bureaucracy. The bureaucratic system in the United States is important, yet it is not pivotal to the government system as is the case in Japan. In France, politicians, bureaucrats, and industrialists co-operate at the top of the power structure, which is decidedly different from the situation in Japan. Japanese bureaucrats scorn politicians and prefer to target industry through regulation and administrative guidance. Even from a sociological viewpoint, the 'iron triangle' in Japan is weak.

Accordingly, if the bureaucratic system collapses, Japan will find itself in a potentially dangerous position. Yet the fact remains that the Japanese bureaucracy has been bewildered by challenges presented by the global scale of current market liberalisation. It seems, however, that during the process of its pragmatic, piecemeal, and occasionally clumsy and mistake-riven adaptation, the Japanese bureaucracy will not lose its pivotal position in Japanese society.

Notes

1. See Takashi Inoguchi, 'Kanryō: The Japanese Bureaucracy in History's Eve', a paper presented, and later revised for the conference on Crisis and Change in Japan Today, Seattle, 20–21 October 1995; 'The Pragmatic Evolution of Japanese Democratic Politics', in Michelle Schiegelow (ed.) *Democracy in Asia*, Frankfurt: Campus-Verlag; New York: St Martins Press, forthcoming; 'Malaise dans la bureaucratie Japonaise', *Le Monde*, 29 June 1996; Takashi Inoguchi, *Japan: The Governing of an Economic Superpower*, Routledge, forthcoming, English translation of *Nihon keizai no seiji unei*, 1993.
2. These will be based on accounts in Japan's major daily newspapers like *Asahi, Nikkei, Yomiuri* and *Mainichi*.
3. Inoki Takenori (1996) *Gakkō to kyōiku* (Schools and education), Iwanami shoten; Hyung-Ki Kim *et al.*, (eds) (1995) *The Japanese Civil Service and Economic Development*, Oxford: Clarendon Press.
4. See Inoguchi Takashi and Iwai Tomoaki (1987) *Zoku giin no kenkyū* (A study of legislative tribes), Tokyo: Nihon keizai shinbunsha.
5. Masao Miyamoto (1994) *The Straitjacket Society: A Rebel Bureaucrat Tells All*, New York: Kodansha America.
6. 'Mr Abe Takashi Argued in his Article that Not Adding Heat is Dangerous', *Mainichi Shinbun*, 17 April 1996.
7. Inoguchi, 'The Pragmatic Evolution of Japanese Democratic Politics'.
8. Stability, cohesiveness, and identity are some key words of those writers who might be called cultural nationalists such as Sakakibara Eisuke, Nishibe Susumu, Ogura Kazuo, and Eto Jun. See Takashi Inoguchi (1993) 'The Emerging Japanese Debate on its Future Course', in *Beginnings of the Soviet-German and the US–Japanese Wars and Fifty Years After*, edited by the Institute of American and Canadian Studies and the Institute for the Culture of German-speaking Areas, Sophia University.
9. Inoguchi, 'Malaise dans la bureaucratie Japonaise' 1996.

7
A story of three booms: from the New Liberal Club to the Hosokawa coalition government

Steven R. Reed

In the general election of 1976, Japan's conservative political establishment was rocked by the Lockheed Scandal. Hearings in the US Senate Committee on Foreign Relations revealed that Lockheed Aircraft had made illegal payments to politicians in several countries, including Japan, as part of a worldwide campaign to boost the sales of its aircraft.[1] The Japanese public was treated to the spectacle of leading politicians repeating the phase 'I have no recollection of that' (*kioku ga nai*) while testifying about their role in the affair. In protest, a small group defected from the ruling Liberal Democratic Party (LDP) and formed the New Liberal Club (NLC). The electorate responded enthusiastically, producing an 'NLC boom'. Due in part to the defections and the NLC boom, the LDP failed to win an outright majority for the first time since it was founded in 1955, though it was quickly able to make up the difference with conservative independents (LDP candidates running without an official nomination). Unfortunately for the NLC, however, the boom produced only seventeen seats and was limited to a single election. After the 1986 election the party was forced to admit failure, and its members rejoined the LDP.

In 1989, in the midst of the Recruit Scandal and controversy over the introduction of a consumption tax, the Japan Socialist Party (JSP), led by Doi Takako, the first female leader of a major party in Japanese history, captured the imagination of the electorate. The 1989 House of Councillors election and the 1990 general election witnessed a 'Doi boom'. More voters chose the JSP than the LDP in the proportional representation vote and the JSP won twenty-three of the twenty-six single-member districts which pitted candidates from the two major parties against each other in head-on contests. The 1989 House of Councillors election was the first actual electoral defeat in LDP history and, followed by the 1990 lower house election, constituted the first break in the pattern of long-term socialist decline which had begun in 1960.[2] Unfortunately for Doi and the JSP, however, this boom failed to last through the next House of Councillors election in 1992. In the next general election in 1993, the socialist vote returned to its previous pattern of secular decline as if nothing had happened.

In 1993, the Kyōwa scandal, the Sagawa Kyūbin scandal, the *Zenekon* scandals and revelations about the financial practices of LDP vice-president Kanemaru Shin once again shook the conservative establishment. The scale of the corruption uncovered reached new heights. Three new parties presented candidates in this election: the Japan New Party (JNP), the Renewal Party (Shinseitō) and the New Harbinger Party (Shintō Sakigake), the latter two being splinters from the LDP like the NLC before them. The 'New Party boom' of 1993 finally brought an end to the thirty-eight year dominance of the LDP. The Hosokawa coalition government formed after the 1993 election included all parties except the LDP and the Communists. The new government enacted a major political reform, something which the LDP had repeatedly promised but never delivered.

Each of these booms was produced by the interaction of an electorate frustrated with the corruption of the ruling conservative regime and the creation of attractive new alternatives. Frustration alone produced no boom because none of the traditional opposition parties could be considered a viable alternative to the LDP. the 1989–90 boom was not a 'JSP boom' but a 'Doi boom'. Doi managed to create a new image for the party, but once she was replaced as socialist leader, the old images returned. The LDP suffered losses of electoral support in the 1983 election which was marked by the 'guilty' verdict handed down on ex-Prime Minister Tanaka Kakuei for his role in the Lockheed scandal. The pattern of LDP losses was similar to that of 1976, but there was no boom in 1983 because there were no attractive alternatives for voters.

The purpose of this chapter is to analyse the interaction between electorate and the elite, between voter frustration and the options offered by political parties in these three boom elections.

Each of these booms produced more change than the one before. The NLC boom helped deprive the LDP of its Diet 'working majority' (enough to both chair and control a majority on all of the committees), producing significant changes in the legislative process.[3] The Doi boom deprived the LDP of its absolute majority, albeit only in the less powerful upper house. Finally, the Japan New Party boom forced the LDP out of power completely, if temporarily, and into coalition with the socialists when it returned. The Japanese party system has been permanently altered, though the new system has yet to take shape.

Given these escalating effects, it would seem reasonable to hypothesise that the electorate grew increasingly frustrated with each new scandal, especially in view of the number and magnitude of the incriminating revelations leading up to the 1993 election. This 'frustration' hypothesis states that the LDP finally lost its control of government when the electorate grew angry enough to kick them out.

A second interpretation is also possible: that the increasing effects of each boom had more to do with the choices offered the electorate than the mood of the voters. It is possible that public ire did not increase significantly, that the electorate was perfectly ready to unseat the LDP in 1976, 1983, and again in 1990 if only it were offered a realistic alternative. According to this 'alternative option' hypothesis, the voters were ready in 1976 but the politicians were not. It took politicians some time to recognise the force of public demand and to organise the new political parties necessary to take advantage of it.

At the simplest level, the 'alternative option' hypothesis is supported by the increasing number of candidates in each boom, covering an increasing percentage of electoral districts. In 1976 the NLC attracted only five LDP incumbents and ran only twenty-five candidates overall. In 1990 the JSP, as an established national party, was able to field candidates in all but three districts, though they failed to nominate enough to form a majority even if all were elected. However, there were no conservative defectors who could bring conservative supporters with them into the anti-LDP camp and the boom was dampened by the reluctance of some conservative voters to express their frustration with the LDP by voting socialist. In 1993, there was a total of forty-six defectors from the LDP, almost ten times the NLC number. There were twenty-five districts with no new party candidate, but many voters, primarily in urban areas, were presented with choices among two or more new parties. In 1993 Japanese voters were offered serious conservative alternatives to the LDP for the first time since 1955.

Using candidate-level data, I will analyse each of these three booms in an attempt to unravel the complex interactions between elite and mass, between parties and candidates on the one hand and voters on the other. My results support the 'alternative option' hypothesis overall but with a surprising twist: the booms started out stronger in urban areas but grew weaker there while gaining strength in rural areas, leaving the overall power of each boom much the same when aggregated to the national level. The NLC boom was stronger in urban areas. The Doi boom was somewhat stronger in rural than urban areas, and the JNP boom was significantly stronger in rural districts. While the 'frustration' hypothesis fits the pattern found in rural districts, the opposite, an 'apathy' hypothesis, fits the pattern found in urban districts.

Analysing Japanese elections at the candidate level

Multi-member districts (MMD, also called the single-non-transferable vote or SNTV) make Japanese elections extremely difficult to analyse. Each district contains several incumbents and several challengers, some of whom have won previous elections. Japanese voters are seldom presented with the same set of options in two consecutive elections. Parties may run in a particular district in one election but drop out in the next or they might increase or decrease the number of candidates in the district. We can solve many of these problems by dropping the analysis from the national to the candidate level. At this level we can estimate 'effective public opinion', the degree to which a party label, issue stand, or other candidate characteristic either increases or decreases that candidate's overall vote.

The dependent variable in the following analysis will be the candidate's vote as a percentage of the district electorate, i.e., the candidate's vote divided not by the total vote but by the total number of eligible voters.[4] This figure controls both for population growth or decline and changes in turnout. When dealing with questions concerning the distribution of seats, the percentage of the vote is the appropriate measure, but when the question involves the response of the electorate to party and candidate strategies, one should treat abstention as a real option and use the percentage of the electorate.

The first independent variable is the candidate's percentage of the electorate in the previous election. We are interested in change so we must control for the candidate's electoral base. We wish to know how much the boom added to that base. This calculation presents no problem for candidates who ran in both the current and the previous election, but we are particularly concerned with new candidates, those who did not run in the previous election. Fortunately, it is usually easy to identify successors to particular retiring candidates and the latter's vote can be used as the baseline for the new candidate. For small parties with only one candidate in the district, coding is easy: the retiring DSP (Democratic Socialist Party) candidate was replaced by the new DSP candidate. The LDP runs more than one candidate per district but the information about which new candidate is each retiring candidate's successor is often included in newspaper reports and is available in the current data set.[5]

New party candidates cause the most trouble, but many did run in the previous election. Experienced independents, usually conservative, are the major recruiting ground for new parties precisely because they come with an established electoral base. Quite a few new party candidates are sons of retiring LDP MPs, and I use their father's vote as the baseline. It might seem reasonable to say that a brand new candidate for a brand new party received zero votes in the previous election but that causes serious problems with the statistical estimation. And, in fact, even brand new candidates normally have some electoral base, often from elections to the prefectural or municipal assembly. We have no estimate for these electoral bases from other elections and must thus exclude these candidates from the analysis. This causes the most problems estimating the votes for the JNP, many of whose candidates had never before run for the Diet.

We must also control for district level factors, particularly the changing number of candidates running from the same party. Most notably, the LDP often reduces the number of nominated candidates and may even be able to prevent conservative independents from running when the party fortunes look dim. LDP candidates may survive scandal elections, or even personal scandals, by picking up votes from retiring conservative candidates. For example, imagine a district with three conservative candidates in 1972, A with 60,000 votes, B with 55,000 votes, and C with 50,000 votes. Candidate A is caught in the Lockheed scandal but C retires with no successor, leaving only two conservatives in 1976. Imagine further that candidate A receives 65,000 votes in 1976. The increase could well be explained by choices made by the 50,000 conservatives who voted for candidate C in 1972, and the fact that candidate A's votes increased by only 5000 under these circumstances could indicate that the voters did indeed punish him or her for involvement in the scandal. I thus coded a variable called the 'district vote' to account for these factors. In this case, the 'district vote' would be 25,000 for both candidates A and B, assuming each candidate has an equal chance of picking up the supporters of candidate C.

The opposite phenomenon also occurs: a party which expects to gain votes tends to run more candidates. For example, in the 1990 election, many JSP incumbents were forced to share the Doi boom with a new socialist candidate running in the same district. Some incumbents' votes fell, not because there was no boom, but because the boom was split between two candidates. When a party increases the number of candidates in a district, the 'district vote' variable is coded as the negative of the votes received by the new candidate divided by the total number of candidates. In the simplest case, the socialists run one candidate in a district in 1986 but two in 1990. If the new socialist received 50,000 votes, the value of the 'district vote' variable for the old candidate is –50,000. In both positive and negative cases, it is important to include the votes of independents from the same camp. A conservative (or socialist) candidate is hurt or helped as much by the entry and exit of a conservative (or socialist) independent as by a nominated candidate.

Both the previous vote and the district vote are control variables, designed to prevent us from misinterpreting the other statistical results. The variables of primary interest are the party labels, each coded as a dichotomous 0 or 1. For example, the LDP variable is 1 for LDP candidates and 0 for all others, including conservative independents. The 'LDP variable' is designed to estimate how much the LDP label helped or hurt a candidate in the average. Conservative candidates may run as independents precisely to avoid partaking in the party image. In other cases, scandal-tainted candidates are denied the official nomination to keep their image from damaging that of the party. I have made an exception to this coding rule for independents from the booming parties. In 1990 many new socialist candidates ran as independents supported by Rengō, the newly unified federation of labour unions. These independents were clearly favoured by the boom, probably even more than nominated candidates. The same logic applies to independents supported by the JNP in 1993 and, with somewhat less force, to conservative independents supported by the NLC in 1976.

Finally, I have coded another dichotomous variable 1 for candidates personally implicated in a scandal of some sort, and 0 otherwise. We wish to know whether voters abandoned individual candidates tainted with scandal above and beyond any tendency to abandon the LDP for one of the booming alternatives.

The New Liberal Club boom

Table 7.1 presents the results of the analysis of the 1976 election. Looking first at the analysis covering all districts, we find first that both the 'previous vote' and 'district vote' control variables are significant and important. Ignoring either factor would have produced inaccurate estimates for the remaining variables. Both the LDP and JSP party labels lost votes, but by insignificant amounts. Surprisingly, LDP candidates did not, on the average, suffer from the Lockheed scandal. On the other hand, the NLC label produced an impressive gain of 5 percentage points or over 34,000 votes per candidates. No commentator could miss a boom of this magnitude.

Table 7.1   Voting in the 1976 election

	All districts		Districts with NLC candidates	
Constant	2.093		2.963	
Previous vote	0.826		0.659	
District vote	0.380		0.187	
LDP	−0.003	(NS)	−0.348	(NS)
JSP	−0.264	(NS)	−0.573	(NS)
NLC	5.071		6.750	
Scandal	−2.489		−3.210	
R-square	0.744		0.653	
N	670.0		117.0	

Scandals cost a candidate 2.5 percentage points of the vote or about 15,000 votes. At the time many commentators missed this phenomenon, focusing instead on the fact that most scandal-tainted candidates were re-elected and that one even gained votes. For example, Blaker argues that 'When the time came to vote,

Lockheed apparently was not in the minds of many Japanese, especially in the rural areas where five of the six Lockheed-associated candidates were successful'.[6] This misinterpretation is based on three errors.

First, one cannot interpret voting behaviour by looking at whether a candidate won or lost. The people speak in votes, not in seats. In the United States, scandal-tainted incumbents also tend to lose votes, but about 75 per cent are re-elected.[7] In Japan, the analogous figure is between 60 and 66 per cent depending on what is counted as a scandal. Japanese and American voters respond to scandals in broadly similar ways, but the effect on candidates is greater in Japan. The difference between Japan and the United States is not in voter attitudes, but is primarily a matter of the greater difficulty of unseating incumbents in the single-member districts used in that country. Second, the total vote received by a scandal-tainted candidate is also misleading. One should not expect voters to forget everything else they know about a candidate, everything that led them to vote for him or her in the past, and evaluate them exclusively on the single new fact of recent involvement in a scandal. The movement of votes, gains or losses, is the best measure of the effect of a scandal.[8] Finally, the effect of scandals is often invisible until one controls for the district vote. A reduction in the number of conservative candidates can compensate for the votes lost because of a scandal. One candidate implicated in the Lockheed scandal actually saw his vote go up. He gained 4.057 votes over his 1972 total, but two conservative independents retired, leaving 50,600 loose votes to be divided among six LDP candidates (district votes = 8,433). To get at the electorate's response to scandals, one must control for the strategic responses of the parties and candidates.

Kabashima and Miyake have each demonstrated that voting behaviour in the 1993 election varied significantly depending on whether a new party candidate was running in the district or not.[9] Voters with a new party option voted differently from those who lacked that option. My analysis confirms their findings not only for 1993 but for earlier elections as well. The right-hand side of Table 7.1 presents the same analysis confined to those districts in which an NLC option was available. When voters were presented with an attractive alternative, they proved much more willing to abandon their previous choice, as indicated by the smaller coefficient for the 'previous vote' variable. They are also more willing to punish scandal-tainted candidates, as indicated by the jump in the coefficient for the 'scandal' variable. Finally, including districts without NLC candidates in the analysis artificially depresses the estimate for the NLC boom.

This boom was very strong. Voters were upset over corruption and ready to move towards an alternative when it was offered. That the NLC had so little impact on Japanese politics is less due to voter apathy than to limited choices. The NLC could have had a significantly bigger impact if it had simply run candidates in more districts. The voters played their part but one cannot vote for a party unless its candidate is running in your district.

The Doi boom

The Doi boom of 1990 proves to be quite similar to the NLC boom of 1976. The boom was somewhat larger overall (5.8 percentage points or almost 39,000 votes) but significantly smaller when limited to districts with a booming candidate (39,000 votes as compared with 42,000). Again we find that including districts in which no JSP candidate was running dilutes the estimate of the boom, indicating that limiting the analysis to only those districts in which a booming candidate is available produces the more accurate estimates. Again as in 1976, we find that voters were more willing to abandon their previous choices when offered a socialist alternative.

Table 7.2   Voting in the 1990 election

	All districts	Districts with JSP candidates
Constant	0.914	1.130
Previous vote	0.814	0.783
District vote	0.401	0.394
LDP	1.068	1.277
JSP	5.789	5.928
Scandal	−1.602	−1.487
R-square	0.834	0.824
N	756.0	744.0

It may be surprising that some LDP candidates actually gained votes in the Recruit scandal election but, by the time of the 1990 election, voters had already vented their anger at the LDP in local and upper house elections.[10] Timing may also explain the lowered coefficient for the scandal variable, almost halved from −3.2 to −1.5. If the first election after the Recruit scandal and after the selection of Doi Takako as leader of the LDP had been a general election, instead of an upper house one, the Doi boom would have had a much greater impact on Japanese politics. The Doi boom was more a uniting of opposition voters behind a single opposition party than a shift of voters away from the LDP. Most of the socialist gains came at the expense of other opposition parties. Nevertheless, this was a serious boom and voters continued to punish candidates for scandals.

The New Party boom

The New Party boom has much in common with both of its predecessors. As in 1976, the LDP label was neither a plus nor a minus. The baseline for socialist candidates is the 1990 Doi boom, so much of the negative impact of the JSP label should be attributed to a shifting of the boom to the new parties rather than a reaction against the JSP. Again we find voters more willing to shift their votes when offered a new party opinion. In districts with such an option, the boom is almost as large as in 1976 (6.5 percentage points or about 39,000 votes). Surprisingly, however, the effect of scandals is smaller than in 1976 and falls into insignificance in districts with new party candidates. The effect of scandals on a candidate's vote deserves a good deal more analysis, but our current findings lend no support to the picture of a rising tide of anger against corruption. If anything, they indicate increasing apathy.

Table 7.3   Voting in the 1976 election

	All districts		Districts with new party candidates	
Constant	0.716		0.861	
Previous vote	0.837		0.768	
District vote	0.314		0.328	
LDP	0.210	(NS)	0.516	(NS)
JSP	−4.263		−3.698	
New Party	5.800		6.528	
Scandal	−1.912		−0.922	(NS)
R-square	0.851		0.709	
N	760.0		598.0	

Our best estimates of the effect of the three booms is 6.75 percentage points or 42,079 votes for the NLC, 5.9 percentage points or 38,741 votes for Doi, and 6.5 percentage points or 39,145 votes for the New Party boom. If we attribute the lower figure for 1990 to the timing of the election, after the electorate had vented its ire in the 1989 upper house election, we come to the conclusion that each of the booms was of roughly equal magnitude. The Japanese electorate had been ready to kick out the LDP ever since 1976. The missing ingredient was not voter anger, but a sufficient supply of attractive alternatives. When politicians finally created enough acceptable alternatives, the LDP's reign ended. While our analysis supports this conclusion overall, it omits the urban-rural dimension of Japanese politics. When we analyse urban and rural areas separately we get a surprising result.

The booms in urban and rural areas

Politics in rural Japan tends to be much more stable than in urban Japan. Personal support organisations (*kōenkai*) and pork barrel politics are stronger in rural districts. Our data confirm this generalisation in that the coefficients for a previous vote tend to be higher in rural areas (analysis not shown). Thus, one would expect booms to be stronger and the costs of scandal to be higher in urban areas. I did each of the above analyses separately for each of the four urban-rural categories defined by the *Asahi Shinbun*. Unfortunately for this study, the number of scandal-tainted candidates within each urban-rural category is insufficient to produce reliable estimates for that variable. We can, however, compare the size of the three booms.

Table 7.4   The booms in urban and rural areas

	1976	1990	1993
Rural	5.671	7.118	10.688
Semi-rural	3.605	5.264	5.955
Urban	7.543	5.888	4.344
Metropolitan	7.460	6.229	6.187

Note: Entries are the coefficients for new party candidates in those districts in which a new party candidate ran

The NLC boom was primarily an urban phenomenon. There is an interesting reversal with the boom in rural districts stronger than in semi-rural districts and, in fact, none of the booms shows a monotonic relationship with the urban-rural dimension, a relatively common but as yet ill-understood finding in Japanese electoral studies.

The Doi boom was stronger than the NLC boom in rural and semi-rural areas, but weaker in urban and metropolitan districts. At the time, the most likely explanation was that the liberalisation of agricultural imports was an issue that worked against the rural LDP in the 1990 election. However, the trend continued in 1993. Not only was the New Party boom stronger than the Doi boom in rural and semi-rural districts and weaker in urban and metropolitan districts, but the estimate of 10 percentage points for rural districts in 1993 is the highest coefficient in the analysis. The New Party boom in rural areas was the biggest boom of all.

Why did each successive boom grow weaker in metropolitan and urban areas? The most likely explanation is growing apathy among voters. As successive booms turned into busts, urban voters found it increasingly difficult to work up enthusiasm for the next boom. In many ways the more interesting question is why booms grew in intensity in rural areas, especially the most rural areas. I will suggest two explanations, one located in the electorate and the other a matter of the choices offered rural voters.

First, rural voters have been disengaging from the LDP. One of the secrets of LDP longevity was a stable rural support base.[11] However, in the late 1980s the party found itself relying too heavily on the declining agricultural sector and moved to expand its urban support base.[12] Liberalisation of agricultural imports became the focus of a general rural dissatisfaction with LDP agricultural policy. One can hardly fault the logic behind this move but first it meant that the LDP had to depend on a more volatile urban electorate, and second, that the rural electorate, dissatisfied with LDP policies, became more volatile. The new strategy was instrumental in staving off defeat and even for producing two conservative revivals. However, the new support base was unstable and meant that booms, instead of being limited to urban areas, would start affecting rural voters as well. Starting around 1980, rural voters began to act more like urban voters; the electorate had become nationalised.[13] In the 1960s and 70s, the LDP was able to survive periods of unpopularity by relying on stable support in rural areas. By the 1980s and 90s, it was no longer able to do so.

By the 1990s, rural voters were prepared to abandon the LDP but they still needed a place to go. They responded to socialists in the Doi boom of 1990 but were particularly enthusiastic about the New Party boom of 1993. In rural areas, the New Party candidate usually came from the Renewal Party and were often established LDP incumbents with strong support bases to begin with. Most notably, the two leaders of the Renewal Party, Hata Tsutomu of Nagano second district and Ozawa Ichirō of Iwate second, both rural districts, brought a large number of personal supporters with them to the new party and benefited enormously from the New Party boom. Removing these two exceptional cases from the analysis reduces the coefficient for rural areas but it remains the largest in the table. Whereas the defectors to the NLC came from urban and metropolitan districts, defectors to the Renewal and Harbinger parties were spread more evenly along the urban-rural dimension. For the first time since 1955, rural voters were offered established conservative candidates from a party other than the LDP. From their response, it would appear that this is exactly the choice they had been waiting for.

Booms and democracy in Japan

The basic story of the three booms is that the people became angry in 1976 and the political system responded in 1993. Based on a simple textbook definition of democracy as a matter of reflecting the will of the people, seventeen years seems an awfully long time. Yet it is difficult to come up with concrete examples of democracy working more quickly in any other country. Most industrial democracies have been suffering in varying degrees from corruption scandals and demands for political reform. So far only three political systems have responded with major reforms: Japan, Italy and New Zealand.[14] In none of these three 'successful' cases did the process look anything like the textbook model, though each looks quite similar to the other two.

Both absolute and comparative standards have their uses. One should not stop striving to make democracy work better simply because no current democracy works perfectly. It is important, however, to use the same standard of judgment for all countries. If one wishes to stress the degree to which Japanese democracy fails to live up to textbook standards, one must also be prepared to give all other democracies failing grades as well. More fundamentally, the story of the three booms and comparisons with other industrial democracies leads me to think that the textbook standard for democracy is unrealistic. We need dynamic models of democracy as messages sent by the electorate, and messages received (or not received) by the parties and candidates.

Why did it take seventeen years for the Japanese political system to respond to demands for political reform? First, the message was not perfectly clear. Each time a major scandal coincided with an attractive alternative, the alternative boomed, but scandal was never the only issue in the election. In addition, election results are subject to varying interpretations. Political scientists fail to reach agreement on the meaning of an election after years of careful analysis of mounds of data. One cannot blame politicians for failing to understand the electorate's message as soon as the returns come in. In fact, of course, voters seldom make clear demands. Japanese voters were upset and wanted change, but they made no precise demands for any particular reforms. A wide variety of party platforms and party images could have attracted an electoral boom in any of these elections (or in 1983). Finding a combination of images and issues that would not only boom with voters but also attract a large number of defectors from the LDP was neither a matter of rational deduction nor of reading the public opinion polls, but of trial-and-error experimentation, and experimentation takes time. The new parties of 1993 had learned from the successes and failures of their predecessors. For example, it was easier in 1993 than in 1976 to convince conservatives to defect from the LDP because by 1993 politicians had witnessed two booms and expected to benefit themselves.

The message not only lacked clarity, but also consistency. The LDP won in 1980 and 1986 and there was talk of a conservative revival after each of these elections. There were major scandals in 1976, 1983, 1990 and 1993, but none in 1979, 1980 and 1986. In fact, it may have required two consecutive scandal elections to unseat the LDP. Momentum, both in the electorate and among the politicians interested in organising an alternative to the LDP, was lost after 1976 but did not have the time to fade between 1990 and 1993.

Was seventeen years fast or slow? It is relatively easy to imagine the political system responding sooner. If the NLC had attracted a few more defectors in 1976 or had offered more candidates overall, they could easily have prevented the LDP from gaining a majority. In fact, the LDP won only 48.7 per cent of the seats and secured their majority only after twelve conservative independents joined the LDP (and one who ran on the LDP ticket left the party). The LDP victory was so thin that random fluctuations in five or six districts could have prevented an LDP majority. Better strategy by the opposition parties could have easily ended the LDP's reign seventeen years earlier than turned out to be the case. One can only speculate on what would have happened after an LDP defeat in 1976, but the odds of the LDP staying in a coalition government were much higher in 1976 than they were in 1993. Such a coalition government would probably not have been able to enact any major political reform simply because the debates over political reform had not yet begun in earnest and consensus-building on such constitutional issues as electoral systems is almost always a long process.

It is also relatively easy to imagine the Doi boom resulting in the defeat of the LDP before 1993. If, as was discussed at the time, there had been a double election in 1989, voting for both upper and lower houses on the same day, the most likely result would have been a JSP-led coalition government. One can also imagine, though with more difficulty, the JSP building on its 1989 House of Councillors victory instead of squandering it. If the JSP had defeated the LDP, instead of being the biggest loser in the election that finally produced an alternation in power, the current coalition and governmental policies would look quite different. The JSP would certainly not be on the verge of falling apart, as is currently the case midway through the 1990s.

The timing of the response affected the substance of the response. A successful boom in 1976 would have produced results different from a successful boom in 1990, and neither would have looked much like the New Party boom that actually succeeded in unseating the LDP.

Finally, one can also imagine scenarios in which the LDP managed to stay in power even longer than it did. A reprieve from the constant flow of corruption revelations between 1990 and 1993 would probably have meant fewer defectors from the LDP and either a smaller boom or no boom at all. If there had been no defectors, the 1993 election result might well have looked like 1976 or 1983. The Hata-Ozawa faction that left the LDP to form the Renewal Party and the Takemura group that left to form the Harbinger Party played a necessary role in bringing about the end of LDP one-party dominance. However, neither of these two groups, nor those who left on their own, were operating in a vacuum. They knew that they would gain votes by defecting and were, in part, responding to popular demands. Previous booms were a necessary condition for major defections from the LDP, and both the defectors and the New Party boom were necessary conditions for overturning the LDP regime.

In the end, I find myself unable to answer the question of whether seventeen years was much too long or reasonably rapid. We have no realistic model of how rapidly a democracy should be able to respond to a public demand of this sort. Neither do we have the comparative studies which would allow us to say whether Japan was faster or slower than other industrial democracies. When measured against realistic expectations, however, Japanese democracy functioned reasonably well.

Notes

1. Terry MacDougall (1988) 'The Lockheed Scandal and the High Costs of Politics in Japan', in Andrei S. Markovits and Mark Silverstein, eds, *The Politics of Scandal*, New York: Holmes and Meier.
2. Steven R. Reed (1991) 'The 1990 General Election: Explaining the Historic Socialist Victory', *Electoral Studies* 10 (3) 10, September, p. 244–55.
3. Ellis S. Krauss (1984) 'Conflict in the Diet', in Ellis S. Krauss, Thomas P. Rohlen and Patricia Steinhoff (eds), *Conflict in Japan*, Honolulu: University of Hawaii Press.
4. Ishikawa Masumi (1984) *Dēta sengo seiji-shi* (Data on postwar Japanese politics), Tokyo: Iwanami Shinsho.
5. Steven R. Reed (1992) *Japan Election Data: The House of Representatives, 1947–1990*, Ann Arbor, MI: Center for Japanese Studies, The University of Michigan.
6. Michael Blaker (1977) 'Japan 1976: The Year of Lockheed', *Asian Survey*, January.
7. John G. Peters and Susan Welch (1980) 'The Effects of Charges of Corruption on Voting Behaviour in Congressional Elections', *American Political Science Review* 74, (3) September, pp. 697–708.
8. Milton Lodge, Marco R. Steenbergen and Shawn Brau (1995) 'The Responsive Voter: Campaign Information and the Dynamics of Candidate Evaluation', *American Political Science Review* 89 (2), June, pp. 309–26.
9. Kabashima Ikuo, *Shintō no tōjō to Jimintō itto yuui taisei no hōkai* (New parties merger and LDP one-party rule collapses), and Miyake Ichiro, *Shintō no shutsugen to kōhosha hyōka moderu* (A model for evaluating candidates and the emergence of new parties), both in *Leviathan* 15, Fall 1994.
10. Steven R. Reed (1991) 'The 1990 General Election: Explaining the Historic Socialist Victory', *Electoral Studies* 10 (3), September, pp. 244–55.
11. Kabashima Ikuo (1984) 'Supportive Participation with Economic Growth: The Case of Japan', *World Politics*, April.
12. Gerald Curtis (1988) *The Japanese Way of Politics*, New York: Columbia University Press.
13. Kobayashi Yoshiaki (1991) *Gendai Nihon no senkyo* (Contemporary Japanese elections), Tokyo: Tokyo University Press.
14. See Mark Donovan, 'The Politics of Electoral Reform in Italy', and Jack Vowles. 'The Politics of Electoral Reform in New Zealand' both in *International Political Science Review* 16 (1), January 1995.

8
Big business and politics in Japan, 1993–95

Akira Kubota*

Japan's economy thrives on big business. The huge bulk of Japanese money is in the hands of the private sector, especially large corporations, rather than the state. With their economic clout, in an environment where money is the basis of political pork barrelling, it is clear that big businesses play a major role in Japan's domestic political processes.

Japan is a highly conservative nation, where political life has been overwhelmingly dominated by conservative forces. Business corporations in Japan, especially the largest, have favoured political conservatism. Thus we find in Japan the coexistence of powerful big business organisations and conservative political culture, producing relatively close working relations between the two.

The roles of Japan's big business and political forces are not, however, fixed and unchanging. During 1992–93, Japanese media exposed to the public a series of seriously corrupt political practices involving some of the country's largest business corporations as

* The author expresses his gratitude to the Japan Foundation and the Academic Development Fund of the University of Windsor for providing financial support to conduct field research and enable preparation of this chapter.

well as some of its most powerful conservative political figures.[1] Big business and major conservative political leaders in general, even those not directly implicated, were consequently subject to severe public criticism. In a major setback for both conservative political forces and the big business community in Japan, in July 1993 came the end of the '1955 system' in which the Liberal Democratic Party (LDP) had continuously and practically single-handedly governed Japan for nearly forty years. The changing political climate could not sustain the relationships that had thrived under LDP rule. In 1994, Keidanren, the Japan Federation of Economic Organisations, chose to end its traditional role as an intermediary for collecting large financial donations from business sources and distributing these funds among the major political parties. The move signalled a shift in relations between big business and government in Japan in an environment where a new mix of political forces had begun to transform the shape of the political system.

In this chapter we consider the relationship between big business and government in Japan during this significant period 1993–94, focusing on the organisations that represent big business in their involvement in political life.

Most studies of business-government relations tend to focus on situations in which business dominates government or government dominates business. Examples of the former can be found in many Marxist analyses of the governing process, and examples of the latter can be found in the thesis of late development capitalism which is often associated with the studies carried out by authors like Chalmers Johnson.[2] In this writer's perception of Japan's political life, the major features of Japan's social structure differ significantly from those of other societies, including Western societies. Since these features have not been easily modified or eradicated by social, political and economic forces that have promoted modernisation throughout the world, the standard explanatory frameworks do not serve us well. Neither of the two approaches pays due regard to the role of the electorate in influencing government-business relations. In Japan, where the electorate is expected to exercise some power in the democratic political system, we can hypothesise that on some occasions, it may vigorously attack both big business and government, and may damage their political positions. I posit this as largely what took place in Japanese national politics in 1993–94.

As I will argue in this chapter, the setbacks of this period by no means indicate that big business in Japan has irrevocably lost political influence, or that it will never regain most or some of its previously significant role in Japan's domestic political process. Nonetheless, it should be conceded that at least throughout

1993–94, big business remained relatively passive politically. Neither do I suggest that political conservatism is largely a spent force in Japan. Indeed, it is unlikely that many of the existing vital characteristics of Japanese politics will shortly disappear. Some pundits even predict that Japan's hitherto powerful conservative political forces will regain most of their former strength in the coming decades.[3] Indeed, a growing number of political analysts in Japan suggests that the new electoral system that includes single-member districts will most likely work in favour of the conservative LDP, and that it has at least a fair chance of regaining its majority status in the next general election.

Big business

We need first to define 'big business' as a key term in this chapter. Big business is a slippery term in most national contexts, though its meaning in the Japanese case seems clearer than in many comparable ones. Here it is useful for us to review two representative interpretations of big business in the Japanese context. First, in Japan 'big business' is used to refer to very large corporations, more specifically the top 10 or 20 per cent of approximately 2000 corporations whose stocks are traded publicly in the Tokyo, Osaka, Nagoya and other local stock exchanges.[4] But limiting big business to these corporations alone is misleading for two reasons: first, the stocks of some of the fully privately-owned corporations, e.g. *Kokudō* (formerly Kokudō Keikaku), are not traded in these domestic markets and so are excluded from this definition despite their size and political significance; and second, many of these corporations whose stocks are listed in the Tokyo and other stock exchanges inside Japan are in fact component members of such massive *keiretsu* (industry conglomerates) as Mitsubishi, Mitsui, Fuyo, Sumitomo and the like, and thus do not operate as fully independent entities as do typical large American and other Western business corporations.

A second meaning for Japan's big business corresponds loosely to the Japanese term *zaikai*, which translates literally as the financial or business world.[5] In the Japanese mass media, the term *zaikai* usually refers specifically to four specific leading national business organisations: the Japan Federation of Economic Organisations (Keidanren), the Japan Chamber of Commerce and Industry (Nisshō),[6] the Japan Federation of Employers (Nikkeiren), and the Japan Committee for Economic Development (Dōyūkai).[7]

When Japanese talk about zaikai leaders, they generally mean the top leaders of these four organisations. These leaders are the heads of Japan's multi-billion dollar corporations. All four are invited to participate in many very important political events in Japan including, for example, state dinners for visiting heads of state.[8] Because these four organisations represent big businesses in Japan and serve as powerful vehicles for their political expression, we will accept this second meaning in our explanation of big business in this chapter.

Keidanren and political fund-raising

In the July 1993 national election, when the LDP was removed from government for the first time in nearly forty years, crucial to its downfall were both the revelations in the mass media that some of the party's most senior leaders were involved heavily in a series of political scandals, and the fall of the LDP king-maker and power-broker, Kanemaru Shin, who was irrevocably implicated. Kanemaru's downfall gave rise to a power struggle over who would succeed him, a bitter feud that in turn led to a sizeable group of Diet members deserting the LDP, causing the party to lose its control of a majority of the seats in the lower house of parliament.[9]

Kanemaru had accepted cash gifts from certain business corporations that were conducting business with government or were seeking favourable administrative rulings. He had diverted some of the monies received from these sources to build his personal fortune in gold bullion and negotiable bonds. The actions of the corporations that had supplied Kanemaru with money in expectation of preferential political treatment inevitably tarnished the image of Japan's big business players. These actions also created an unfortunate public image for big business in Japan, since it became very clear to the public that corporate political contributions could inevitably distort the democratic political process. During 1993 and 1994, not only political commentators and politicians but also business people themselves, began seriously to explore the possibility of banning corporate political donations entirely, and replacing them with public funding of elections, with an increased emphasis on individual donations.

Despite the conjecture, by the time a set of political reform bills was approved by the Diet in December 1994, corporate donations to political parties were once again permitted, though with some

Table 8.1   Public funds received by political parties, 1994

Party	Amount (US dollars at the Rate of 100 yen = $1.00)
Liberal Democratic Party	65.993 million
New Frontier Party	43.383
Social Democratic Party of Japan	29.581
New Party Sakigake	3.624
Clean Government Party	2.656
Democratic Reform League	2.837
Liberal League	0.879
Peace-People	0.549
Total	149.503 million

Note: The Communist Party of Japan declined to accept any
      public funds
Source: *Asahi Shinbun*, 21 July 1995

limitations. A major plank of the new reform measures was the introduction of public funding for political activities. For the first time in Japanese political history, a significant portion of the funds used to support the election campaigns for politicians and other activities of political parties was to be supplied by the public treasury, i.e. from taxpayers' money. The new legislation set the annual total budget for public funding of election campaigns at approximately $300 million. These funds are to be paid twice a year, and the first round of these payments was made in late July 1995. On 20 July, the first payment of approximately $150 million was made for the first half of the 1995 calendar years as shown above.

   At this point it should be noted that when we consider all types of political fund-raising in Japan, Keidanren's intermediary role is relatively minor. The total annual amount of political funds handled by Keidanren in this process usually ranged from $120 to $140 million per year.[10] A large portion of all the funds used by political parties in Japan has always been given to politicians and parties at both national and local levels without passing through the formal channel of Keidanren, even when it played an active role as mediator. However, as long as Keidanren was involved in the political funding process, it usually handled the single largest amount of money in any year. Furthermore, a critical advantage of the Keidanren collection was that it was seen by the general public to be relatively 'clean' money and likely to be free of the potential or real economic gains to be made by 'special interest' groups seeking to secure their particular business, regulatory on other interests with the government. The exact formula for calculating the amount of donation from each regular member of Keidanren was developed over the years by Hanamura Nihachirō, taking into consideration such factors as the amount of capital and regular profit of the firm involved, the current status in terms of the business cycle as well as the general position of each of the industrial sectors involved.[11]

The negative public image of corporate political contributions during 1993–94 prompted Keidanren to give up its intermediary role of collecting and distributing political donations.[12] Yet public pressure did not compel Japan's biggest firms and key trade organisations to give up their corporate donations to political parties outside the Keidanren channel. Instead, as December 1994 approached and the Finance Ministry began the final stages of drafting the nation's annual budget, these major firms and associations readily resumed their traditional practice of direct political contributions to parties, factions and other key political players, bypassing the intermediary step formerly undertaken by Keidanren. It is therefore significant to note that available data suggest there was only a small reduction in the total amount of political contributions made in Japan during 1993–94, even without Keidanren's mediation.

In reaching its decision on the issue in 1994, two compelling factors made it difficult for Keidanren not to relinquish its role in political fund-raising. One was the difficult precedent arising from a public utility company that had made indirect political contributions, and the other was the finding of a Keidanren international survey on comparable institutions and practices in the West.

In October 1993, it was publicly revealed that the Tokyo Electric Power Company (TEPCO) was making disguised political contributions. As in most nations, in Japan public utility companies, such as electric power, telecommunications, and gas, are permitted to monopolise their assigned markets and are therefore regulated tightly by government in the rates that ordinary consumers and business corporations are asked to pay for their services. In other words, the amount of profit that a Japanese public electric power company makes is largely determined by the price list fixed by government, or more precisely by a government commission. It is clearly improper for such a company to make monetary political contributions that could influence the party in government.

Precisely on these grounds, the TEPCO had been reproved by consumer groups in the 1980s for making political contributions. Soon the company publicly announced its decision to stop making political contributions often recognised as unethical. Yet in 1993 it was discovered that TEPCO had in fact continued to make clandestine political contributions in a cleverly disguised manner. The company simply purchased advertising space in the LDP newspaper, *The Liberal Star*, instead of making regular direct cash political donations. A critical advantage of this indirect method of funding was that since purchasing advertising space was not classified as a political donation, it did not need to be reported to the relevant government agency responsible for overseeing political contributions.

The Board Chair of TEPCO was then Hiraiwa Gaishi, who was also the Board Chair of Keidanren. Inevitably, both Hiraiwa and TEPCO were driven into the situation where they had no alternative but immediately to end this practice of making hidden political contributions. Hiraiwa dealt with this problem on both the TEPCO and Keidanren fronts simultaneously. With TEPCO, Hiraiwa arranged for a public announcement by the company that it had ceased secret political contributions. At the level of Japan's big business, with the support of the then-Board of Directors of Keidanren, Hiraiwa announced a more sweeping strategy, ending entirely the role of Keidanren as mediator in collecting political funds from its member corporations and trade associations and distributing funds among those political parties which would be willing to co-operate with Keidanren on important business and other issues.

The second reason leading to Keidanren's withdrawal from its role as intermediary involved the conclusions of a report submitted by a team of leading business people who Keidanren had sent abroad in the fall of 1994 to survey comparable institutions and practices in other advanced industrial nations. It was discovered that in many nations there was no Keidanren-like body that represented only the top layer of business (i.e. all or most of the nation's biggest business corporations and key trade associations). Even if there was such an organisation, it was found that it generally did not play a formal role as an intermediary for collecting and distributing political funds. This latter finding strengthened the personal view of Hiraiwa that Keidanren should relinquish this role altogether.

Despite these imperatives, two other factors made it difficult for Keidanren to give up its role as intermediary in political fund-raising. First, some saw it as impractical for business corporations to cease their political contributions entirely. In this view, it would still be necessary for some representative business organisation to co-ordinate fund collections from big business, and Keidanren is one of the very few organisations that appears to be eminently qualified for such a task, for the nation as a whole, and for all industrial sectors.[13] Second, some key career staff of Keidanren appeared to prefer preserving this role, so that tension developed between them and its *zaikai* leaders. Probably as a result of this division within Keidanren, some of the top Keidanren career staff were let go at the end of June 1995.[14]

In pre-World War II Japan, a very large portion of political funds was provided by Japan's leading *zaibatsu* groups such as Mitsui, Mitsubishi, Sumitomo, Yasuda and Furukawa. When World War II ended, the *zaibatsu* were broken by the Allied Occupation. In most of the post-1945 period, when Keidanren played a leading role in handling political contributions, it has conducted many useful studies on major issues affecting Japan's big business, presenting its policy recommendations to successive Japanese Cabinets. In both political funding and policy recommendation, Keidanren has generally tried to act on an aggregated basis for all Japan's big businesses and key industrial sectors, not on the basis of any one particular corporation or industrial sector. Accordingly, the impact of Keidanren on basic policy formulation in Japan has been more effective than that of a typical lobbying group in North America, such as a political action committee, which tends to act on an unaggregated basis for a single business interest or a business sector. Keidanren's move to abandon its intermediary role in political fund-raising appears quite remarkable to some who judge that through this move Keidanren has chosen voluntarily to reduce its potential influence in Japanese politics.

This is especially so when we note that of Japan's four principal *zaikai* organisations, only Keidanren played a publicly acknowledged role in collecting funds from leading Japanese corporations and major trade (or sectoral, *gyōkai*) organisations, distributing these funds mainly among Japan's conservative political parties. In this sense, Keidanren's function in political fund-raising was exceptional even within Japan's *zaikai* context. Nevertheless, we must appreciate that while a given *zaikai* organisation may insist that it is not officially involved in the political fund-raising process, this does not necessarily mean that it does not in fact play a limited informal role. Many of those who are familiar with the funding of Japanese politics believe that the hierarchies of individuals who largely correspond to the structure of a typical *zaikai* organisation or a part of it, sometimes informally assist aspects of political fund-raising, although the original formal organisations officially maintain a position of non-involvement. When a politician sells tickets for his or her fund-raising party, they may well be sold unofficially through these individuals using an informal person-to-person organisational structure. One well-known example is the case of the Sōka Gakkai and the Clean Government Party where it is widely assumed that the former provides ample political funds to the latter, although the Japanese Constitution (Article 20) proscribes a separation of religion and state.

Whether or not Keidanren would continue to reject its former role in political fund-raising was not clear as of December 1995. While publicly Keidanren's key officials have insisted unequivocally that the decision to abandon its intermediary role in political fund-raising is final, it is nevertheless undeniable that a few business leaders and Keidanren staff members were not fully satisfied with the decision. These dissenters provide support for the position that corporate and sectoral political donations from business are bound to play a critical role in Japanese politics; and that some organisations must play a role of rationally and equitably assigning the amount to be paid by each large corporation and trade association to fairly divide the financial responsibility of the Japanese business community for the political process. According to these dissenters, Keidanren naturally occupies this strategic position.

Political activity beyond fund-raising

The involvement of *zaikai* organisations in Japan's political life is naturally not limited to political fund-raising. Each of the four *zaikai* organisations performs a relatively distinct role. Keidanren's membership consists of large business corporations whose stocks are publicly traded at the first division of the Tokyo Stock Exchange as well as numerous trade organisations representing sectors of the Japanese economy, such as steel, manufacturing, construction, banking, insurance, transportation, energy, telecommunications, wholesale, retail and leisure. Keidanren deals with issues that directly affect such a membership. Because of its emphasis on big business, it focuses on national issues such as foreign trade and taxation, avoiding agriculture and fisheries or other commercial fields that are handled primarily by small or medium-sized business entities.

Nisshō is a corporate entity established under special government legislation to oversee and regulate national, regional and local chambers of commerce. Nisshō's membership consists of business entities of all sizes, including large, medium-sized and even small corporations, as well as other incorporated commercial entities. It thus has a more official and formal status than Keidanren and is more closely controlled or supervised by appropriate government organisations. Nisshō tends to complement Keidanren by focusing on medium-sized and small enterprises. As large corporations tend to advocate free trade internationally while medium-sized or small corporations tend to support protectionism *vis-à-vis* the continuing process of global trade liberalisation, Keidanren and Nisshō do not fully agree with each other on foreign trade issues, nor on the extent to which internationally uncompetitive enterprises in Japan outght to be tolerated or even supported and subsidised by the government. The views of the two also tend to differ with respect to the impact on the Japanese economy of *kūdōka*, the 'hollowing out' of Japan's manufacturing industry.

Nikkeiren's membership consists mainly of relatively large business firms, and it deals almost exclusively with issues pertaining to industrial relations or employer-employee relations. It conducts extensive studies on education, recruitment, employment practices, wages, bonuses, pensions, fringe benefits and other personnel matters. Since almost all Japan's wage negotiations are dealt with through the annual spring offensive or *shunki tōsō (shuntō)*, a comprehensive report compiled by Nikkeiren and made public immediately prior to each shuntō exerts enormous influence on the outcome of the subsequent annual shuntō.[15] While most of the membership of Nikkeiren's key committees consists of senior executives of major corporations, these relatively prominent business people are invariably assisted by a professional staff who are employed on a career-long basis by Nikkeiren, with professional researchers employed by government research institutes and universities. When the Chair of Keidanren speaks, he tends to represent the interests of large business corporations or top officers of such corporations. When the Chair of Nisshō speaks, he tends to represent the interests of medium-sized or small business firms. When the Chair of Nikkeiren speaks, he tends to represent the interests of average industrial workers.

Dōyūkai is quite different. Unlike the other three organisations, Dōyūkai's membership consists of individual business people and not businesses or trade organisations. Dōyūkai is more like a club of business people who are interested in carrying out in-depth studies of important issues affecting not only Japan's business community but also its economy as a whole or almost any major issue which might influence the entire state of Japan or Japan's role in the international community. Since Dōyūkai was not formed specifically to represent the interests of any specific business group in Japan, its proposals and recommendations tend to be more imaginative and innovative than the other organisations.

Conversely, such proposals and recommendations by Dōyūkai tend to be taken less seriously by the government and are less likely to be incorporated into official policy.

Since the LDP's fall from government in July 1993, Japan's conservative political forces have regained much of their lost ground, to the point where by early 1996 an LDP Prime Minister, Hashimoto Ryūtarō, retook the national helm. Under these circumstances Japan's big business is likely to regain some of the political influence it lost in 1993–94. Even if it does not completely regain its former clout, it is likely to continue as a fairly potent or potentially powerful political force in Japan for years to come. If the political influence of Japan's big business declined significantly in the long term, it is still likely to remain greater than that of comparable groups in the United States or Canada, for several reasons. First, it appears that each of these four *zaikai* organisations remain structurally intact and will survive much as they are now for some time to come. Second, top Japanese business leaders are likely to continue to devote a large amount of their time to matters that are national in scope and far broader than particular concerns directly related to the specific corporations that continue to pay their salaries. Third, to a significantly larger extent than others, Japanese elites prefer to participate in one kind of meeting or another in the field in which they specialise or in related fields, in order to solidify and expand their social contacts. Fourth, it appears that many of Japan's top business organisations show a strong tendency to develop close ties with groups whose immediate interests appear quite different from their own, demonstrating a Japanese characteristic of expanding or building as large a group of connections as possible on the basis of what many Westerners might regard as minimal common interest.

On the one hand, Japan's big business is unlikely to influence Japan's political process as crudely as a simplistic version of Marxism might suggest. Japan's big business is likely to recognise the special skills that are essential in effective politicking and will avoid meddling in those matters which are generally considered to be the exclusive prerogative of political leaders — such as filling key political positions (including ministerial appointments) or bringing together particular political parties to form a governing coalition. On the other hand, Japan's big business is sufficiently concerned with issues which profoundly affect not only their own future but also the future of the Japanese nation as a whole, such as maintaining social and political conditions that promote economic prosperity and continuing to maintain close political and military relations with the United States.

In this sense, we need carefully to separate what is merely being said about the *zaikai* from what it is actually doing. Japan's mass media has often reported in recent years that the *zaikai* is no longer *ichimai gan* (one chunk of rock) or solidly unified. Although some Western analysts assume that different sectors of Japan's big business cannot fully agree with each other because their basic interests are different, in the socio-cultural context of Japanese business life, different industrial sectors are expected to reach agreement with each other on potentially diverse issues because of an exceptionally strong Japanese tendency to reach harmony and consensus. Media reports have told us that the *zaikai* has not been functioning effectively, and have suggested ways to restructure or reform it in coming years, just as we have been witnessing restructuring of the *seikai* or political world since the summer of 1993.

Yet it is also significant to note this talk remained as mere talk during 1993–94. In this period and later, neither a concrete nor sustained movement nor a specific study emerged to restructure Japan's *zaikai*. Since each of the four *zaikai* organisations was performing a distinctive set of functions, there was relatively little that could be considered as overlap. The Japan Chamber of Commerce and Industry is based on a particular piece of Diet legislation. It therefore cannot easily be combined with any of the other *zaikai* organisations, which are organised on the basis of different legislation covering a wide variety of non-profit legal entities in the economic and other fields. In addition, these four *zakai* organisations tend to maintain reasonably friendly relations with each other and to co-operate closely on many matters, including those which may not fall neatly into the jurisdiction of one *zaikai* organisation or another.[16] One can detect little evidence in today's *zaikai* that any one of the four is assertive enough to try to replace or absorb any of the remaining three. Indeed, the four organisations have good reason to try to work jointly to promote the basic interests of the Japanese business community as a whole, in a manner and to a degree which can rarely be achieved in Western nations.

Moreover, it would appear to be very much against the general grain of Japan's contemporary *zaikai* to try to consolidate or amalgamate existing organisations, reducing the number of top *zaikai* positions. Although it is said to cost a few million dollars a year for a corporation to send out one of its most senior officers as a *zaikai* leader, these positions are being actively sought by Japan's top business leaders. Naturally there is little interest among Japan's top business leaders to consolidate the present four basic organisations, reducing the number of top *zaikai* positions available to them.

Government and big business relations at work

Let us now turn to consider specific topics pertaining to big business as it is active in Japan's political life. First we will evaluate *zaikai* involvement in one of the most sensitive contemporary political issues, US-Japanese trade negotiations. Next we will consider their role in supplying political funds to major parties and politicians. Some of the events discussed below have taken place beyond the 1993–94 period, but as they are particularly instructive to our understanding of *zaikai* involvement in 1990's Japanese politics, we shall briefly review them here.

Japan's big business and US-Japan trade negotiations

By early 1995, it became increasingly clear that the US government had become firmly committed to a diplomatic approach of pressuring Japan to accept specific numerical targets on many products that Japan imported from the US,[17] thereby reducing the US trade deficit with Japan. Instead of employing less direct approaches such as asking the Japanese government to increase its spending on public works or to streamline Japan's distribution system, the US government opted for the direct approach of making the Japanese government responsible for importing fixed amounts of designated items from the United States. From the standpoint of US grassroots democratic politics, it might be speculated that since Japan was hesitant in opening up its domestic market, there was no other effective approach to solve America's trade deficit with Japan than to mechanically impose on it well-defined numerical quotas.

A technical problem in this high-handed diplomatic approach on the part of the United States is that it possibly violated the basic principles of the World Trade Organization (WTO). The suggested numerical targets measures conflicted with the principle of the market mechanism, one of the most basic organising doctrines of Western studies of economics. Many Japanese political, economic, bureaucratic and academic leaders were steadfastly opposed to this US approach and urged the Japanese government to reject such a request firmly and definitively.

By June 1995, the Japanese government had only two viable options in responding to the US request. One was to categorically reject the approach, thus running the risking of driving the matter into the WTO dispute-settling mechanism, while progressively aggravating already difficult US-Japanese relations. The other option was reluctantly to accept some of the specific demands being made by the United States after an extended and difficult series of negotiations, thus retaining a small possibility of both enabling the US government to persuade grassroots Americans that it had succeeded in opening up Japan's market to some degree, and reducing the chance of creating irrevocably and unmanageably hostile US-Japanese relations.

Both the American and Japanese governments continued to issue mutually contradictory interpretations of what they had agreed in June 1995. It is conceivable that an international debate on the basic substance of this agreement may persist for many years to come. Nevertheless, it seems possible to draw a tentative conclusion: the Japanese and American governments offered two different explanations for two different political audiences. The Japanese government was trying hard to convince the Japanese public and others outside Japan, that it had successfully defended its anti-numerical target principle when it negotiated with the American government. The American government was trying equally hard to convince its people that its 'no nonsense' approach to Japan had essentially worked, because the Japanese government had in fact accepted some of its key demands. Although the American position of demanding numerical targets may have violated some of the basic principles of WTO, it would have been difficult for Japan to exert diplomatic pressures on the United States to alter its position, given the realities of Japan's present dependence on the United States for its national security and other vital matters.

There is a precedent for supporting such an interpretation. Involved in an earlier stage of trade conflict were semiconductors. When the American and Japanese governments signed an agreement on semiconductors in September 1986, the Japanese government insisted that it had successfully rejected the American demand for Japan to accept numerical targets. Yet, it was revealed about a year-and-a-half later that the Japanese government in fact handed over to the American government an informal, unofficial letter acknowledging that it had accepted some of the key numerical targets demanded by the Americans at that time. This was done by Kuroda Makoto, then a senior MITI official, who was widely acknowledged in Japan to be a 'tough negotiator' with the US. Since this revelation, the Japanese government has maintained that the letter was simply a gentlemen's agreement, and not legally binding. From the American perspective, however, this became the beginning of a series of enforceable *de facto* numerical agreements on semiconductors between Japan and the United States.

A significant feature of the June 1995 automotive products agreement between these trade partners is that Japan's *zaikai* informally stepped into the process of negotiation, and by pressuring the Japanese government to accept some of the key American demands, managed to avert the implementation of the list of sanctions on Japan which had already been announced by the American government. At least, this was the kind of information that the CIA (Central Intelligence Agency) was able to intercept by tapping telephone conversations among members of the Japanese negotiating team. It should, however, be added that the assessment that the Japanese automobile manufacturers were beginning to soften their position had already been reported in the Japanese mass media when these negotiations were taking place, and that many specialists on these matters were aware of this development many months prior to the media report in October 1995 of the CIA findings.

In general, trade frictions between America and Japan have been treated as a relatively grave international issue by the people of Japan, and certainly by key leaders of Japan's *zaikai*. Some of Japan's top business leaders are realistic, acknowledging that few viable options are available to American politial leaders in terms of domestic politics, and that given the commanding position of automotive products in America's trade imbalance with Japan, the June 1995 agreement was unavoidable.[18] In this writer's view, as long as Japan seeks American help with respect to national security matters — and it appears that it will continue to do so in the foreseeable future — it has in the final analysis little option but to give in to some, if not all, of the basic demands made by the United States. This is so even though such demands violate prevailing international trade rules and even though such a policy works against an increasingly powerful nationalist trend now emerging in the Japanese electorate.

On matters such as this, it is incumbent upon Japan's *zaikai* and other key leaders to exercise some critical leadership. Many of Japan's *zaikai* and other key leaders appear to realise the vital importance of maintaining at least minimally harmonious relations with the United States. This is surely more fundamental than the fact that the Chair of Keidanren at the time in question happened to be Toyoda Shōichirō, Board Chair of the Toyota Motor Company, or the fact that the Japanese automobile manufacturers would have suffered a greater economic loss had the Japanese government continued to resist American pressures, thereby driving the dispute into implementation of the announced American sanctions. At its heart, this issue is about how to avoid a possible national calamity. More specifically, it is about averting a fatal collision between the two largest economies in the world today. Since it is highly likely that Japan and the United States will continue to face trade frictions for at least another decade or more, these two nations are bound to continue to face many difficult diplomatic issues. If so, it looks inevitable that Japan's *zaikai* will play an increasingly critical role in Japan's external relations.

Also important is the future role of Japan's *zaikai* in political fund-raising and, more particularly, the intermediary function of Keidanren. As this writer assesses the circumstances involved, including the weight of Japan's cultural tradition, there is a considerable probability that this intermediary function, or a variation of it, will ultimately be revived. One possibility is a revival in substance if not in form of the earlier strategy, thus making it possible for Keidanren to continue to insist that it has definitively abandoned its traditional role as an intermediary in political contributions. In any event, there are two specific reasons why *zaikai* will most likely resume such a role in some form or other. First, Japan is a nation where the exchange of gifts plays a critical role in maintaining satisfactory and reliable interpersonal relationships. This practice of gift exchange takes place in many areas where there is no such practice in the West, or where such a practice is deemed unethical. Electoral process in Japan tends to be significantly more expensive than elsewhere, partly because if politicians are to be taken as serious candidates, they have no choice but to hand out gifts in one form or another, in ways that are rarely practised in Anglo-American democracies. Further, it is unlikely that the electoral-district system to be implemented in the next general election for the lower house will significantly reduce the cost of campaigning in Japan.

North American politicians may be obliged to give 'goodies' to their constituencies in the form of job creation, obtaining government grants, or sending out a book on child-rearing when a new baby is born. But Japanese politicians often go significantly further in gift-giving, and this is especially so when they try to thank their 'volunteer' campaign workers. They sometimes sponsor subsidised group tours which would otherwise be quite expensive; they occasionally subsidise English conversation schools or other cultural activities; and they regularly send out flowers and donations on the occasions of weddings, funerals and other events involving their key supporters. Election campaigning in Japan tends to be so extravagant that no amount of public funding of the electoral process is likely to cover all the money that serious and effective political candidates need to cover the expenses they see as necessary for electoral success and for sustaining loyal interpersonal relationships. Thus, in order to succeed in politics, one has to raise a very large amount of money. Since big business corporations are one of the few sources that can meet such a strong demand for massive funds, it is very difficult for politicians not to approach them. In addition, by using the Keidanren channel, politicians recognise that they can profit by being removed from specific benefits that individual corporations might currently be seeking from government.

There is a stronger tendency in Japan than in other societies for heterogeneous individuals, groups and organisations to develop closer ties with one another. One type of relationship is a parent-role child-role (*oyabun-kobun*) relationship. This seems to be the type of relationship between the zaikai and major political parties in Japan. Many political bosses (*oyabun*) regularly give out money to politicians, *kobun*. The former may be the leader of a major LDP faction while the latter may be members of that faction. This money is often referred to as *mochi dai* (rice cake cost), the money necessary to take care of one's basic needs. Most Japanese do not view as illegal this practice of money changing hands among Japanese Diet members. By contrast, we rarely hear of politicians in North America accepting money from other politicians directly or indirectly. The *oyabun-kobun* relationship can also be seen in formal relationships among members of a given *keiretsu*. As these business corporations create quasi-familial relationships with each other, in a similar vein Japan's *zaikai* creates quasi-familial relationships with some of the most powerful political parties in Japan. Given these relationships, it is difficult for the zaikai not to lend or give money to the LDP and other pro-business political parties, just as a typical Japanese father finds it difficult not to lend or give money to one of his sons, as long as he can afford it and as long as it is clear that the latter obviously needs it. There is of course some danger in over-stretching the analogy of the father-son relationship, though surely similar feelings and motivations are at work.

It is very likely that the *zaikai* will continue to sustain close relationships with major pro-business political parties in Japan and that the extent of this bond will continue to be strong, and will remain stronger than comparable bonds which might exist in many of the advanced industrial Western nations. By November 1995, Keidanren already appeared to be moving in the direction of resuming its role as an intermediary in political fund-raising. Keidanren insisted vehemently that it was not reviving its traditional role, but was simply trying to take care of outstanding debts, worth $100 million, that the LDP had incurred in June 1993, since Keidanren had served as a guarantor at that time. Nevertheless, a growing number of Japanese observers reached the conclusion that Keidanren had in fact resumed its historical role of acting as an intermediary in raising political funds, in substance if not in form.[19]

Both the *zaikai* and the LDP sustained a series of major setbacks during 1993–94. Here we see how the Japanese electorate will treat both the *zaikai* and the LDP when it is pushed beyond certain limits. In the extremely long run, both the *zaikai* and the LDP may lose a considerable part of their traditional strength. Nonetheless, in the immediate future and for some time to come, some of the most basic relationships enmeshed in Japan's social and political structures are unlikely to change drastically. *Zaikai* will remain relatively tightly allied with the LDP, and is likely to play a role in Japan's domestic politics that is at least as important as hitherto. Furthermore, Japan's *zaikai* will play an increasingly significant role in the nation's external relations, particularly in American-Japanese relations, their political and military as well as their economic dimensions.

Notes

1. Corporations included Sagawa Kyūbin, Shimizu Construction Corporation, the Kashima Construction Corporation and other large corporations, while one of the political figures involved was Kanemaru Shin, then Vice-President of the LDP.
2. See, for example, Chalmers Johnson (1982) *MITI and the Japanese Miracle: The Growth of Industrial Policy, 1925–1975*, Stanford, California: Stanford University Press.
3. For example, by the spring of 1996, which is beyond the scope of the present study, we once again found a conservative LDP Prime Minister in Japan and a growing possibility that Keidanren might resume its role in political fund-raising. For discussion of my theoretical position, see Akira Kubota (1990) 'Social Familism: A Structural Model of Japanese Society', in Don J. Daly and Thomas T. Sekine (eds), *Discovering Japan: Issues for Canadians*, North York, Ontario, Canada: Captus University Press, Akira Kubota (1994) 'Japanese Politics: A Reflection of Social Familism', in Jacob Kovalio (ed.), *Japan in Focus*, North York, Ontario, Canada: Captus University Press, and Akira Kubota (1995) *Nihon shakai kōzō no samazamana moderu* (Various models of Japan's social structure), a paper prepared for delivery at the Society of Eastern Studies in Tokyo, on 27 May 1995.

4. As of April 1993, 2,128 corporations were listed on these exchanges.

5. *Zai* means 'wealth' and *kai* means 'world'.

6. The Japan Chamber of Commerce and Industry is more likely to be misunderstood than the other three *zaikai* organisations for two reasons: First, in terms of personnel, physical office space and other resources that the Japan Chamber of Commerce and Industry uses, it is almost identical to the Tokyo Chamber of Commerce and Industry. Second, two other organisations have names that sound similar, even though they are both entirely separate from the Japan and the Tokyo Chambers of Commerce and Industry. These are Zenkoku Shōkōkai Rengō Kai (the All-Japan Federation of Associations of Commerce and Industry) and Zenkoku Chūshokigyō Dantai Chūōkai (the All-Japan Headquarters of Federations of Small and Medium-sized Enterprises).

7. Full official Japanese names are Keizai Dantai Rengō Kai, Nihon Shōkō Kaigisho, Nihon Keieisha Renmei, and Keizai Dōyū Kai respectively. All four *zaikai* organisations maintain extensive regional and local branches nationwide, though legally these regional and local branches constitute separate entities. When *zaikai* is used in Japanese mass media, the reference is taken to mean the national headquarters of these organisations which are in Tokyo, and not regional and local branches, although the headquarters usually try to reflect he views and preferences of the branch organisations.

8. Except for Dōyūkai, it is the corporations and associations (themselves legal entities), that constitute official members of the *zaikai* organisations. Nonetheless, Japan's mass media, politicians, and others who work with *zaikai* leaders tend to treat them as though they are largely independent of the bodies they represent. Accomplishments that *zaikai* leaders achieve while in these positions tend to be attributed neither to the zaikai organisations they represent nor to the particular business corporations in which in fact they are employed, but rather to the specific business individuals involved.

9. For details see Akira Kubota, 'A Genuine Reform?': The June–August 1993 Upheaval in Japanese Politics', *Asian Thought and Society: An International Review* 18 (53–54), May–December 1993, pp. 93–125.

10. The range of amounts expressed in the Japanese currency generally surpassed 10,000,000,000 yen, but rarely exceeded 20,000,000,000 yen.

11. See, for example, Iwai Tomoaki (1990) *Seiji shikin no kenkyū*, Tokyo: Nihon Keizai Shinbunha.

12. Since the New Frontier Party came into existence during the last phase of Keidanren's intermediary role in political contributions, it appears that Keidanren did not give a substantial amount of money to this party.

13. The particular political fund-raising process that Keidanren gave up in 1994 was originally created in 1961. To avoid a situation where particular business corporations donate funds to particular political organisations or politicians, where a basic mechanism for outright

bribery could be suspected, Keidanren and other organisations decided to channel this process into a single generalised national stream.

14. One of the highest of these executives was Fusano Natsuaki, who had been the most senior officer in Keidanren, specifically charged with the task of collecting and distributing political funds. His immediate predecessor was Hanamura Nihachirō, who developed the famed Hanamura list with a formula to determine the specific amounts of donations to be made by individual Keidanren members.

15. It is significant to note that even a large portion of government employees are included collectively in this nationwide management-labour negotiation process.

16. Horizontal cross meetings are not limited to the highest levels. We have already mentioned that the top leaders of the four *zaikai* organisations meet frequently and regularly with each other. In addition, some of the top professional staff of different *zaikai* organisations also meet regularly with each other, largely to exchange information and co-ordinate the large variety of tasks that each of these four *zaikai* organisations continuously perform.

17. Also included in these numerical targets is the number of dealers in Japan of automobiles imported from the United States.

18. '[Nichibei jidōsha] ketchaku ni iron', *Nihon Keizai Shinbun*, 28 July 1995, p. 5.

19. 'Keidanren, kenkin assen saikai', *Asahi Shinbun*, Evening Edition, 16 November 1995, p. 1 and *Keidanren no kenkin assen fukkatsu*, *Asahi Shinbun*, 3 December 1995, p. 4. One unconvincing aspect of Keidanren's explanation in late 1995 was the fact that when it announced that it had decided to cease acting as an intermediary in political fund-raising in 1993, it did not indicate then that it would have to raise as much as $100 million two years later. At the time of the announcement, Keidanren gave the impression that within a year or so, it would finish up its remaining fund-raising tasks, which did not amount to a great deal of money.

9
Tax policy in Japan after the demise of conservative dominance

Junko Kato

Tax and politics are inextricably linked. In Japan in recent years, the interplay of one with the other is instructive. In 1989, Japan's long-term incumbent Liberal Democratic Party (LDP) suffered a critical decline in its support in the elections for the House of Councillors. One important reason was public antipathy toward the consumption tax that was introduced in April that year after ten years of effort by the Japanese government. The Socialist Party (SDPJ or Social Democratic Party of Japan), which had been suffering a long-term decline in support, regained ground in these elections with its opposition to the new tax. Subsequently, public opposition to the new tax waned, as consumers became accustomed to the new system and the LDP regained its foothold in parliament.

In June 1993, four years after the critical defeat in the Upper House elections, factional in-fighting split the LDP and helped to weaken its grip on government. Thirty-eight years of conservative dominance were ended by the formation of a coalition government that excluded the remnant LDP following the general elections that summer. In summer 1994, about a year after it lost dominance, the LDP came back to office, but this time allied unexpectedly with the SDPJ and Sakigake. Under the LDP-SDPJ-Sakigake coalition government, a decision was taken to increase the consumption tax rate from 3 to 5 per cent effective from April 1997. For the first time, the SDPJ as a party showed its support for the consumption tax system, despite intra-party opposition.

The value added tax, which has been named a consumption tax (*shōhizei*) in Japan, is now an indispensable part of the Japanese tax system. However, the process through which it was introduced is a history of continuous political battle. In 1979, the tax was proposed in the name of a general consumption tax, but this proposal not only brought about electoral losses for the LDP, but also caused discord inside the party. After the second proposal (this time presented as a sales tax) failed to pass through the Diet in the mid-1980s, the consumption tax bill finally passed into legislation early in 1989, incurring severe political costs for the LDP.

Even after the loss of conservative dominance, the consumption tax remained a focus of policy disagreements. Disagreement between and within coalition parties over the consumption tax increase helped to break the first non-LDP coalition government. The decision to increase the consumption tax rate was made but immediately withdrawn by the first coalition government in February 1994, while tax policy disputes intensified.

The introduction of the consumption tax has much to tell us about Japan's political system, not only because the issue was contentious for politicians, but because it sheds new light on the power relationships between politicians and bureaucrats. Although the bureaucrats' fiscal conservatism appears to be consistent with the introduction of the value-added tax, incumbent politicians are expected to oppose such an unpopular tax. In an earlier study I have examined why this tax was introduced.[1] Here I focus on the relationship between bureaucrats and party politicians by reviewing the tax reform case after the loss of conservative dominance.

For this purpose, I take up the following questions. Why did the coalition government, which included the former incumbent LDP and the SDPJ, decide to increase the tax rate in autumn 1994? Did the major political changes attendant upon the LDP's 1993 ouster influence the tax decision? Were there significant changes in the power relationship between the party politicians and bureaucrats? In answering these questions, I argue that the tax case reveals that the power of financial bureaucrats is declining. My argument runs counter to the conventional view that after the demise of conservative dominance, bureaucratic power has increased. To frame my argument, I briefly review the ten-year process through which the value-added tax was eventually introduced. I then examine the tax policy process after the end of LDP dominance.

Framing the key question about political-bureaucratic ties

Many studies have been made of tax politics at the national level, with specific national governments as examples. There are likewise many studies of relationships between politicians and bureaucrats at the national level. The intersection of these two fields of study in the Japanese case is particularly informative because of two distinctive features of Japan's political system. First, Japan has long been known for its strong bureaucracy. Second, the nation was ruled by one party, the LDP, from 1955 to 1993, well after the consumption tax was introduced. In other words, the Japanese case of tax reform provided a clear example of a situation in which bureaucrats faced a long-term incumbent party. Moreover, the Ministry of Finance (MOF), the ministry in charge of tax policy, is regarded as one of the strongest within the Japanese bureaucracy, and the introduction of the value-added tax was closely related to its organisational interests.[2]

The tax policy became an issue, that allowed the LDP ultimately to increase its influence over the bureaucrats. It is, then, a major puzzle as to why the LDP, which had gained enough policy expertise to comprehend a highly specialised and complicated policy such as this, accepted a tax proposal made by the MOF. The introduction of the value added tax was unpopular and ultimately electorally costly for the LDP. Considering the high level of policy expertise among experienced LDP politicians, it is hard to imagine how the MOF could force the LDP to accept it.

To solve this puzzle, we need to consider the changes in policy agenda under which the introduction of the value added tax was proposed. First, in the late 1970s, the tax was proposed by Prime Minister Ohira, who insisted that the new tax was necessary to solve the deficit finance problem.[3] At the time, the MOF, which had been planning since the beginning of the 1970s to introduce a value-added tax, was totally dependent upon Ohira's assurance to convey the ministry's tax proposal. Despite Ohira's support, the proposal, which had been decided upon formally by the LDP leaders, was thwarted by opposition from inside and outside the party.

The MOF challenged a proposal for major tax reform again in the mid-1980s under the leadership of Prime Minister Nakasone. An austerity campaign in the early 1980s and chronic public debt changed public opinion, which had regarded the new tax on consumption as a symptom of the government's fiscal irresponsibility. Public opinion did not support a tax increase through the introduction of a value-added tax, but recognised the need to cope with the budget deficit. This time, the MOF attempted to persuade the public to accept the new tax by emphasising that its introduction was a means of reforming the revenue structure. More specifically, the bureaucrats proposed that it was necessary to shift revenue reliance from direct to indirect taxation by introducing a broad-based tax on consumption. The MOF's proposal first appeared to be strong because it was consistent with Prime Minister Nakasone's desire to cut income tax. However, this revenue-neutral reform (i.e. a reform package including the same amounts of tax increase and reduction) was not implemented. The public suspected that the government had concealed a future tax increase in the guise of massive income tax reduction, and voiced criticism that the introduction of the value added tax was inconsistent with Prime Minister Nakasone's public promise made during his election campaign. The government's compromises with the firms and distributors were expected to produce inconsistent and discriminatory treatment among them. The public regarded these as distortions of the new system and blocked the second proposal.

In the third proposal, from 1987 to 1988, the government emphasised both the rectification of tax inequities and the need to secure revenue for Japan's ageing society. The government countered public mistrust by proposing a net tax reduction. Income tax reduction in the reform package would exceed increased revenue raised by introducing the new tax. Though these attractive agendas for tax reform swayed public opinion, and prevented it from blocking the tax proposal, the LDP government suffered public criticism of the new tax system after it was implemented. The government lost its majority in the upper house elections, held a few months after the introduction of the consumption tax.

This review of the process shows that the reform agendas under which the new tax was proposed were important for understanding the consequences of the proposals. The agenda setting does not, however, explain the full picture. It is especially unclear why the incumbent LDP accepted such an unpopular tax proposal.

We can explain this by investigating the bureaucratic and party organisations. First, bureaucratic organisations can devise a mechanism to create consensus on a policy and co-ordinate members' behaviour to pursue that policy, provided the policy objective is clearly consistent with the organisation's interests. This mechanism worked in the case of introducing the consumption tax. Introducing a value-added tax was consistent with the MOF's critical organisational interest — its discretion over budget decisions and public finance. Furthermore, a stable revenue source from a value-added tax was expected to sustain the MOF's control over public finance.

Second, party politicians tend to have different interests in making policy. This is especially the case when these politicians need to secure their re-election independently of, and at times in competition with, other politicians from the same party. For example, the LDP politicians pursued distinct electoral interests under the medium-sized election district system which was used during most of the post-war period, until 1993. In the case of tax reform, this difference in interests had special significance. By the 1980s, the LDP had increased its members, who were eager to gain more specialised policy knowledge to promote their influence inside the party through policy-making. For example, the experienced ones were more likely to be concerned with their reputation as policy experts. They were also concerned about what policies would be needed to maintain their rule in the long run. In the tax reform case, the LDP leaders were interested in securing a financial source to continue the public investment program and maintain welfare expenditures; the broad-based tax on consumption was considered an effective means to reform the tax system and secure the financial source. They felt they could afford to support an unpopular policy if it would augment their own reputations as policy experts and satisfy policy needs, even though such a policy was counter to the interests of other members with a weak electoral base. LDP leaders of course care about re-election of their followers in order to secure their status as leaders of the incumbent party. It needs to be noted, however, that the leaders take more risks than their followers, who are preoccupied with their re-election in specific election districts, and this gap is likely to cause a different attitude to an unpopular policy such as a new tax on consumption. The experienced party members accepted, or even actively advanced the proposal for the new tax, in spite of risking the re-election of other LDP members. The introduction of the value-added tax was regarded by the leaders as a technical solution to improve the allegedly inadequate Japanese tax system.

Third, relating to both the first and second points, bureaucratic influence could work effectively not just because of the bureaucrats' domination of policy expertise and knowledge. Bureaucrats also gained their influence by obtaining support for their policy proposal from incumbent politicians. To muster political support, the bureaucrats needed to reveal policy information and share policy ideas. This process runs counter to the conventional wisdom that bureaucratic influence is derived from the bureaucrats' monopolisation of policy information and expertise.

These findings on the tax reform case from the late 1970s to the late 1980s[4] suggest that the relationship between bureaucrats and politicians on the tax issue was influenced by conditions under the LDP's one party rule. This implies that there should have been a change in bureaucratic influence on the tax policy process after the LDP's fall from government. If the above line of analysis is applied to the coalition governments that succeeded the LDP regime, coalitions in which there have been fewer politicians with policy expertise, the bureaucrats should have had more difficulty pushing desired policies. This hypothesis runs counter to conventional wisdom concerning power relations between politicians and bureaucrats under the 1990s coalition governments. We shall also consider more broadly the impact of subsequent political change on tax policy decisions. First, I will review the tax policy process under the two non-LDP coalition governments, and then under the coalition government that includes both the LDP and SDPJ.

Politics against bureaucratic expertise: process

In 1993, the split from the LDP of two renegade groups and their subsequent formation into two splinter conservative parties unexpectedly led to the demise of conservative rule. The actions of the LDP defectors, including their absence from the parliament and votes of support, ensured that the no-confidence motion against the Miyazawa Cabinet proposed by the opposition parties passed through the Diet. In the general elections in July 1993, which followed the dissolution of the lower house after the passage of the no-confidence motion, the LDP almost kept its pre-election number of seats, and remained a plural party. But it could not restore the majority that it lost in the pre-election exit of many members. Seven parties comprising five former opposition parties and the two LDP breakaways formed the first non-LDP Cabinet since 1955. They were the Japan Socialist Party (SDPJ), the Clean Government Party (CGP), the Democratic Socialist Party (DSP), the Federation of Democratic Socialists (FDP), the Japan New Party (JNP), the Renewal Party, and the Sakigake. Hosokawa Morihiro, who had formed the JNP about one year before, was chosen as Prime Minister in August.

The first major issue for the non-LDP coalition government under Hosokawa was political reform, i.e. reform of the election system and control of political funding. However, after this issue was resolved in January 1994, the tax issue emerged as a major policy problem. On February 3 1994, Prime Minister Hosokawa proposed about six trillion yen of tax reduction and an increase in the rate of the existing consumption tax.[5] Hosokawa explained that the tax reduction, especially five point three trillion yen of income and inhabitant tax reduction, would be implemented retrospectively to the previous month, January. He also proposed that the tax increase be implemented from April 1997, about three years after the tax reduction, by replacing the existing 3 per cent consumption tax with a 7 per cent people's welfare tax (*kokumin fukushizei*). According to his proposal, the tax reduction would be financed temporarily by the issue of a special kind of deficit bond, which would be paid back within two years.

Among the socio-economic conditions that were the context of the tax policy, the critical downturn in the Japanese economy was important. From the end of 1994, an economic depression had increased political pressure for income tax reduction, and even the MOF bureaucrats, fiscal conservativists, recognised its necessity. The biggest problem was how to finance the tax reduction. The MOF wanted to increase the rate of the consumption tax to avoid the issue of deficit bonds. The previous November, the Government Tax System Research Council had issued a mid-term reform report which had proposed income tax reduction and the future increase of the consumption tax, though it had not specified when the reform would be implemented. It was apparent that the proposal of the Tax Council was consistent with the view of the MOF which worked as its secretariat.

Opposing the MOF's strong inclination to increase the consumption tax, some party politicians, especially those in the SDPJ, supported the issue of deficit bonds and resisted an increase in the consumption tax rate. Prime Minister Hosokawa agreed to propose the tax increase, however, because the leaders of the Japan Renewal Party (JRP), who agreed with the MOF, persuaded him. Hosokawa proposed in February 1994 to postpone the tax rate increase; to emphasise the use of increasing revenue sources for welfare expenditure; and to redeem the bonds issued for financing the tax reduction within two years. The public was surprised with the government proposal, which was clearly aimed at the consumption tax increase. Immediately after the proposal was publicly announced, its unpopularity became apparent. This package had not even been accepted inside the coalition government, and some parties and politicians had expressed strong opposition to it. The proposal was immediately withdrawn, but the incident intensified policy disputes inside the coalition.

The tax proposal made coalition members aware of their different views on various policy issues. The SDPJ and the Sakigake especially suspected that the JRP leaders had increased their influence over Prime Minister Hosokawa and had tried to alienate the two parties from decision-making. The SDPJ and the Sakigake, which were cautious about implementing a tax increase by raising the consumption tax rate, had not been consulted by Prime Minister Hosokawa about the tax proposal. So disharmony over the tax issue contributed to the dissolution of the Hosokawa Cabinet in April, and creation of the minority Hata Cabinet in May. The latter was short-lived. Socialist Prime Minister Murayama formed a Cabinet in June, and the unexpected coalition between the LDP and SDPJ was formed, with the Sakigake as a mediator.

The tax issue was still an important policy problem. Because the Hosokawa government had decided only on the income tax reduction without securing a revenue source, the new government needed to service this unwanted inherited problem. The same conflict that had occurred under the Hosokawa Cabinet arose again between the SDPJ and the MOF under the Murayama cabinet. The MOF wanted to finance the tax reduction with both short-term deficit bonds and consumption tax increase. It insisted on including a measure to enhance tax revenue in the same Bill as the one planned for tax reduction. The SDPJ did not mind financing tax reduction by deficit bonds, but opposed the consumption tax increase. The SDPJ continued to show opposition to the consumption tax five years after its introduction, and insisted on separating any decision on tax reduction from financing measures. The LDP also assumed a cautious attitude towards the consumption tax increase. Immediately after the formation of the Murayama Cabinet, the LDP's position had been closer to the MOF than the SDPJ and Sakigake to the Ministry. The LDP had appeared more supportive of combining the same amount of tax cut and increase in the same package, although it advocated that the tax cut should precede the tax increase. The LDP became worried, however, about the undesirable effects of the tax increase, since especially during an economic recession, the unpopular tax increase might prove fatal for the party which had managed to return to office but was still suffering from its weakened political standing.

The LDP also became suspicious of the MOF which had worked so closely with the JRP under the Hosokawa Cabinet to propose the tax increase. More importantly, the experienced LDP politicians who had worked closely with the MOF under the LDP's one party rule did not have sufficient incentive to support the MOF position, because showing their policy expertise was no longer a means to gain influence in the coalition government. Ironically for the MOF, the non-LDP coalition parties, (especially the JRP), which had supported the consumption tax increase from 3 to 7 per cent in the Hosokawa Cabinet, were more sympathetic towards the MOF than the LDP.

The compromise among the coalition parties came from an unexpected direction. The SDPJ and Sakigake proposed combining a temporary fixed rate reduction and a permanent measure in the income tax cut package. The LDP began to pay attention to this as a compromise. By this two-step tax cut, the permanent income tax cut, making the progressive tax structure flatter, would remain about 60 per cent of the total cut, and subsequently the consumption tax rate increase would be suppressed. The MOF, which intended to shift the revenue reliance from an income to a consumption taxation, did not like this hybrid tax cut, but was forced to accept it because the LDP considered it necessary to make the SDPJ and Sakigake accept the future tax increase. Also, the tax cut would precede the tax increase by three years (instead of two) because of the deep recession in the Japanese economy. As a result, the tax reduction would be implemented retrospectively to the 1994 fiscal year and the consumption tax rate would increase from 3 to 5 per cent from the 1997 fiscal year, from April 1997.

The MOF's concession to the incumbent parties, however, was not limited to acceptance of the *ad hoc* tax cut. The SDPJ wanted to have a 'reason' to accept the increase in the consumption tax which the party had formally opposed since the late 1980s. It resisted including the tax reduction and tax increase in the same Bill, which was scheduled to be enacted in 1994. Two compromise measures emerged at the last moment. The first was securing the expenditure specifically for the welfare program. The MOF managed to allocate a total of three hundred billion yen for the 1995 and 1996 fiscal years for welfare expenditure and to secure five hundred billion yen from the 1997 fiscal year, when the consumption tax rate would be increased. This compromise was mainly made between the MOF, the SDPJ and Sakigake; the LDP did not clarify its position. For the LDP members who were familiar with the tax issue, such an *ad hoc* Budget appropriation was not desirable. However, these LDP leaders let the SDPJ make the demand because maintaining the coalition with the SDPJ was imperative for the LDP to keep its hold on power. Securing welfare as a financial source for the tax increase was regarded as a good justification by the SDPJ, which was also forced to accept the tax increase in order to maintain the coalition.

The second compromise measure was to institutionalise the local consumption tax system, upon implementing the tax rate increase in 1997. Although the substantial administrative work to collect the tax will remain in the hands of the tax authority at the national level, local governments will have the discretion to use the tax revenue coming from 1 per cent of the 5 per cent tax. This measure was especially welcomed by the SDPJ and Sakigake, which had advocated the autonomy of local government. The measure was also supported by politicians who had strong ties with the labour unions of the employees of local government.

The incumbent coalition parties agreed in September 1994 on the tax reform package, and subsequently submitted the Bill to the Diet in October; it was passed in November 1994. Consequently, the income tax structure (five brackets from 10 to 50 per cent) was to be made less steep, by lowering the minimum income threshold to which the tax would be applied. The inhabitant tax rate structure was to be graded by a similar measure. For the consumption tax, a 5 per cent rate will be implemented from the 1997 fiscal year, allocating 20 per cent of this revenue to the local consumption tax system. At the same time, special tax calculation measures and special tax exemptions will be modified to make the taxation more effective.

Politics against bureaucratic expertise: explanation

There are two opposing views of bureaucratic influence over the tax reform in 1994. One explanation regards this as a result of the influence of the MOF which still persisted after the demise of conservative dominance. According to this view, the MOF succeeded in raising the consumption tax rate despite a high level of uncertainty in party politics. The compromises that the MOF made are interpreted as 'inevitable' considering that there were three coalition governments in only one year from late 1993 to late 1994. The MOF bureaucrats are considered to have taken advantage of former opposition politicians' unfamiliarity with policy-making and of the demise of the conservatives. Another view regards the reform as a defeat of the MOF bureaucrats, and bases its interpretation on the compromises that the MOF made. Although it pays attention to the same factors as the first view, the uncertainty of the political situation, it concludes that the bureaucrats fell short of using their expertise in policy-making while they faced unpredictable political changes.

These seemingly opposing views are parallel in the sense that both claim the way technocratic bureaucrats cope with an uncertain political situation determines whether the bureaucrats preserve or lose their influence over tax policy. Neither view contradicts the conventional one that regards bureaucratic influence as a direct product of monopolisation or control of policy information and expertise. Both views consider political uncertainty a challenge to bureaucratic control; one concludes that policy expertise remains even under political strains, while the other holds that the influence of technocratic bureaucrats was overshadowed by political uncertainty.

It is necessary, then, to examine the compromises made in the 1994 reform, comparing them with those made at the time of the introduction of the consumption tax in 1993. I will then critically examine these two views and present a different interpretation of the tax reform under the coalition government.

The first major issue of the 1994 tax reform was the scale of the tax increase. A consensus was reached on the necessity of an income tax reduction because of the economic recession which has been the most severe in the post-war history of the Japanese economy. How to finance the tax cut, by deficit bonds or tax increases, was the major issue. The reform had a mixed result in terms of these different options. First, deficit bonds were to be issued, but they were supposed to be redeemed by the time the tax increase was implemented. At the same time, the tax was increased but the rate of increase was suppressed, and the excess tax increase was replaced by revenue neutrality, that is, the same amount of tax cut as tax increase.

Let me examine more closely the MOF's attitude to the tax increase. The MOF did not want to implement the tax cut without a financing measure, or entirely by the issue of deficit bonds. However, it did not mind choosing the revenue neutrality reform instead of the excess tax increase. This meant that the MOF defended the minimum imperative to confine the tax cut to an amount that could be financed by a tax increase in the near future. If the tax cut and tax reduction were simultaneously decided (in the same bill) without relying on deficit bonds, the MOF's purpose would be fulfilled. Three years' delay for a tax increase would also not hurt the MOF.

This interpretation shows that ways to increase the tax were more important than how much revenue was to be obtained. This interpretation is further supported by the MOF's attitude to the income tax cut. Although the coalition parties under the Murayama Cabinet were eager to make roughly half the tax cut as a temporary measure, the MOF wanted to institutionalise the cut through a structural change in the income tax rate brackets. If the MOF bureaucrats had wanted to suppress the tax cut *vis-à-vis* the tax increase they would have welcomed the coalition parties' proposal. Instead, the MOF was hesitant to include the temporary measure, although the Ministry eventually accepted it because of political pressure. This shows that the MOF clearly intended to shift the revenue reliance from income to consumption taxation. The MOF in 1994 clearly aimed at a structural reform instead of *ad hoc* revenue enhancement. The MOF pushed the permanent income tax cut, financed by the consumption tax increase. The idea that a smaller cut in the permanent income tax might relieve the tight budgetary condition but replace it with an *ad hoc* tax cut measure was unacceptable to the MOF. In this sense the MOF resisted political pressure for the net tax cut. Inclusion of the *ad hoc* tax cut, however, made it fail to implement structural reform.

The last two compromise measures, that is, promising welfare expenditure and institutionalising the local consumption tax, involved more controversies. Both issues are especially interesting because they were also discussed in the process through which the value added tax was implemented, in the late 1980s. Enhancing the financial source for the welfare program has been the major issue in the tax reform. For example, even in the late 1970s when the first value added tax (the general consumption tax) was planned, some conservative politicians favoured financing welfare expenditure by consumption tax revenue. More importantly, when the consumption tax was finally introduced, securing the financial source for providing welfare to a future ageing society became an important reason advanced to deflect public opposition. Until 1994, the MOF had avoided institutionalising a linkage of the revenue raised by the consumption tax with the welfare program.

The amount which the MOF promised to spend on welfare in 1994 may not be large, especially for the first two years of the reform (1994 and 1995). The MOF also stipulated that the allocation of the consumption tax revenue was not a budget allocation for expanding the welfare program (named the New Gold Plan) by the Ministry of Health and Welfare. In other words, the MOF tried not to commit itself to financing the welfare program expansion while at the same time implying that the revenue increase would serve to finance welfare expenditures for Japan's ageing society. The Ministry of Health and Welfare also did not regard this appropriation as a promise to finance a major welfare program. The amount that the MOF promised to spend was only three hundred billion yen for the first two years and five hundred billion yen for the third year; in total these sums fall far short of financing the program.[6]

In this way the MOF avoided committing itself to starting this massive welfare expansion. However, the promise to link consumption tax revenue with the welfare program may force the hands of the fiscal bureaucrats in future budget making. As I have explained elsewhere,[7] the MOF continued to fight against pressure to designate revenue in the general account to a specific expenditure or program to allow room for discretion over budget allocation. In this sense, the MOF's appropriation of the consumption tax revenue for welfare expenditure is a step forward from the organisation's previous position, and thus is regarded as a small but substantial compromise.

The institutionalisation of the local consumption tax system is regarded as a larger compromise to the MOF's discretionary power over public finance. When the consumption tax was introduced, ways to allocate the tax revenue became a major controversy between the MOF and the Ministry of Home Affairs. The MOF allowed the allocation of the tax revenue to local governments which were expected to lose revenue they had hitherto gained from commodity taxes and those on specific services at the local level. But the MOF avoided giving actual authority to local governments and maintained a system through which the fiscal authority at the national level allocated the designated amount of tax revenue to each local body. Full control over the consumption tax revenue and its allocation were important for the MOF's control over public finance. In this sense, the institutionalisation of the local consumption tax ran counter to the MOF's interests. It had long resisted this proposal, reasoning that the local consumption tax would undermine the consistency and simplicity of taxation. But the MOF's opposition was surpassed by pressure from various political sources which supported an increase in the autonomy of local governments.

This examination of the content of the 1994 reform shows that the MOF made substantial compromises in its aim to achieve structural reform.[8] If one pays attention only to the consumption tax system, the MOF succeeded both in diminishing or repealing the special tax measures that were to calculate the amount of the tax, and in employing a more effective tax calculation method, the invoice method. However, in the entire reform plan, the MOF needed to withdraw its proposal for a change of the revenue structure while being subject to the measures that were expected to constrain its discretion over public finance.

The crucial question remains: why did the MOF accept such substantial compromises on the tax reforms under the coalition governments, and in the absence of conservative LDP dominance? One of the views presented at the beginning of this section explains that the MOF's concessions were the result of the political uncertainty brought about by its difficulties in predicting the responses of the parties in and out of power, as well as by the relatively frequent changes of governing coalitions. However, this explanation is not convincing. Even under LDP dominance, the MOF spent ten years before the eventual introduction of the consumption tax. It became a seasoned player in the struggle. Specifically, the first proposal, the general consumption tax, and the second proposal, the sales tax, were blocked by political opposition. The level of the political uncertainty is not the only factor that determines bureaucratic influence over a policy: some uncertainty had always prevailed.

It will be useful, then, to compare the 1994 reform process with those that took place from the late 1970s to the late 1980s. In the following section I will pay special attention to why the first attempt to raise the tax rate under the coalition government in February 1994 was immediately rejected, and why the second attempt under the socialist prime minister was accepted barely several months later, with considerable concessions made by the bureaucrats. To answer this question, I refer back to the tax reform process during the conservative dominance.

Comparison of the tax reform process before and after 1990

Comparing the tax reform process before and after 1990, it is obvious that there is a very important parallel between the proposals for the general consumption tax in 1978 and 1979, and for the people's welfare tax in February 1994. Both proposals were similarly withdrawn in response to political opposition, without being deliberated in the Diet. But, in addition, the two failed proposals contained several common elements despite the fact that the former was made under the LDP cabinet and the latter under the non-LDP coalition. First, both proposals relied on the reports of the Government Tax System Research Council which has close ties with the MOF. The Council first proposed the necessity of tax reform, with the introduction of the general consumption tax, in 1978, and increase in the consumption tax in 1994.

Second, both proposals were made with the support of a small number of incumbent politicians. In the case of the general consumption tax, the senior members of the LDP Tax System Research Council had made the earlier general consumption tax a formal party decision despite expected intra-party opposition. Prime Minister Ōhira at that time continued to support the proposal until public opposition forced it to be shelved immediately before the general elections in 1979. In February 1994, the leading politicians in the JRP and the CGP persuaded Prime Minister Hosokawa to go ahead and make the tax proposal without obtaining approval from the lay members of their own parties as well as the other coalition parties such as the SDPJ and the Sakigake. In other words, in both cases, the MOF capitalised on the strong support of a small number of politicians to put the tax reform which they favoured on the policy agenda, but the politicians' support proved to be ineffective. The leaders could plan and propose the reform without informing the other politicians and the public, but the opposition from the public as well as from within the incumbent party or coalition eventually caught up with them and prevented the reform from being implemented.

These similarities between the two reform proposals cannot be found in the proposals for the sales tax and the consumption tax which were made from the mid-1980s to the late 1980s under LDP rule. First, the tax reform proposal was substantially initiated and drafted by the LDP Tax System Research Council while excluding the Government Tax System Research Council from decision-making. This shift in the balance of power between the two tax councils was caused by the rapidly increasing policy expertise, and intervention in policy-making of the LDP politicians. Second, the support from the incumbent LDP leaders not only helped put the tax proposals on the political agenda in the 1980s, but also served to suppress opposition inside government. Although the proposal for the sales tax was thwarted, this was mainly because of public criticism on the alleged breaking of a public promise made by Prime Minister Nakasone.

The discussion above implies that tax policy making during the coalition government reverted back to the style that prevailed before the 1980s when the LDP institutionalised a system in which policy expertise gained importance and party leaders could discipline party members. Without the presence of experienced incumbent politicians who at the same time supported and sponsored their tax proposal, the bureaucrats could not expect it to be implemented as they desired. What is to be noted here is that this situation was not changed by the LDP's return to office as a coalition member. Unlike in the 1980s, experienced LDP politicians could not expect to benefit from co-operating with the bureaucrats in the coalition government in 1994. Their active alliance with the bureaucrats was expected to threaten the maintenance of the coalition. This is why the tax reform in 1994 under the LDP-SDPJ-Sakigake Cabinet involved measures that required substantial compromises by the MOF, as described in the previous section.

Conclusion

In this chapter I have briefly reviewed the tax reform process from the late 1970s to the late 1980s, as well as the process in the 1990s. I have compared the earlier experience with the system that shaped tax policy decisions in the 1990s. My findings have been largely counter to the conventional picture painted of the Japanese policy process. The tax reform under the LDP-SDPJ-Sakigake coalition government in 1994 imposed substantial concessions on the MOF, but these were not attributable entirely to political instability after the demise of conservative dominance. In comparing the tax reform process before and after the 1990s, we have seen that the bureaucrats similarly benefited from political support, and were disadvantaged when it was weakened. More specifically, the findings of this chapter confirm my hypothesis, generated by the reform cases of the late 1970s to the late 1980s, that the MOF bureaucrats gained influence when the leading incumbent politicians who shared policy information and expertise with bureaucrats supported their proposal, despite opposition inside the party coalition. In this regard, the monopolisation or control of policy expertise and information is not of itself a reliable means for bureaucrats to advance their influence, even in a coalition government in which there are few politicians who are experienced in policy-making.

Notes

1. Junko Kato (1994) *The Problem of Bureaucratic Rationality: Tax Politics in Japan*, Princeton: Princeton University Press.
2. In my book, I argue that a value added tax is consistent with the MOF's interests because it provides more stable revenue than a progressive income tax which is influenced by economic conditions (Kato, *The Problem of Bureaucratic Rationality*, pp. 73–80). On the value added tax used in other countries, especially in Europe, see H.J. Aaron (ed.) (1981) *The Value Added Tax: Lesson from Europe*, Washington DC: Brookings Institution; H.J. Aaron (ed.) (1982) *VAT: Experiences of Some European Countries*, Deventer, Netherlands:

Kluwer Law and Taxation Publishers. To understand recent developments in the theory and practice of tax systems, see the discussion in J.A. Pechman (ed.) (1980) *What Should be Taxed: Income or Expenditure?*, Washington DC: The Brookings Institution; J.A. Pechman, ed. (1988) *World Tax Reform: A Progress Report*, Washington DC: Brookings Institution; D.F. Bradford (1986) *Untangling the Income Tax*, Cambridge: Harvard University Press. On the development of the Japanese tax system, see H. Ishi (1993) *The Japanese Tax System*, Oxford: Oxford University Press; H. Miyajima (1986) *Sozeiron no tenkai to Nihon no zeisei* (Developments in tax debates and Japan's taxation system), Tokyo: Nihon Hyōronsha.

3.   In the early literature on public debt problems, see H. Ando (1987) *Seikinin to genkai (Ge)* (The regulators and their limits), Tokyo: Kinyū Zaisei Jijō Kenkyūkai, H. Miyajima (1989) *Zaisei saiken no kenkyū: Saishutsu sakugen seisaku o megutte* (A study in reconstructing the tax system: Towards a policy for reducing annual expenditures), Tokyo: Yūhikaku.

4.   Several important works on the Japanese tax system and tax reform process were published after my 1994 book. For the Government Tax System Research Council see K. Kinoshita (1992) *Zeisei chōsakai* (Examination of the tax system), Tokyo: Zeimu Keiri Kyōkai. For a chronological description and insider observation of the process for introducing consumption tax, see M. Mizuno (1993) *Shūzeikyokucho no sensanbyakunichi* (1,300 days in the Tax Bureau), Tokyo: Okurazaimu Kyokai; N. Takeshita and S. Hirano (1993) *Shōhizei seido seiritsu no enkaku* (A history of how the consumption tax came into existence), Tokyo: Gyōsei. For the current problems of Japanese public finance, see A. Miyawaki and T. Miyashita (1995) *Zaisei shisutemu kaikaku* (Reform of the tax system), Tokyo: Nihonkeizai Shinbunsha. See more detail on 1994 in Chapter 8, J. Kato (1997) *Zeiseikaikaku to Kanryōsei* (Tax reform and bureaucracy), Tokyo: University of Tokyo Press.

5.   On the process and consequences of the proposal for a tax increase in February 1994, also see Nihonkeizai Shinbunsha, ed. (1994) *Renritsu seiken no kenkyū* (A study of the political power of coalition governments), Tokyo: Nihonkeizai Shinbunsha; Asahi Shinbun Seijibu (1994) *Renritsu seiken mawaributai* (Coalition government does the rounds), Tokyo: Asahi Shinbunsha, 1994, pp. 270–87; F. Igarashi (1995) *Ōkurashō kaitairon* (On dismantling the Finance Ministry), Tokyo: Toyo Keizai Shinpōsha.

6.   The Ministry of Health and Welfare estimated that about 3.7 trillion yen was necessary to finance the new program for five years.

7.   Kato, *The Problem of Bureaucratic Rationality*, Chapter 2.

8.   The content of the tax reform was reviewed in 1996, and the final decision was made under the Hashimoto Cabinet to implement it from the 1997 fiscal year.

10
Heisei labour politics: a long and winding road

Toru Shinoda

The leading actor on the landscape of labour politics in the Heisei period is Rengō, the Japanese Trade Union Council. Rengō was established as a new national centre for Japanese trade unions in November 1989, the first year of the Heisei period. Rengō is a creature of Heisei not simply in the temporal sense, but also of its politics. Rengō's development has been complex. Let us consider the road that Rengō has taken in the first six years of labour politics in the Heisei period. This will provide a rich account of developments in the politics of the labour movement in Japan at this time.[1]

Certainly, after six years as a unified body, Rengō remains an influential institution on the political front — a voice for labour under politically volatile circumstances. Political volatility and economic stringency through the 1990s have served to keep alive and potentially divisive the continuing tensions between traditional supporters of Left and Right. Rengō appears to have moved full circle, from participative democratic strategies to political democratic strategies, and back again.

The rise of private sector unions

We cannot appreciate Rengō's stormy political path without understanding the history of the post-war labour movement in Japan, especially the National Council. We shall therefore begin with a brief review.[2]

Formation of blocs (1945–64)

In the post-war period, the first National Council to lead the Japanese labour movement was Sōhyō (the General Council of Trade Unions of Japan), which was established with backing from SCAP (Supreme Commander for the Allied Power). Sōhyō's stance on the pressing national issues of a peace treaty and Japan's involvement in the Korean War were in opposition to SCAP's plans to make the National Council and anti-Communist body. Sōhyō supported the Leftist group within the JSP (Japan Socialist Party) when the party split over irreconcilable views on these issues. Inspired by a Marxist–Leninist view of class struggle, Sōhyō pushed for demonstrations and strikes that culminated in mass protests over renewal of the Japan-US Security Treaty, and the Miike Coalmine Dispute in 1960.[3]

The radicalisation of Sōhyō, however, brought internal cleavages. The Rightist unions, which repelled Sōhyō's stance on the peace treaty issue, quit the organisation and later established Dōmei (the Japan Council of Labour) with other Rightist unions in the early 1960s. With a climate of conflict between Sōhyō and Dōmei, the non-affiliated unions formed Chūritsurōren (the Federation of Independent Unions of Japan). Another small National Council, Shinsanbetsu (the National Federation of Industrial Unions) composed of a few independent unions, was also established. In this way the 'Four National Councils' regime was established in the early 1960s.

During this period, each National Council formed blocs with a political party. Sōhyō formed one with the JSP (Japan Socialist Party) after earlier narrowly supporting the party's Left wing. Sōhyō established an internal JSP Membership Council composed of the party's mainstream faction leaders. The Council came to serve as a base for power struggles between the pro-JSP rank and the pro-JCP (Japan Communist Party) rank within Sōhyō. On the other hand, former officers of affiliated unions, particularly public sector unions (PUU), increased their number, standing as JSP candidates in the national elections. PUU provided all the funds for their officers to stand as JSP candidates in return for its contribution to representing the PUU's interests in the Diet where the wages of public employees were decided through the national budget.

Dōmei, on the other hand, supported the DSP (Democratic Socialist Party), which the former JSP Rightists had established. Although Domei sent officers from its affiliated unions to stand as candidates for the DSP, their number was lower than for Sōhyō's JSP candidates. This was because affiliated unions were composed mainly of private sector unions (PRU) that needed less political lobbying activities than the PUU. Furthermore, Domei did not need to form an organisation such as the JSP Membership Council in Sōhyō since Dōmei was politically more homogeneous than Sōhyō. After all, Dōmei had expected that the DSP would function as a check on the radicalisation of the JSP, rather than act as an outright replacement for it. In this way, by the middle of the 1960s, Japan's labour movement was divided into two main blocs alongside the other smaller National Councils.

The first movement for labour front unification (1964–73)

The movement for labour front unification (MLFU) began in the middle of the 1960s.[4] This was initiated by the PRU when it was faced with quite a new environment. In the 1960s the PRU increased their membership with some unions affiliated to Dōmei and others that had left Sōhyō, discontented with Sōhyō's actions that they felt tended to favour the PUU. In this period, the ruling LDP succeeded in changing its image by turning public attention towards the nation's high economic growth. Meantime the JSP failed to transform itself from a resistance-oriented party to one capable of governing. The formation of Kōmeitō (Clean Government Party) and the rising popularity of the JCP in urban areas divided the opposition.

The establishment of the JC (Japan Council of Metalworkers' Unions) in 1964 was virtually the starting point of MLFU. The metalworkers' unions were separately affiliated across the four National Councils. These unions sought to realign the National Councils in order to deal more effectively with the adverse consequences of internationalisation of the Japanese economy upon their members' working conditions. The metal industry, as the key export industry, was that most influenced by the liberalisation of trade, for which the national government made key policy decisions. Metalworkers' unions were composed of typical big business unions whose members' working conditions, most importantly their continuing employment, depended on the development of solid enterprise. With so much at stake, these unions sought unity to protect the future of the industry.

The establishment of JC shook both Sōhyō and Domei. In 1967, discussions about an MLFU began in earnest at the initiative of a major union leader from Sōhyō who advocated forming a JSP government through this MLFU. After this initiative, the chief secretaries of major unions in the four National Councils formed a liaison organisation. Not long after, when the JSP suffered a crushing defeat and the JCP made remarkable progress in the 1969 general election, the big business unions in various industries established liaison organisations locally and nationally to support the new reformist group across the four National Councils. In 1970, leaders of the major unions agreed on their need to unify, and a conference about this was held in 1972. It reached deadlock, however, during discussions of participation by the PUU. Sōhyō had by then turned against unification, after the JSP and the JCP made progress while the DSP suffered a crushing defeat in the 1972 general election. The first MLFU failed with dissolution of this conference in 1972.

The second movement for labour front unification (1973–86)

The second MLFU began when the PRU formed the Joint Action Council of Private Unions (JACPU), which demanded the national government take effective measures to deal with inflation after the 1973 oil shock. In 1976 the Joint Action Council was transformed into the *Seisuikaigi* (Trade Union Council for Policy Promotion). In this way, conditions were set for reconsidering unification. The nature of the Sōhyō-JSP bloc had also changed significantly, losing strength and forcing Sōhyō to concede to the MLFU to escape isolation. Sōhyō had lost out in the major strike it had organised for the PUU's right to strike and was deprived of its hegemony in *shuntō*, the annual spring wage bargaining round. This outcome for Sōhyō was related to the JSP's switch in political strategy from links with the JCP to links with DSP and Kōmeitō in 1980.

Thereafter, the MLFU progressed well. In 1980, the agent unions of the four National Councils established a Conference for

Promoting Unification and drafted a basic plan for this, though from this point the JCP and the Leftist JSP-related unions moved to break away from the MLFU. In 1982, *Zenminrōkyo* (Japanese Private Sector Trade Union Council) was established on the basis of the plan. It was dissolved in 1987 to form Japan's Private Rengō (Private Sector Trade Union Council) as the National Council of the PRU. At the same time, Dōmei and Chūritsurōren disbanded, with Shinsanbetsu following the next year. Thus the PRU were able to concentrate their power as a unified body ahead of the PUU.[5]

The demands for policy change and institutional reform (DPCIR)[6]

If MLFU was the main stream in the birth of a new National Council, the activities known as Demands for Policy Change and Institutional Reform (DPCIR), which the PRU had developed in the period of Seisuikaigi, Zenminrōkyo and Private Rengō, might be termed the 'underground stream'. In its DPCIR activities, the National Council annually makes demands and proposals concerning government policies, and lobbies among administrations, political parties and bureaucracies to realise its aims. These are linked with the DPCIR of industrial federations and local centres by co-opting their demands.

Why had the PRU developed DPCIR? First, after the oil shock, the PRU regarded the security of 'real' wages as important. The PRU were aware of the strong influence of government policies over the employment and overall lives of union members, conditions which industrial relations practices within enterprises could no longer completely cover. Second, the growth of policy concerns within the PRU added to their complaints over the segmented bloc politics between the National Council and the political opposition which failed to function effectively for policy promotion. Third, DPCIR were influenced less by the idea of political democracy, where unions realise their demands through links with political parties, than by the notion of industrial democracy, where unions influence policy making and implementation by sending their representatives to administrative organisations. Fifth, unions sought to break the conventional movement by formulating and implementing policies that would be appreciated by the full workforce, not just union members. All in all, DPCIR were a solution for one of the principal concerns of the PRU since the 1960s, the political autonomy of unions.

The process and therefore the outcome of DPCIR were inevitably influenced by the political situation of the time. Seisuikaigi's actions had been supported by the close relationship between the PRU and the LDP following the 1975 shuntō. In that, the JC and the Fukuda administration shared views on price and competitive power, and had co-operated to hold down wage increases. The PRU were then struggling to propel the MLFU and DPCIR, and the LDP was up against its opposition in the Diet, so both were keen to have support from unaffiliated bodies. Thereafter, government-labour talks on DPCIR could proceed, and Seisuikaigi was treated on an equal footing with the National Council.[7]

The relationship between the Fukuda administration and the PRU was further deepened through a body known as the Gathering for Friendly Discussion on Industrial Labour Problems. This was a private advisory committee to the Minister of Labour, modelled on West Germany's Concerted Action for free discussion between government, unions, employers and scholars on current economic problems. When the number of government representatives on this committee increased, the PRU requested that the body be upgraded to an official board.[8]

The PRUs' commitment to administrative reform in the first half of the 1980s was also significant. Seisuikaigi originally stressed administrative reform because the PRU, which had been forced to rationalise operations after the oil shocks, complained about irresponsible management of the public sector. Therefore, when the Suzuki administration established *Rinchō* (the Second Special Investigative Committee for Public Administration), the PRU quickly sent their representative and formed a popular movement to support it. The PRU also advocated Rinchō's goals of reconstructing public finance without a heavy tax burden, limiting tax within the social security system and privatising public corporations (National Telephone and Telegraph, tobacco, and the national railway company), in opposition to the stance of the PUU.[9]

These actions by the PRU had some important implications for labour politics in this period. First, the PRU played a key role in supporting the LDP-dominant regime in the middle of the 1980s. Second, PRU's sympathy with neo-liberalism came to an end. Third, Rinchō politics, driven by Prime Minister Nakasone, set up the PRU as a new political force. Rinchō had needed a new supporter to legitimise its actions, because it had to take an alternative political route that impinged on important vested interests.[10] In this way, the MLFU and DPCIR were entirely under the control of PRU.

The scene changes (1986–90)

The 1986 shock

The second half of the 1980s saw enormous change in Japan's political economy. By 1986, the economy had recovered from the turbulence of the 1970s oil shocks. However, another turbulent period was about to begin. Its starting point was negotiations between the Japanese and American governments directed at opening Japanese markets in 1985. Since then, the basic pattern of Japanese politics has continued, domestic politics being affected by pressures from foreign countries on the country's internal economic policies.[11] In 1985 a meeting of the finance ministers and governors of the central banks from the world's five largest economies (G5) agreed on strengthening co-operative intervention in the exchange market. Its result, the Plaza Accord, facilitated the transition from a strong dollar to a strong yen, with serious negative consequences for the Japanese economy. As a response, in 1986 the Research Council on Economic Structural Adjustment for International Co-operation established by the Japanese government presented the *Maekawa Report*. This became a guideline for national policy-making, and emphasised the need to steer a national course away from a 'production oriented' economy toward a 'living oriented' one. The value of the yen skyrocketed in the Tokyo foreign exchange market from 1986 to 1987.

Tax reform had become a pressing and highly contentious issue. Successive governments struggled to deal with the urgency of the financial crisis, and another which loomed, the rapidly ageing society. The first in a series of shocks for the Japanese public was the setback for the Nakasone administration in attempting in 1987 to introduce a sales tax. In 1988 news of the Recruit Scandal broke, revealing that this burgeoning information service and real estate company had bribed scores of LDP politicians and bureaucrats, many key political players among them. As this sordid saga unfolded, the Takeshita administration forced legislation to introduce a consumption tax through the Diet. Backlash forced the Cabinet to resign. The Recruit scandal and the consumption tax, plus the issue of liberalising rice imports under foreign pressure, damaged the LDP. In the 1989 election for the House of Councillors, the LDP was defeated decisively and lost its upper house majority for the first time since the party had come to power in 1955.

Grand unification[12]

Indifferent to this turbulence in Japan's political economy, the MLFU reached its final consolidation. Private Rengō set out for the PUU in both Sōhyō and Dōmei the conditions for a grand unification, including respect for the principle of Private Rengō, and sorting out the anti-unification unions. Both groupings of the PUU consented to these conditions and Sōhyō proposed that the schedule for grand unification be moved forward a year.

During this period, the PUU chose to affiliate to new National Councils at each convention. However, the JCP faction in the All Japan Prefectural and Municipal Workers' Union (*Jichirō*) and the Japan Teachers' Union (*Nikkyōsō*) opposed the unification. These two factions boycotted and split the conventions.[13] Despite these setbacks, in 1989 the grand unification of Private Rengō and the PUU to form the new national council, Rengō, was finally realised after twenty-five years of struggle and effort. At the same time Sōhyō disbanded.

In one sense unification had come too early. The PRU had originally considered that the process would take much longer. Sōhyō, Dōmei and Chūritsurōren had each left it up to their successor organisations — Sōhyō Centre, Yuaikaigi and Chūren — to deal with subjects that were too complex to bring immediately onto the agenda of the new National Council. Such subjects included political activities and local organisations.[14]

A turn to the Left

The DPCIR of Private Rengō during the second half of the 1980s were again influenced by changes in the nation's political and economic circumstances. The DPCIR were also shaped inevitably by the grand unification. In 1987, Zenminrōkyō planned to make a statement similar to the *Maekawa Report* as a basis for DPCIR. At the same time, the contents of DPCIR were changing.[15]

For example, the statement for DPCIR of 1986–87 stressed the need to reform the unfair tax system and reduce income tax for salaried workers. That of 1987–88, however, emphasised the need for structural adjustment in production and consumption. In the following year this developed beyond structural adjustment into full systemic change. The statement for that year had a social democratic tone, and called for establishment of a welfare vision for an ageing society, reduced working hours and correction of the disparity in working conditions between large and small-scale enterprises. Private Rengō produced a publication titled *General Welfare Vision for an Ageing Society*, which included measures for extending social welfare.

Thus the trend of the DPCIR in this period was a 'turn to the Left', in contrast with the previous period, which had seen a 'turn to the Right'. These changes in DPCIR were mainly a product of the strategic adjustment by Private Rengō to its own change in circumstances. In the background, however, were the ideas of Sohyo which the grand unification had introduced.

Unexpected political success

Since the days of Seisuikaigi and Zenminrōkyo, which had held periodic meetings with ministries, sent representatives to governmental councils and influenced policy making in the bureaucracy, the 'participative democratic strategy' of the PRU matured with the advent of Private Rengō. Many proposals were incorporated into the DPCIR. Among these were that new policy making councils, consisting of representatives from all the concerned bodies, including unions, should be formed. Another was that workers' representatives should be drawn into established government councils. Furthermore, in the general welfare vision mentioned above, the governmental council system was considered an effective organ to compensate for weaknesses in the parliamentary system.

In the 1989 election for the House of Councillors, however, the political situation of Private Rengō changed completely. It stood twelve candidates and unexpectedly won a great victory, forming *Rengō Sangiin* (Rengō Upper House Group) as a group within the House. This outcome was not what Private Rengō had been seeking. Rather, it was the consequence of pressure upon this national body by the newly established Local Private Rengō, which had responded to political changes at the grassroots level.[16] Consequently, national Private Rengō, which had a wide network because it contained groups with different political backgrounds became involved in its own political struggles. This came about within Private Rengō itself, without a clear political strategy.[17]

Rengō's debut (1989–92)

Leaping ahead as a new national council

On 21 November 1989, Rengō, the Japanese Trade Union Council, held its inaugural convention. The book of proposals prepared for the convention was full of the determination of the new National

Council to function as the most comprehensive of all the councils in Japan.

Among its basic goals were to achieve equality of the sexes in the labour force (which had not been a goal of Private Rengō), as well as restoring basic labour rights under law for public sector employees. Environmental safeguards were proclaimed forthrightly under the heading 'Subject and Mission'. The terms 'comfort', 'affluence' and 'fairness', that Sōhyō had first used a few years earlier and that Rengō had been using in its 'total life improvement' plan, also appeared in its 'Action Plan'. As well, in Rengō's new secretariat, an office was established for small and medium-sized enterprises, aiming to remove the disparity in working conditions between large-scale enterprises and smaller ones.

In taking account of social issues such as gender, equality and environmental protection, this 'living oriented' stance of Rengō was influenced by social trends following the release of the *Maekawa Report*. This stance also reflected Rengō's intention to create a new National Council identity that was in keeping with the times.[18]

Blowing in the wind

The early days of Rengō were blessed with the favourable conditions that then prevailed. Although Japan's 'bubble economy' began to deflate from 1990, the issue of greatest concern in those days was the abnormal way of life arising from unusual overwork and an extraordinary rise in real estate prices, rather than issues arising from serious economic recession that preoccupied the following period. Rengō's DPCIR and shūntō activities during this time were enhanced by the Council's opportunity to seize the times. In particular, it set a goal of reducing the number of work hours per year to 1,800, by 1993. As Rengō embarked on its campaigns, the trend towards reduced working hours had already strengthened rapidly after the government also incorporated this goal into its five-year plan for economic management, as part of the 1988 structural adjustment.

For shuntō. Rengō included the reduction of working hours as well as wage increases, and it moved affiliated unions to action. At the same time Rengō pressured political parties into laying the groundwork for reducing working hours, and urged government bodies to make institutional arrangements for promoting this goal.

Consequently, a large number of unions made great headway on the issue of reduced working hours in the 1991 and 1992 shūntō. Rengō succeeded in incorporating a reduction of annual work hours to 1,800 by 1996 as a goal in the government's new economic plan, the Five-Year Plan for Advancing Quality of Life, that was adopted in 1992. Rengō was also successful in its push to enact the Temporary Measures Law to Promote Reduced Working Hours, to take effect on an industry-wide and regional basis. Rengō was also behind the 'Declaration of Comfort', which affirmed the decision to reduce work hours in the Diet and in a number of local assemblies. In addition, Rengō contributed to the enactment of laws on child-care leave, a holdings tax, promoting regional employment, and securing labour for small and medium-sized enterprises.[19]

Political drive

Although Private Rengō had unexpectedly become an important political actor in the 1989 House of Councillors election, it did not have a firm policy steering its political activities. At its inaugural convention, Rengō came up with aphorisms such as its role of 'triggering political change', 'leaving choice of support for political parties to each affiliated organisation' and 'limiting co-operating political parties to Rengō Sangiin, JSP, DSP, Kōmeitō and Shaminren'.

Rengō moved to set in place a comprehensive policy after a series of talks on forming a coalition with JSP, DSP and Kōmeitō. These talks followed the 1990 House of Representatives election in which the JSP performed strongly while the DSP and Kōmeitō performed miserably. In 1991 Rengō's political committee published its *Report on the Political Policy of Rengō*, which moved well beyond its usual ideas about the relationship between unions and political parties.

First, the report attached importance to 'social justice' and 'international co-operation' in a section on 'political ideas', to 'superiority of public interest' and 'system change' in a section on 'expected politics', to 'policy-based choice of political party and politicians' in a section on 'relationship between unions and political parties' and to 'the representatives of working people' in the section 'the political role of Rengō'. These ideas were as new and fresh as the general political opinion that had begun to surface in Japanese society. The report heralded the transformation of the dominant labour politics paradigm from the bloc-based and conflict politics model, to a network-based consensus model. The report gave as its aims: promoting functional separation between unions and political parties, and forming voluntarily supportive relations between parties, politicians and union members to replace traditional relationships based on support for a specific party as determined by the affiliated unions.[20]

Immediate attempts were made to partially implement the report. In 1992 for the House of Councillors election, Rengō made preparations for a larger-scale effort than ever under the slogan, 'Changing Government through a New Political Force', after Rengō's candidates had defeated LDP candidates in a few by-elections. In this election, it fielded new candidates with whom the electorate was unfamiliar. These included businessmen, an officer of the national agricultural co-operative, an actor and so forth. It also supported candidates running for the JSP and the DSP.

Rengō discussed the national issues to be put forward in its basic policy, reaching consensus among its members on both foreign and defence policies. It was able to obtain concessions from affiliated unions, particularly public sector ones. Nevertheless, Rengō's candidates were soundly beaten in this election. The LDP had aimed its attack at Rengō, lured the DSP and Kōmeitō by co-operating with them on the divisive United Nations Peace Keeping Operations issue, and had also helped cause a split between the JSP and the DSP.

This defeat caused Rengō virtually to give up the idea of reconciliation between the JSP and the DSP. The defeat also prompted among the major affiliated private unions a much firmer commitment to re-alignment with parties, in order to bring in a new government through a new political force.[21] In this way, Rengō pursued a 'political democratic strategy', a shift from the 'participative democratic strategy' it had favoured in earlier times.[22]

Local Rengō begin

From 1989 to 1990, Local Rengō were formed one after another in each prefecture. They served as new local centres for affiliated local unions. The successor organisations of local Sōhyō and Dōmei retained responsibility for political activity that had not been subsumed by Rengō, due to the severe conflicts between these bodies in the past.

The central members of Local Rengō were the unions of influential local industries such as electricity, telecommunications, retail and electrical machinery, as well as local government unions.[23] In all Local Rengō, there were cleavages even bigger than in national Rengō, between ex-Sōhyō related unions and ex-Dōmei ones, and between public sector unions and private ones. Hence Local Rengō needed to tackle various tasks with vigour and sensitivity in order to forge a new identity for themselves locally.[24]

National Rengō's nationwide 'reduction of working hours' campaign gave impetus to the Local Rengō initiatives. The first DPCIR of Local Rengō urged each prefectural authority to make preparations for participation by Local Rengō representatives, while the process of DPCIR had made Local Rengō aware of prefectural politics. Some Local Rengō used the DPCIR as the start of their attempts to seek a social partnership with local government and employer associations.

The political events that most decisively influenced the development of Local Rengō were, however, elections. In particular, the 1989 and 1992 House of Councillors elections in which almost all Local Rengō were involved brought out the bright and dark sides of election influences on these local organisations. The 1989 election solidified the relationship between ex-Sōhyō related unions and ex-Dōmei ones, while the 1992 election alienated the two streams within each Local Rengō. Such experiences gave each Local Rengō the incentive to decide for itself the most appropriate line of political activity according to local conditions.

On the other hand, elections for prefectural governors during these years had rather different implications for the conduct of political activity by Local Rengō. On this electoral scene, the power orientation of Local Rengō appeared clearly. Increasingly it saw Rengō supporting winning candidates virtually irrespective of the candidate's party. All the while it was the intention of Local Rengō to achieve their various policy demands smoothly, and prevent their organisations from splitting internally.[25]

The height of Rengō's glory (1992–94)

Widening political links to the Right

After the 1992 House of Councillors election, major affiliated unions which had supported the JSP and the DSP over a long period began to re-examine their support for political parties. Both parties had fared poorly. A few leaders of these unions had connections with Ozawa Ichirō, the central power broker and ex-Secretary-General of the LDP, with whom some of the private sector unions had co-operated in the 1992 election for Governor of Tokyo. The major unions' search for alternative ways to support political parties intensified when Ozawa and his cohort from the Takeshita faction split from the LDP. After that, much of the political manoeuvring among Rengō, the affiliated unions, politicians and political parties proceeded in the name of political reform.

The first institutionalised move was reform of the electoral system. This had become the focus of political reform since the autumn of 1992. The leaders of Rengō and major affiliated unions planned their strategy so that they would first urge the reformist group within the JSP to participate in Diet discussions about reforming the electoral system. They had expected the JSP to split and form part of 'the new political force', after Rengō President Yamagishi Akira had agreed with Ozawa Ichirō in early 1993 about the need to reform the electoral system for political re-alignment.[27] There were also, however, other union leaders who conspired with the leaders of the DSP, Kōmeitō, and the newly-formed JNP (Japan New Party). There was also LDP renegade Takemura Masayoshi who was soon to head another new party, Sakigake, and other LDP politicians beyond the Ozawa group who were interested in forming 'the new political force'. At the 1993 general election, 'the nine union group' of the major ex-Sōhyō and ex-Dōmei unions supported candidates from all three of the newer parties, the JNP, Sakigake and Ozawa's party, JRP (Japan Renewal Party), in addition to the JSP, DSP and Kōmeitō. All were non-LDP candidates. Meanwhile the names of JSP politicians who opposed electoral reform were removed from the list of members to be supported by these nine unions.

After the election, in which the LDP lost its parliamentary majority, Rengō President Yamagishi worked judiciously behind the scenes, particularly with the JSP, to help form a non-LDP coalition government.[28] Rengō and the nine unions group were naturally delighted with the establishment of the Hosokawa administration, almost as if the coalition had been their own doing.[29] At the annual meeting of those major unions in the summer of 1994, the leaders of all the coalition parties (JNP, Sakigake, JRP, JSP, DSP, Kōmeitō and Shaminren), were invited as guests. In Rengō's meeting the following autumn, Hosokawa gave the first address to be given by the Prime Minister in Japanese union history.

The effect of non-LDP government

Because Rengō had played a major role in the birth of the Hosokawa administration, it found this administration more responsive than had ever been the case under LDP administrations. Rengō and the affiliated unions by no means expected the new government to deliver everything they requested. In fact the union players from Rengō often had to be content to remain behind the scenes of the administration. This was largely because views on the Hosokawa administration within Rengō were mixed, and because Rengō and the unions had anticipated many problems given the unwieldy nature of this seven-party patchwork coalition.[30]

Certainly, Rengō's DPCIR under the Hosokawa administration did not make great strides forward. For many of the Bills approved in the Diet during this period, Bills that Rengō saw as the result of DPCIR, many arrangements for their passing had already been made before Hosokawa came to government.[31] Rengō and the unions could not stop their political manoeuvrings simply because the LDP had been ousted from government. On the contrary, Rengō was forced to work hard in order to build consensus among the seven coalition partners on the new government's policies, since it alone had the means to persuade all these parties to a particular point of view. When political reform legislation was approved by the coalition parties in January 1994, Rengō and the affiliated unions urged the coalition's Diet members to agree, even at the cost of sidelining a few 'dissident' members, and in spite of the unsatisfactory content of this legislation.[32]

The reform of the public pension system was a case that typified parliamentary process during the Hosokawa administration. After initial failure in the House, this Bill was eventually carried over to the next sitting. Rengō, the Ministry of Health and Welfare and the ruling parties continued to approach the issue from different perspectives, right to the end. In fact these players were taking good care of each other throughout the long-winded approval process, even though officially they appeared to be arguing back and forth.[33]

The reduction of income tax, however, was quite a different matter for Rengō. This was the only real demand that Rengō made upon the Hosokawa administration. It had pushed this claim, expecting from the outset that the outcome would take effect under domestic economic conditions of recession and a slump in wages. Nevertheless, in drafting the 1994 budget, the Ministry of Finance joined forces with Ozawa to insist on a package to reduce income tax and increase consumption tax simultaneously. This was in opposition to Rengō's view that the income tax reductions should be introduced before any increase in the consumption tax. Rengō was angered by the National Welfare Tax plan pushed by the Ministry of Finance and Ozawa, and pressed the coalition parties to co-operate with its demand. In the end, a plan was put forward to reduce income tax without the welfare tax in February 1994, at the behest of the coalition parties. This case lit a political bonfire among Rengō, the affiliated unions, the coalition parties and the Hosokawa administration.[34]

Labour's depths of despair (1994–   )

Political schism

The conflict over reducing income tax brought with it a sense of the impending political crisis. The influence of the Ozawa group was expanding within the Hosokawa administration. The ex-Sōhyō union leaders and particularly Yamagishi were inclined towards forming a 'third pole' based on 'the concentration of social democratic and liberal forces' in the Japanese political landscape, and including the JSP, DSP, Sakigake and a part of the LDP.[35]

After the JSP chose not to join the second non-LDP coalition, making it a minority government, the relationship between the ex-Sōhyō affiliated unions and the ex-Dōmei unions became more contorted. Rengō was caught up in this, and was forced to declare a policy of being 'fair and square' to the ruling administration.

In the wake of these developments, the movement which had concentrated social democratic and liberal forces began to divide. One stream was oriented towards the Hosokawa coalition, the other towards the Murayama one. The former comprised Zentei (organised by postal service workers), Zendentsū (organised by telecommunications service workers) and the major ex-Dōmei unions. The latter comprised Jichirō (organised by local government workers) and other bodies.

Zentei, Zendentsū and Jichirō were all major ex-Sōhyō unions with a strong influence on the JSP. Zentei and Zendentsū had supported the centre of the 'reformists' in the JSP, but were seriously concerned at discussions in the political and business world about privatising the postal service and dividing NTT (the national telecommunications body). These two put their faith in Ozawa's political clout. On the other hand, Jichirō considered the social democratic parties in the West European countries as their idea of an appropriate political force and therefore had the 'conservative' members of Diet, including the JSP's Murayama, within their organisation. The fate of the Murayama administration depended heavily on the consequences of this conflict.[36]

It peaked at the end of 1994 and the beginning of 1995. Zentei and Zendentsū had been hasty in supporting the formation of Shinshintō (the New Frontier Party or NFP) to unify most of the opposition parties under one umbrella in December 1994. They were also involved in a plan to split the JSP in January 1995. This plan was foiled when the JSP Diet members who had intended to resign from the party re-thought their position and the consequences of their actions for the national government, after both were rocked by the Kobe earthquake.[37] To avoid isolation, Zentei and Zendentsū moved to reconcile with Jichirō and other union bodies. Meanwhile, in the background, the LDP dangled before their eyes the threatening prospect of privatising the postal service and dividing NTT.[38]

On the other hand, after the DSP joined the NFP, the ex-Dōmei unions became the mainstay of the new party, alongside Sōka Gakkai, the religious organisation that supported Komeitō. Before long the power of the newly formed umbrella party was brought home to the people. In the 1995 House of Councillors election, the NFP scored a sizeable victory and the candidates supported by the ex-Dōmei unions performed very well. Immediately after that the parties in the Murayama coalition, particularly the LDP, denounced Sōka Gakkai as an abnormal religious organisation, in order to weaken the NFP. This did not cause real unrest among the ex-Dōmei unions. At the end of 1995, Ozawa replaced ex-prime minister Kaifu to lead the NFP. Ozawa nominated an ex-chief secretary of the DSP as the NFP's new secretary-general. These circumstances suggest that the ex-Dōmei unions intend to continue their support for the NFP for the time being. Yet with the ex-Dōmei unions supporting the NFP, this has led to a sense of rivalry among the ex-Sōhyō unions.

The ex-Sōhyō unions had helped repair relations between Zentei, Zendentsu and Jichirō. After the JSP's crushing defeat in the 1995 upper house election, these unions sensed an impending crisis in the next general election. They decided to push forward to form a new party to replace the JSP in order to make the 'third pole', based on a concentration of social democratic and liberal forces. Certainly, the result of the 1995 upper house election had been decisive enough to expect the appearance of a conservative two-party regime under the small constituency electoral system which will take effect with the next general election. The ex-Sōhyō and ex-Dōmei unions thus fought the election without compunction. Although these unions at one time had manoeuvred in earnest, the movement to form a new liberal party reached a deadlock at the end of 1995 due to disagreements within the JSP and Sakigake. The unions concerned are therefore seeking co-operation from the LDP in the next general election.

The effect of a 'fair and square' approach

Although Rengō adopted an attitude of 'fair and square' after the brief interlude of the Hata administration early in 1994, this stance did not lead to a slump in DPCIR. This was because Rengō could choose between the measures devised to deal with DPCIR offered by both the ruling and opposition parties, using to its own advantage the situation in which the parties supported by the affiliated unions were split into two.

As mentioned earlier, Rengō was successful with its push for amendments during deliberations on a Bill concerning the public pension system in autumn 1994. It got the opposition parties on side and by jolting the JSP into allegiance, forced the LDP to make concessions.[39] This happened again during the deliberations on the Bill for nursing leave.[40] In the background was the intention of both the LDP and the NFP to curry favour with Rengō.[41] Meanwhile, Rengō has held periodical conferences about DPCIR with the NFP as well as the JSP, Sakigake and the LDP.

Although the LDP attempted to recover its earlier closeness with Rengō, by the end of 1995 there had been no conspicuous change in the relationship. Rengō's anti-LDP policy continues to present obstacles. Yet the relationship between Rengō's affiliated unions and the LDP has been a different matter. The greatest beneficiary has been Jichirō, as I shall explain.

The short history of Rengō's DPCIR under review here reveals that they have made a great contribution to improving the social welfare system in a difficult climate of economic recession and budget curtailments since 1990. For example, in addition to the successes mentioned above, Rengō's DPCIR have helped establish or revise laws and policies concerning part-time workers' employment and insurance for those of advanced age, job security for nurses, a ten-year plan for welfare for the aged, a five-year plan for child care and so forth. These DPCIR have been especially effective under the Murayama administration. Needless to say, providing better social welfare for an ageing society involves expanding the public sector. Jichirō had been expected to provide some social welfare services as part of a plan to decentralise power away from the national level, and could therefore play a key role in realising Rengō's demands by making full use of its links with the JSP, LDP and related ministries. In the process it could secure Rengō's own interests such as the right of fire fighters to organise.[42]

The teachers' union, Nikkyōsō, has been another beneficiary of the LDP/JSP coalition. In autumn 1994, Nikkyōsō virtually changed its stance from antagonism to partnership with the LDP and the Ministry of Education on the issue of educational reforms. Nikkyōsō has entered into dialogue with the LDP, the Ministry of Education and related associations one after the other, keeping in mind the success of Jichirō.[43]

Denryokusōren (the electrical workers' union) has also taken good care of its relationship with the LDP, despite its history as a major ex-Dōmei union. Managers within the electrical industry have been more than mere friends with the LDP. Their industry was closely connected with politics from the start, since electricity is a public utility. Denryokusōren supports nuclear electric power generation, and so has felt a closer affinity to the LDP than the JSP. And with the potential for the management to increase electricity bills, labour has felt could not antagonise the ruling party.

The unions representing the workers in export industries such as steel, electrical machinery and automobiles were disgusted by the extent of Denryokusōren's power during the Murayama administration. These industries had suffered heavily under policies that promoted, or at least allowed, a strong yen. What they had desired most during this period was deregulation. Certainly, while Rengō continued to criticise the indecisiveness of successive administrations towards deregulation and administrative reform, it did not itself reach an internal consensus on these matters. Conflict arose not only between public and private sector unions, but also among those representing workers in the processing, materials and energy industries.[44]

The unions representing workers in export industries, whose centre is the JC (Japan Council of Metalworkers' Unions), were irritated with this situation. These unions formed a united front with Nikkeiren (Japan Federation of Employers' Associations), which took a strong stance on promoting deregulation. For example, when Nikkeiren's President Nagano criticised the government for increasing public utility charges in 1994, the JC cheered him on. In discussions concerning shuntō, 'self-determination of industrial federations' appears as the key catchphrase. JC has used this in order to admonish the low productivity industry unions that have taken a free ride on the wage improvements that the high productivity unions have struggled to achieve. At the same time, Nikkeiren put the blame for the meagreness of the wage increases on delays by the government in market deregulation.

Nikkeiren's stance shifted with a change of presidency from Nagano (from manufacturing), to Nemoto (from transportation). For example, under Nemoto, Nikkeiren and JC co-published *The Big Ten Proposals by Labour and Management for Correcting the Overvalued Yen and Stopping Deindustrialization*. However, the content of this tract had been toned down from the original, which had been prepared during Nagano's presidency. The situation is all the more serious for JC because in Japan, as in many industrialised economies, employment opportunities are waning.

The decline of local Rengō

Local Rengō have been disturbed by national Rengō's political preoccupations during this period. When the Hosokawa administration came to power, Local Rengō were at a loss. They faced rapid change in the political environment with unfamiliar political parties and allowances.[45] After the Hata administration took office, Local Rengō were further troubled by political splits and the withdrawal of some parties from this coalition government. The tenacious Local Rengō tried to maintain the framework of the original non-LDP coalition and planned to form what was virtually to be a new party out of Local Rengō.[46] Clashes between the LDP and NFP and disorder within the JSP after the 1995 House of Councillors election destroyed the plan and Local Rengō were buried in a political landslide.[47]

Meanwhile, strategies for taking power at the local level changed fundamentally. In nationwide local government elections in 1995, in crucial electorates such as Tokyo metropolis, amateur independent candidates defeated the professionals who Local Rengō co-supported with almost all political parties. Mass media generally explained this result as the electorate's disillusionment with all existing political parties and presented Local Rengō unfavourably as the ringleaders of co-sponsored elections.[48] At this point, midway through the 1990s, most Local Rengō malfunction or cannot exercise real political influence beyond the relatively low level of the prefectural assembly.

Rengō held its fourth convention in 1995. Many affiliated unions and Local Rengō had expected that at this convention a decision would be taken to unify the diverse political policies of Rengō bodies. This idea was shelved. The move was seen by many to manifest the powerlessness and apolitical disposition of the new Rengō president, Ashida Jinnosuke, who had taken over from Yamagishi the previous autumn.

Also at this time, the Action Program to Build an Overall Consensus-Oriented System had gained a bad name. There had been little struggle over the issue.[49] The idea of building all-round consensus was reflected in the 1995–96 DPCIR in the context of identifying the original idea behind DPCIR, emphasising particularly the need for wide policy consultation — with the administration, the political parties and the appropriate ministries — in other words, democratisation of the Administrative Council. In this DPCIR, the terms 'advanced welfare society' and 'decentralisation' were offered as important goals of Japanese society. A concrete example of these ideas is the thinking outlined in a Rengō publication released towards the end of 1995. Titled *Toward our New Nursing System*, it is full of a vision of general welfare, as outlined above.

Conclusion

As we enter the second half of the last decade of this century, Rengō appears to be steering a course away from political democratic strategies, back toward participative democratic strategies. In this way it appears to have returned to its roots. Through the first six years of the Heisei period, Japan's party politics have taken off in directions largely unforeseen as the nation began to cast off its Showa heritage in 1989, when Rengō began its life at the forefront of Japan's labour politics. The volatility in party politics, and the trend towards conservatism in the labour movement in the past few years, have fundamentally shaped what Rengō has set out to achieve and what it can achieve as a voice for organised labour in Japan. Rengō has lurched along a winding, bumpy road through the Heisei years. The challenges are enormous as it faces the future.

Notes

1. In earlier articles I have treated some of the issues surfacing during this period. See Toru Shinoda, 'The Tale of Cain and Abel? — A Study of the Contemporary Japanese Labor Politics', *Japan Labor Bulletin* 34 (11) 1995; Toru Shinoda, 'Rengō and Policy Participation — Japanese Style Neo-Corporatism?' in Mari Sako and Hiroki Sato (eds), (forthcoming), *Japanese Management and Labour in Transition*, London: Routledge.
2. For an outline of the post-war labour movement, see Hisashi Kawada, 'Workers and Their Organizations', in Kazuo Okochi, Bernard Karsh and Solomon B. Levine (eds) (1974) *Workers and Employers in Japan — The Japanese Employment Relations System*, Tokyo: University of Tokyo Press and Princeton: Princeton University Press; T.J. Pempel and Keiichi Tsunekawa (1979) 'Corporatism Without Labor?' in Phillipe C. Schmitter and Gerhard Lehmbruch (eds), *Trends Toward Corporatist Intermediation*, London: Sage; Andrew J. Taylor (1989) *Trade Unions and Politics — A Comparative Introduction*, London: Macmillan. On post-war Japanese national elections and political parties, see Norihiko Narita (1995) *The Diet, Elections and Political Parties*, Tokyo: Foreign Press Center.
3. On the influence of Marxism-Lenism on Japanese unions, see Taishiro Shirai 'Japanese Labor Unions and Politics', in Taishiro Shirai (ed.) (1983) *Contemporary Industrial Relations in Japan*, Madison: University of Wisconsin Press.
4. For detail on MLFU, see Rōdō Undōshi Kenkyūkai (ed.) (1996) *Shiryō rōdō sensen tōitsu — Sōhyō, Dōmei kara Rengō e* (Data on labour front unification — from Sōhyō and Dōmei to Rengō), Tokyo: Rōdō Kyōiku Center.
5. On the establishment of Private Rengō, see Michio Nitta, 'Birth of Rengō and Reformation of Union Organization', *Japan Labor Bulletin*, 4 February 1988.
6. On the situation of DPCIR in these periods, see Shinoda Toru (1989) *Seikimatsu no rōdō undō* (The labour movement at the end of the century), Iwanami Shoten; Shinoda Toru (1992) '"Rengō" jidai ni okeru "Seisaku sanka" no genjo to tenbo' (The present situation and prospects of policy participation in the "Rengō" era) in Hōsei Daigaku Ohara Shakai Mondai Kenkyūjyo (ed.), *Rengō jidai no rōdō undō* (The labour movement in the Rengō era), Tokyo: Sōgō rōdō kenkyūjo.
7. For further detail on labour politics in this period, see Shinkawa Toshimitsu (1993) *Nihongata fukushi no seijikeizaigaku* (Political economy of Japanese-style welfare), Tokyo: Sanichi Shobo, pp 203–16; Ikuo Kume, 'Changing Relations Among Government, Labor, and the Business in Japan after the Oil Crisis', *International Organization* 42 (4), Autumn 1988.
8. Inagami Takeshi (1980) *Rōdōsha sanka to shakai seisaku* (Workers' participation and social policy), in Aoi Kazuo and Naoi Yu (eds),

Fukushi to keikaku no shakaigaku (Sociology of welfare and planning), Tokyo: University of Tokyo Press; Tsujinaka Yutaka (1986) *Gendai Nihon seiji no kōporatizumuka — rōdō to hoshu seiken no futatsu no senryaku no kōsaku* (The corporatisation of modern Japanese labour politics: A mixture of strategies by labour and conservative governments), in Uchida Man (ed.), *Kōza seijigaku III Seiji katei* (Lectures on political science: 3 — political process), Tokyo: Sanreishobo.

9. Omi Naoto *Gendai Nihon no makuro kōporatizumu: Chingin kettei to seisaku sanka* (Macro-corporatism in contemporary Japan: wage negotiation and policy participation) in Inagami Takashi, *et al.* (1994) *Neo koporatizumu no kokusai hikaku* (Comparative research in neo-corporatism), Tokyo: Nihon Rodo Kenkyu Kiki.

10. For detail on these points, see Takeshi Inagami 'Labor Front Unification and Zenmin Rōkyō: The Emergence of Neo-corporatism', *Japan Labor Bulletin*, 1 May 1986; Shinoda, '*Rengō* jidai ni okeru '*seisaku*' sanka'; Yutaka Tsujinaka, *Rōdōkai no saihen to 86 nen taisei no imi* (Labour realignment and the significance of the '86 regime), *Revaiasan*, Autumn 1987.

11. A detailed explanation of this point is made in Sasaki Takeshi (1987) *Ima seiji ni naniga kanōka* (What can politics do now?), Tokyo: Chūō Kōronsha.

12. On the grand unification, see Michio Nitta, 'Grand Unification of Japan's Labor Movement — Formation of New Rengō', *Japan Labor Bulletin*, 1 February 1990.

13. For detail on the anti-Rengō movement, see Kinoshita Takeo (1992) 'Taikōteki nashonaru sentā no keisei ni tomonau sangyō betsu zenkoku sōshiki no bunretsu to saihen' (The making of opposition national centres and splits and realignments of industrial organisations) in Hōsei Daigaku Ohara Shakai Mondai Kenkyujo (ed.) *Rengō jidai no rōdō undō.*

14. After that, Sohyo Center and Yuaikaigi were succeeded by simpler organisations. They are, however, still active.

15. *The Course of Japan*, which Rengō settled on in 1993, was the fruit of this plan. See Shinoda Toru (1994) 'Ima mata kōporatizumu no jidai nanoka — mezo kōporatizumu to sono Nihonteki tenkai' (The era of corporatism again? Meso corporatism and Japanese style development), in Inagami Tsuyoshi *et al.*, *Neo kōparatizumu no kokusai hikaku* (Comparative research in neo-capitalism), Tokyo: Nihon Rōdō Kenkyū Kiko.

16. Yamagishi Akira (1995) '*Renritsu*' *Shikakenin* (The instigator for coalition), Tokyo: Kodansha, 1995.

17. For detail on this House of Councillors election, see Narita (1995) *The Diet, Elections and Political Parties.*

18. Inoue Sadahiko (1996) 'Seikatsu taikoku gokanen keikaku' (The five year plan for advancing quality of life), in Kazuyoshi Kōshiro and Rengō Sōgō Seikatsu Kaihatsu Kenkyūjo (eds) *Sengo 50 new: sangyō koyō rōdō shi* (Fifty post-war years: industry, employment and labour history), Tokyo: Nihon Rōdō Kenkyū Kiko.

19. On the results of *shuntō* in this period, see Nihon Rōdō Kenkyū Kikō, *Rōdō undō hakusho (kakunenban)* (Annual white paper on the labour movement), Tokyo: Nihon Rōdō Kenkyū Kikō, 1991, 1992, 1993.
20. For detail on the political policy of Rengō, see Michio Nitta (1991) 'Probing Rengō's Political Policy', *Japan Labor Bulletin* 30 (4).
21. Yoshimura Yōsuke and Takagi Ikura (eds), (1994) *Rengō Now: 21 seiki rōdō undō no tenbō* (Rengō now: Perspectives on the labour movement in the 21st century), Tokyo: Rōdō kyōiku Center.
22. On this change in political strategy, see Takashi Hikohiro (1993) 'Seiji kaikaku ron no sai kosei' (Reconstruction of the political reform argument), in Takahashi Hikohiro, *Sayoku chishikijin no riron sekinin* (The theoretical accountability of leftist intellectuals), Tokyo: Mado sha.
23. Shinoda Tōru (1992) 'Chihō sōshiki no saihen — sono bunseki shikaku ni tsuite' (Realignment of local organisations — an analytical perspective), in Hōsei Daigaku Ohara Shakai Mondai Kenkyūyō (ed.), *Rengō jidai no rōdō undō*.
24. On the new identity of Local Rengō, see Shinoda Tōru, 'Saki o kaku 'Rōdō' — sangyō, chiiki o meguru kōzō chōsei to sei rō shi kankei no imi' (Labour taking initiatives — the implications of structural adjustment and tripartism across industry and region), *Economics and Labor* 92, special issue on labour, 1993.
25. For background on Rengō's commitment to the governors' elections, see Shinoda Toru (1994) 'Rodosha ni kagirinai aijo o' — aru chiho rosei no monogatari' (Give workers unlimited love — A tale of local labour politics), in Kataoka (ed.). *Gendai Gyosei Kokka to Seisaku Katei* (Contemporary administrative state and the policy process), Waseda Daigaku Shuppankai.
26. On the relationship between unions and the political world before and after the Hosokawa administration, see *Asahi Shinbun*, 15–19 March 1994; *Asahi Shinbun*, 18 March 1994 and 19 October 1994.
27. Yamagishi Akira (1995) *Ware kaku tatakaeri* (I fought like this), Tokyo: Asahi Shinbunsha, pp. 6–9.
28. Yamagishi, *Ware kaku tatakaeri*, pp. 12–21.
29. For political opinions on the affiliated union leaders of Rengō immediately after the 1993 general election, see Yoshimura Yosuke and Takagi Ikurō (eds) (1994) *Rengō Now: 21 seiki rōdō undō no tenbō* (Rengō now: Perspectives of the labour movement in the 21st century), Tokyo: Rōdōkyōiku Centre.
30. Yamagishi (1995) *'Renritsu' shikanenin* (The instigator for coalition), Tokyo: Kōdansha.
31. For detail on the result of DPCIR in this period, see Rengō (1994) *Seisaku seido no torikumi to kekka* (The measures and results of the policy system), in *Rengō seisaku shiryō* (Rengō Policy Documents) 76.
32. 'Seirō' (Politics and Labour), *Asahi Shinbun*, 18 March 1994; Yamagishi, *Renritsu*, pp. 169–95.
33. For detail on this political process, see Shinoda Toru, 'Shakai hosho seisaku ni okeru seiji katei — hitotsu no dessan (the political process of social security policy — a sketch), *SOCIUS*, 1, 1994.
34. Yamagishi, *Renritsu*, pp. 169–95.

35. Ibid.
36. 'Sentakushi o kangaeru Rinen no mosaku' (Thinking about alternatives — Seeking ideas), *Asahi Shinbun*, 19–28 October 1994; Sasaki Yoshitaka, 'Shakaito, rodokai, Ozawashi no kankei' (The relationships between the SDPJ, labour unions and Mr Ozawa), *AERA*, 24 October 1994.
37. 'Rengō naibu isshoku sokuhatsu ni' (The explosive situation in Rengō), *Nikkei Shinbun*, 18 December 1994.
38. 'Toshutsu sake soshiki boei' (Avoid prominence, protect organisation), *Asahi Shinbun*, 22 February 1995a.
39. 'Rengō naibu isshoku sokuhatsu ni' (The explosive situation in Rengō), *Nikkei Shinbun*, 18 December 1994.
40. *Saihen no ashimoto* (The underlay for realignment), *Asahi Shinbun*, 4 March 1995.
41. 'Sentakushi o kangaeru', *Asahi Shinbun*, 18 March 1994.
42. Ibid.
43. *Nikkyōsō, Monbusho to patona ni* (Nikkyōsō, toward partnership with the Ministry of Education), *Asahi Shinbun*, 19 October 1994.
44. *Nikkei Shinbun*, 13 February 1995.
45. *Sei, rō — saihen teiryū* (Politics and labour: An undercurrent of political realignment), *Asahi Shinbun*, 15–19 March 1994.
46. On the Liberal Kinki as a distinctive case, see Nagumo Takashi (1994) *Michi kewashii shamin seiryoku kesshu* (Difficult concentration of social democratic forces), *Asahi*, 5 February 1995.
47. 'Saihen no ashimoto' (The underlay for realignment), *Asahi Shinbun*, 22 June 1995.
48. *Asahi Shinbun*, 4 March 1995.
49. Egami Sumio (1995) *Shikai futōmei na Rengō* (The invisible prospects of Rengō), Tokyo: Shukan Rōdō Nyūsu, 9 October 1995.

11
Japan's agricultural politics at a turning point

Tomoaki Iwai

The changing face of agricultural politics

Since the mid-1980s, agricultural politics in Japan has been in the process of major transformation. Throughout the post-war years, the conservative Liberal Democratic Party (LDP) keenly pursued the farmer's vote. As a consequence, farmers have been able to wield strong influence over agricultural policy in Japan. The overwhelming majority of Japanese farmers are members of the National Federation of Farmers (Nōkyō). Nōkyō's Central Committee (Zenchū) has led farmers in lobbying activities with the aim to maximising benefits for farmers across the nation. Since many of the nation's farmers grow rice, the national rice price policy has been a significant target of Zenchū's political strategies, and it has often attempted to influence this policy by intense lobbying when important policy decisions are being made.[1]

One clear example of this occurs each year when the rice price deliberative council meets to determine the summer price. During that month, farmers across the nation participate in meetings, petitions and other activities. At other times, such large-scale activity is rare. The price deliberative council has been a target of these activities, though Zenchū's main target has been the LDP during its thirty-eight years of continuous rule. Under the LDP, decisions are often made by the party rather than by a neutral government deliberative council. Zenchū could often achieve farmers' objectives by using the strength and size of their vote as a political weapon.

Zenchū's tactics have transformed the producers' rice price from a specific policy issue into a broader-ranging political one. Zenchū has used the strength of the farmers' vote to reinforce its demands to the LDP, and the party has invariably responded favourably, not only in order to secure their vote at election time but also financial support from farmers. In election years, Zenchū sends a questionnaire to all election candidates to determine their position on rice price policy and other agricultural issues. After the election, Zenchū chases up promises made by the winning party, to make sure they are fulfilled. Because of the political strength of the agricultural lobby, the rice price policy became a highly politicised issue. There were even some election years when the LDP's Minister for Agriculture, Forestry and Fisheries attempted to make a deal with Zenchū ahead of the election.[2]

In the short term, then, Zenchū's activities, emphasising the rice price policy, were very successful. Until the mid-1980s, the producers' rice price increased annually and farming districts grew wealthy through protection policies that included subsidies. Agricultural policy continued to provide strong protection for the farming sector despite the fall in the proportion of Japan's farming population from 40 per cent in the 1950s to below 10 per cent in the 1980s. This indicates how influential the agricultural lobby has been in Japanese politics as a unified body led by Zenchū.

Japan's agricultural politics became centred on a distorted policy that favoured agricultural producers despite their numerical decline. Tactics that focused on the rice price policy prevented the rationalisation of Japan's agricultural sector. They served to raise the price of Japan's agricultural produce, particularly rice, to incredible heights, leading to consumer dissatisfaction. Over-protective agricultural policies have also intensified friction in international trade by impeding progress towards an open domestic agricultural market. Zenchū's tough tactics have caused some Japanese to see it as a self-centred radical organisation. The LDP's weakness in the face of pressure from Zenchū has lost the party support among urban populations, since the LDP came to be viewed as the champion of the nation's agricultural interests.

Pressure on the LDP to take action against farming interests mounted both domestically and from foreign sources, with demands for a complete overhaul of Japan's agricultural policy. From the second half of the 1980s, calls from foreign agricultural suppliers and their governments (particularly in the United States) to allow access to Japan's agricultural markets were heard alongside stronger demands from Japanese consumers for reasonably priced agricultural products. Pressure was also applied directly to Zenchū, from internal as well as external sources. Farmers in Nōkyō were themselves becoming increasingly dissatisfied with the central committee of their federation. A 1986 report issued by Zenchū's board of directors identified the major problems facing Nōkyō members: slow movement of prices for agricultural produce overall; a drop in the share price of domestic agricultural produce; cutbacks in the national budget allocation for agriculture due to the government's tight fiscal policy; reduced incomes from farming due to an ageing farming population; increased participation of farmers in other lines of work; and growing competition with Nōkyō's general business. The report also acknowledged that Nōkyō's inability to respond effectively to these problems had resulted in increased dissatisfaction among its members.[3]

Although Zenchū itself had acknowledged this sense of dissatisfaction, until the 1990s little was done to implement policy measures to address these problems. One exception was the government's decision to remove official restrictions on imports of oranges and beef into Japan, as a palliative to mounting trade tensions. The issue on which the government held out most firmly was opening Japan's rice market. Here the Diet made clear its position on protecting agricultural interests, by passing two unanimous resolutions aimed at keeping the Japanese rice market closed to outside competition. While this may have given reassurance to Japanese rice farmers, the move also succeeded in aggravating trade tensions between Japan and the United States and was harshly criticised inside Japan by consumers, financial circles and the mass media.

The political transformation of 1993 that occurred under these circumstances fundamentally changed the face of agricultural politics in Japan. Following the breakaways from the LDP and the party's loss of government at the general election of July 1993, the non-LDP coalition came to power under the leadership of Prime Minister Hosokawa with 'Responsible Reform' as its slogan. With overwhelming and unprecedented support from 70 per cent of the Cabinet, the Hosokawa government announced its decision partially to liberalise the nation's rice market. It thereby helped bring to a successful conclusion the Uruguay Round of the General Agreement on Tariffs and Trade (GATT), in December 1993.

The decision was reached very quickly, not even allowing Zenchū the chance to offer significant opposition. Zenchū had limited access to the non-LDP Hosokawa Cabinet, since its past lobbying had been focused exclusively on the LDP.

Some of the political parties that comprised the Hosokawa government, such as the Renewal Party, of course contained former LDP members. However, the decision to support rice market liberalisation by party Secretary Ozawa Ichirō, who had engineered the rise to power of the Hosokawa government, was taken with the knowledge that since the general election had been held in July of that year, it would be some time until the next election. Furthermore, there was considerable support for liberalising the rice market among the general population and, apart from a few Diet members, opposition was minimal. Its main source was, ironically, from the Socialist Party which was transforming itself from an urban-style political party towards a rural one. However, its decision to give priority to maintaining the coalition in a bid for political reform, in the end forced the socialists to accept the Hosokawa government's decision.

The LDP was at first ready to apply for a vote of no confidence in the government on the grounds that the Hosokawa government's decision to liberalise Japan's rice market violated earlier Diet resolutions. However, strong support for the Hosokawa administration and the view that the LDP would itself have reached the same decision had the party been in power, meant that opposition was relatively muted. If anything, LDP members saw that with a non-LDP government taking this step, the LDP could avoid responsibility for problems arising from the decision, problems that their party had been incapable of resolving while in power. They could see it would be politically convenient for the LDP to leave these decisions to the Hosokawa Cabinet. As a result, problems over liberalising the rice market that had plagued Japanese politics for seven years were solved almost overnight, with only a small amount of political confusion.

There was, of course, solid opposition to this decision from farmers across the nation. The new government's action clearly indicated the severe limitations of the political influence of the farming lobby under the coalition administration. Party politicians who had traditionally supported the protection of agricultural interests and who had hitherto opposed liberalising the rice market, suddenly acquiesced. Under the coalition government, minority and majority parties alike had either openly accepted or given tacit approval to the decision. The relative ease with which such a decision was reached in the Diet, despite Zenchū's strong opposition, caused farmers to have serious doubts about it as a political force. We see, then, that the sweeping changes of 1993, both in government and in agricultural policy, dramatically changed the nature of agricultural politics in Japan, its strategies, aims and outcomes. The upheaval forced farmers to reconsider how best to protect their interests, given that their old strategies were clearly ineffective.

Growing distrust in Nōkyō

The future of Japanese agricultural politics will be affected by the actions of players beyond Zenchū. Farmers are questioning the relationship between agriculture and politics, and seeking to identify new ways of expressing their political interests. At a time when agricultural interests are struggling to make their political voice heard, it clarifies our understanding to know how farmers view institutional politics and their place within it.

National surveys of public attitudes towards politics have naturally included farmers as members of the general population and information concerning farmers' attitudes has been treated in this context. But there are limits to this type of analysis. With Zenchū's co-operation our survey team carried out the first survey exclusively of farmers' attitudes towards politics, questioning 1,982 Nōkyō members affiliated to Zenchū. The purpose of the survey was to ascertain the attitudes of farmers towards politics, given the splits within the LDP and the seven-party coalition's rise to government.[4]

The first issue raised in the survey is farmers' views on liberalising the rice market. The second concerns their views on the changing political environment. The third asks for their ideas on how they can most effectively achieve their future goals.

As anticipated, results on the first question revealed that many farmers were unhappy with the government's decision to liberalise the rice market (Table 11.1). However, less than 36 per cent totally disapproved of liberalising this market, while nearly 30 per cent said that they were resigned to the move. This indicates that partially opening the rice market was expected among the agricultural sector, and that many farmers were prepared for it. At the same time, the level of criticism from farming households was directly related to the proportion of their total income derived from farming. This means that in the present situation where just under 16 per cent of all households engaged in farming pursue farm work full-time, while just under 70 per cent also pursue some type of other work and derive less than half their income from farming, there is likely to be much less criticism than generally anticipated.

Table 11.1 Evaluation of the Uruguay
Round of GATT
Q: What is your view of the agreement reached
during the Uruguay Round to partially open
Japan's rice market?   %

	%
Strongly disagree	35.8
Somewhat disagree	27.9
It can't be helped	29.8
Agree	1.5
Don't know	5.0

The section of the survey where farmers are separated according
to their main line of produce reveals a subtle difference in their
opinions (Table 11.2). Farmers who criticised market liberalisation
were generally engaged in rice, livestock and dairy production,
whereas farmers engaged in vegetable, fruit, and flower and tree
production were usually uncritical of this move. Strong criticism
from rice farmers had been anticipated; nevertheless the criticism
that came from livestock and dairy farmers was stronger. Rice
farmers did not react strongly to the moves for partial rice market
deregulation to a very limited degree (5 per cent), since for them
complete deregulation had not yet become a reality. The rice
liberalisation debate had been part of the mainstream for the previous

Table 11.2 Evaluation of the impact of the Uruguay Round (by
producer's product)

	Grain %	Live- stock %	Vegetables %	Fruit %	Dairy %	Flowers and trees %
Strongly disagree	40.8	44.2	32.9	27.3	49.5	22.0
Somewhat disagree	8.8	26.7	30.3	30.2	20.6	35.2
It can't be helped	24.4	20.9	29.0	34.3	20.6	31.9
Agree	1.0	3.5	1.1	1.6	3.1	3.3
Don't know	5.0	4.7	6.7	6.5	6.1	7.7

seven years, and to some extent the majority of rice farming house-holds had taken steps to prepare for this liberalisation. Consequently, the impact on the rice farmers of the decision partially to open the rice market was relatively small. Opposition was in fact stronger from livestock and dairy farmers, since they had already experienced the effects of liberalising beef and orange markets and understood the costly implications for farmers. It is possible, then, that the effects of rice market liberalisation will be greater than many farmers had thought initially.

The agricultural sector's dissatisfaction with agricultural trade policy was not particularly high before the government's decision to liberalise the rice market (Table 11.3). Farmers' complaints focused mostly on such regulations as changeover of crops. The main grievance for rice farmers was the acreage regulation policy that aimed to regulate the extent of paddy that farmers could plant. Rice farmers had also made strong demands for an increase in the producer's rice price, which had been held constant for the previous ten years. We find that the decision reached just before the closure of the Uruguay Round to liberalise rice markets internationally did not push this issue to the forefront of Japanese farmers' concerns. Rather, they saw their main concern as the absence of concrete results after the government had pledged 6 billion yen to support agricultural production. This apparent failure by the government to fulfil its pledge caused a great deal of distrust among Japanese farmers in the agricultural policies of their government.

One can also detect a change in farmers' attitudes toward Nōkyō, the representative body that for years had been pivotal in bringing

Table 11.3 Dissatisfaction with agricultural policies (by policy area)

	%
Rice price policy	37.8
Production co-ordination (crop change-over)	47.6
Maintenance (land improvement/regeneration)	6.7
Agricultural (produce) trade policy	26.0
Expansion (growth) support strategy	8.5
Strategy to address lack of farming successors	14.3
Sales and distribution policy	25.3
Strategy for farming in valleys	17.2
Regulation of agricultural land	12.9
Nothing in particular	1.6

political pressure to bear in their interests (Table 11.4). More than half the farmers who took part in the survey thought that Nōkyō should put more emphasis on supporting actual farming practice in the form of agricultural technical guidance, as well as on supporting their sales of produce. In relation to farmers' expectations of regulating crop production and rice policy, mentioned earlier as their principal concerns, less than 30 per cent wanted Nōkyō to undertake more political lobbying. During the 1980s, before the move to liberalise rice markets, farmers had been firmly behind Nōkyō's lobbying strategies. Political organisations were set up across the country in each prefecture and the National Farmers Political Council (Nōseikyo) was created within Zenchū to devise more effective lobbying tactics. Yet for all its efforts, Zenchū was unable to stop the government from liberalising the rice market and farmers' expectations have diminished. The major shift in policy has led to significant change in the once-strong relationship between the farmers and Nōkyō, as the survey results indicate.

Table 11.4 Activities that Nōkyō should strengthen
Q: Which Nōkyō activities do you think should be given more emphasis? Choose two from the following.

	%
Sales	48.8
Purchasing	10.7
Credit	8.4
Mutual aid	5.9
Farming methods	60.4
Livelihood activities	7.2
Agricultural policy	28.6
Public relations	4.7
Various consultations	14.0
Cultural activities	2.9
Nothing in particular	3.8

Farmers' political consciousness

This section explores how farmers understood their political position after the collapse of LDP rule and the rise to government of the non-LDP coalition. In the past, the voting rate of farmers has been extremely high, at just over 90 per cent (Table 11.5), while the average voting rate among the general population in lower house

Table 11.5   Voting in the past
Q: Have you voted in past national elections?

	%
Always	90.5
Usually	7.2
Sometimes	1.8
Usually not	0.4
Hardly ever	0.2

elections has been around 70 per cent. The high turnout rate of farmers at elections was in fact a crucial element in their ability to gain strong political influence, since it meant that their political preference would almost certainly be registered. However, when we separate survey results according to the districts where farmers live, we find that though their voting rate is very high in purely agricultural districts, in the urbanised rural areas on the outskirts of cities, the rate tends to fall closer to that for the general population. This is because a large number of farmers in these areas pursue farming as a second job, and their livelihood is therefore less dependent on income from farming than is the case for full-time farmers. As more farmers move to urban or semi-urban areas in search of work and have less vested interest in supporting agricultural interests at the polls, the number of full-time farmers voting is likely to drop.

In Table 11.6 we see respondents' views on the main factors that determine their vote. Most important is the individual candidate, followed by policy, with only about 20 per cent claiming to attribute special significance to the political party. Placing heavy emphasis on the qualities of the individual candidate is common throughout Japanese society, though compared with the rest of the voting population, farmers tend to take the candidate into greater account as an individual, and less account of the party.

This situation is largely the result of an electoral system in which election campaigns focus on individual candidates. But it is also a result of the apparent irrelevance of candidates' party affiliation. Unanimous opposition from all political parties to opening the nation's rice market and unanimous support for increasing the producers' rice price meant there was little to choose between the policies of the parties. Farmers' recognition of these circumstances is clear from the relatively low priority they have given to 'political party'. These circumstances are also reflected in the lower emphasis respondents have given to 'policy'. Agricultural policy is actually extremely important to farmers. However, lack of difference between

Table 11.6   Voting criteria
Q: Which of the following was most important in determining your vote?

	%
Political party	20.8
Policy	27.7
Individual	38.4
Local interests	9.7
Family's view	0.5
Work group's view	1.7
Influence from outsiders	0.4
Other	0.8

political parties and individual candidates in their agricultural policy stance has made 'policy' less of an issue in voting, even though it is of vital concern for them. Because of the virtual sameness of parties and their policies, it is 'individual candidates' who really make a difference at the polls, and is therefore the area of greatest concern.

This attitude was also reflected in the association that farmers have with the support organisations of individual politicians. More than half the respondents were involved with such a political support organisation in some capacity or other (Table 11.7). This far exceeds the rate of involvement by the general population as revealed in the National Electorate Awareness Survey.[5] The large number of farmers who place high importance on the qualities of individual candidates when deciding their vote is no doubt associated with their relatively active participation in the support organisations of individual politicians. The relationship between farmers and politicians thus moves beyond the normal clientelist relationship between politicians and their supporters to become more like a relationship founded in 'the land'. Notwithstanding this, given the relatively cool attitude of politicians towards their decision on rice market liberalisation and their inertia over implementing reforms to the electoral system, farmers can expect considerable changes on the domestic policy front.

Neither family, farming colleagues nor second-workplace colleagues had substantial influence on farmers' votes (Tables 11.8, 11.9, 11.10). The tiny influence of farming colleagues is one indication that Nōkyō does not control farmers' votes. As we saw in the earlier tables, it is the personal relationship between politicians and farmers that heavily determines farmers' votes. Therefore, from the politicians' perspective, gaining the recommendation of Nōkyō and gaining farmers' support are two separate issues. At a glance farmers appear

Table 11.7   Involvement in support group activities
Q: Are you, or your family, actively involved in activities to support a particular politician?

	%
Very involved	14.7
Slightly involved	37.1
Not very involved	27.7
Not involved at all	20.6

Table 11.8   Family influence on vote
Q: Has your family's opinion been important in determining your vote in the past?

	%
Yes, very	18.2
Yes, somewhat	51.4
No	30.4

Table 11.9   Farming colleagues' influence on vote
Q: Has information obtained from farming colleagues been important in determining your vote in the past?

	%
Yes, very	12.8
Yes, sometimes	41.1
No	46.1

Table 11.10   Influence from second workplace upon vote
Q: Has information obtained from your second workplace been important in determining your vote?

	%
Yes, very	7.9
Yes, sometimes	33.5
No	58.6

to be acting in political unison to protect agricultural interests. But it is not the case that all who identify themselves as farmers share the same political interests, nor the same voting preferences. Thus while most farmers are members of Nōkyō, farmers do not necessarily constitute a solid political bloc unified by Nōkyō, and nor is Nōkyō a political organisation that can express the political will of all farmers.

This points to a factor that is crucial in understanding the transformation now underway in agricultural politics in Japan. As more full-time farmers have been forced to supplement their income from non-farm sources of employment, their interests can no longer be seen as monolithic. There are ever-fewer farmers who can speak with one voice exclusively in the interests of 'agriculture'. Farmers' collective clout, as a voting bloc and as a political lobby, has been seriously eroded.

Let us now turn to see how farmers' views of voting considerations translate into voting behaviour, in terms of parties they have supported hitherto and those they think they will support in the future, as of December 1994.

Farmers' political support over the years up to the LDP downfall had been overwhelmingly in favour of the LDP (Table 11.11). This figure is congruent with the results of other national surveys.[6] From this we can again see that the LDP was the accepted party representing the agricultural sector, and as such it was exceedingly protective of agricultural interests. In contrast, there was minimal support among farmers for the Socialist Party and almost no support for urban-style parties such as the Clean Government Party or the Japan New Party, despite these parties also supporting the protection of agricultural interests. However, while support for the LDP was strong, it was entirely dependent on the relationships between farmers and individual politicians.

Table 11.11   Past party support
Q: Which political party have you supported in the past?

%

Liberal Democratic Party	71.3
Socialist Party	11.8
Clean Government Party	0.7
Democratic Socialist Party	1.7
Communist Party	1.7
Japan New Party	1.4
Other	3.2
None	8.1

As we see in Table 11.12 on the issue of future party support, the change in government and its consequences have clearly shifted much of this former affection and loyalty away from the LDP. We see support for the LDP dropping almost by half, from 65.7 per cent to 36.9 per cent, paralleling a considerable drop in support for the Socialist Party, from 11.8 per cent to 6.9 per cent. When we compare past with future support, we have an indication of the extent of distrust that developed among farmers for these two major parties. Even though the newly-formed Renewal Party and Harbinger Party (Sakigake) appear to have attracted some of the farmers' vote, they have absorbed only a small proportion of the vote that had previously supported the LDP. We see a dramatic increase in the number of farmers who claim they will not support any party, or who were still uncertain about which party to support. From this we see signs of the considerable confusion created for them by the LDP's internal splits and ultimate fall from government. We see that a fairly large bloc (17 per cent) of farmers have abandoned their faith in political parties completely, while many others were still undecided about party support more than a year after the LDP's downfall.

Continuity in party support (or ruptures to it) also reveal a significant shift in farmers' political disposition (Table 11.13). We see that almost 30 per cent of former supporters of three of the smaller parties, the Clean Government Party, the DSP and JNP, have shifted their support to another party. Both the LDP (at 14.3 per cent) and the Socialist Party (at 19.7 per cent) have also lost support to other parties. Another striking message is that the Socialist Party retained fewer traditional supporters than any other

Table 11.12   Future party support
Q: Which political party do you intend to support in the future?

	%
Liberal Democratic Party	36.9
Socialist Party	6.9
Clean Government Party	0.7
Democratic Socialist Party	1.2
Communist Party	1.9
Renewal Party	12.7
Japan New Party	1.6
Harbinger Party	4.3
Other	1.1
None	17.0
Don't know	15.7

Table 11.13 Continuity in party support (political party supported in the past versus future support for a political party)

Political party supported in the past	Continuous support %	Switch to other political parties %	Support no parties %	Undecided %
Liberal Democratic Party	57.8	14.3	10.9	15.7
Socialist Party	36.6	19.7	22.3	20.1
Clean Government Party	61.9	28.6	9.5	0.0
Democratic Socialist Party	44.7	28.9	15.8	10.5
Communist Party	77.3	9.1	6.8	3.4
Japan New Party	37.5	28.1	12.5	21.9

party; almost one-quarter (22.3 per cent) of former Socialist Party supporters will no longer support any party.

Clearly the farmers' political support which was once strongly in favour of the LDP became fragmented after the party's fall from government. The fundamentally conservative nature of farmers' political persuasion did not change. There has been, however, a dramatic increase in the number of farmers who do not support any party or who are uncertain about which, if any, party to support. The survey results indicate on the one hand recognition by many farmers that their mutually beneficial relationship with the LDP has ended with the end of one-party LDP rule. On the other hand, these results indicate farmers' increased distrust in established political parties. That so many former party supporters are either uncertain or no longer support any party reflects the confusion created by the recent momentous political changes in Japan.

This confusion is also reflected in respondents' views of their preferred ruling party/ies (Table 11.14). Despite farmers' strong support for the LDP in the past, only 16 per cent answered that they want exclusive LDP rule. Almost one-third favoured an LDP/Socialist coalition. This can be attributed to the fact that both are now

Table 11.14 Preferred party/ies in government

	Whole nation %	20s %	30s %	40s %	50s %	60s %	70 years and over %
LDP	16.0	11.1	18.7	17.5	18.9	19.5	21.0
LDP/Socialist Party coalition	32.1	14.8	16.3	24.2	28.7	36.0	31.7
Renewal Party/ Clean Government Party	9.9	7.4	6.7	6.5	8.2	9.6	10.7
Not LDP	5.5	9.9	5.7	4.3	6.1	4.0	6.2
Conservative coalition	18.7	16.0	14.8	19.0	20.0	17.1	21.8

rural-style parties, and that the farmers expect these parties will look after agricultural interests. By contrast, only some 5 per cent answered that they want a government without the LDP, such as the Hosokawa and Hata governments. This may be due to farmers' intense opposition to the Hosokawa governments on the grounds that it was this government that took the decision to liberalise the rice market. The majority of those aged under sixty favoured a conservative coalition, whereas the older generations tended to favour LDP one-party rule or an LDP/socialist coalition. These data reveal a difference of opinion between different generations as to which party/ies should rule.

Nōkyō's inability to stop liberalisation of the rice market not only increased farmers' distrust in it, but also raised their doubts about which parties they ought to support. As a consequence, the view among farmers strengthened that neither Nōkyō nor the political parties they had traditionally supported would be able to protect their interests.

The view that farmers need to create their own political party in order to protect farming interests grew increasingly popular. Specifically, the Farmers New Party (Nōminshintō) movement grew, aimed at setting up a single-issue party to pursue this goal. Support for this movement was said to be centred around the younger members of Nōkyō, particularly in the Tōhoku district where rice production is heavy. However, Zenchū has been cautious on this issue, since it is acutely aware of the potential risks involved in farmers creating an independent party.

However, nearly half of the Nōkyō members surveyed (46.1 per cent) saw a need for a new political party for farmers (Table 11.15). This proportion is far greater than Zenchū had predicted. From these data we can see signs of farmers' awareness of the limitations of their earlier involvement in politics, and their urges to take action to correct this.

Table 11.15 Perceived need for a farmers' political party
Q: Despite the financial burden, do you think it will be necessary to create an independent political party for farmers in the future?

%

Yes	46.1
No	30.3
Don't know	23.6

When we look at farmers' responses by the prefecture where they live, again we find some variation in attitudes (Table 11.16). More than half the farmers surveyed from Shiga, Fukuoka and Kumamoto saw a need for an independent political party. This compares with roughly one-third of respondents from Toyama and Shizuoka. This variation in opinion appears to depend on the scale of livestock and fruit farming in each district. As mentioned earlier, liberalising the beef and orange markets had already taken a serious toll on these sectors, and those who had suffered were

Table 11.16 Perceived need for farmers' political party (by respondents' prefecture)

	Necessary %	Not necessary %	Don't know %
Hokkaido	45.6	26.5	27.9
Akita	40.8	36.2	23.0
Ibaraki	41.2	22.0	36.8
Toyama	35.5	40.0	24.5
Nagano	47.5	33.9	18.6
Shizuoka	31.6	37.4	31.0
Shiga	52.1	23.0	24.9
Shimane	49.0	29.1	21.9
Tokushima	44.7	31.6	23.6
Fukuoka	54.2	24.6	21.2
Kumamoto	59.2	21.7	19.1

deeply concerned about the critical situation that might occur if the rice market was to follow these two markets. A large number of farmers from the affected areas saw the need for an independent party so they themselves could protect agricultural interests.

While it was expected that the drive for a new independent party in Tōhoku and other regions had strong support from the younger sections of Nōkyō, these survey results reveal that middle-aged farmers in fact form the backbone of this support (Table 11.17). If anything, the younger farmers are less supportive, or equivocal. This result is most likely because younger generations are less attached to farming than their parents and are more often engaged in second jobs outside agriculture. Farmers in their fifties and above who form the backbone of the movement are committed to farming as their livelihood and are more aware of potential crisis.

Table 11.17   Perceived need for a farmers' political party (by respondents' age)

	Necessary %	Not necessary %	Don't know %
20s	22.0	23.2	54.9
30s	36.6	28.8	34.6
40s	43.6	25.8	30.6
50s	48.1	26.1	25.8
60s	47.7	29.2	23.1
70 years and over	42.2	32.1	25.7

However, while nearly half the farmers surveyed saw a need for an independent farmers' party, only around one-third answered that they would definitely vote for such a party (Table 11.18). If the farmers who answered that they would probably vote for an independent farmers' party are taken into account, this new party would obtain well over half their vote. However, the fact that there is a difference in numbers between those who see that there is a need, and those who answered that they would definitely vote for a farmers' new party, indicates that the future of such a party is not necessarily guaranteed.

In the past, farmers' political activities have been closely tied to their involvement in the support organisations of individual politicians. Therefore, while they may have felt strongly about the need for an independent farmers' party, they were hesitant to follow this idea through, since it interfered with their sense of obligation to individual politicians.

Table 11.18   Likelihood of voting for
a farmers' political party
Q: If a new farmers' political party was
formed, would you give it your vote in
elections?

%

Yes definitely	34.4
Probably	30.7
Don't know	29.3
Probably not	3.0
No	2.6

Conclusion

The Hosokawa government's decision to liberalise the Japanese rice
market undeniably roused fears about the future of agricultural
policy in Japan. The step forced the nation's farmers to reconsider,
and ultimately acknowledge, the weakness of their long-standing
political ties with Nōkyō, with established parties and with politicians.
Farmers have begun to seek a new independent system to achieve
their political goals, as we saw in the data concerning respondents'
views on the need for a new party for farmers. However, integration
of farmers into the existing political system has helped curtail their
commitment to creating an independent means of expression.
Such a concept has hitherto been completely foreign to farmers,
since they have known only the system created by long-term LDP
one-party rule. This is one indication of how entrenched the
system created by the LDP regime had become.

The collapse of LDP rule and formation of several coalition
governments have naturally affected more than just agricultural
interests. Japan's money-fuelled political system was thrown into
confusion by these events. In the political climate that subsequently
took hold, private sector organisations were uncertain where to
cultivate political favour, and moved away from party politics.
The majority of industrial groupings that in the past had given
their full commitment to the LDP, also adopted a less partisan
approach to politics. Generally, the strategy of industrial groups
has become one of staying on good terms with all the leading
parties as a way of guaranteeing the interests of their members.

In an environment where the trend among private sector
organisations is to move away from active politicking with parties,

only organisations from the agricultural sector are increasing their pressure on the parties. This is most likely because agricultural concerns are thought of as a complex political issue rather than a specific policy issue. Agricultural organisations feel unable to sever their ties with politics. This reveals the vulnerability of Japanese agriculture to the vagaries of politics.

For many years Japan's agricultural production, especially rice, was protected through conservative politics. Zenchū used the strength of the farmers' conservative vote to gain bargaining power, making both Nōkyō and farmers important to political parties and individual politicians alike.

Yet by the late 1980s, mounting pressures from Japan's important strategic and trade partners, particularly the United States, escalated into serious trade conflicts. This pressure from external sources forced decisions on agricultural policy beyond the narrow ambit of domestic political interests, which had for so long seen agriculture as a protected industry. Zenchū did not have the clout to overcome international lobbying and prevent deregulation of Japan's agricultural markets. For some years this had been seen as an inevitable outcome, as the LDP staved off outside interests to protect an important benefactor group. Zenchū's failure invited farmers' distrust, and the movement to create a farmers' party and other means of independent political expression. It is anticipated that a new law on foodstuffs passed in Autumn 1995 that deregulates rice distribution will further highlight Nōkyō's ineffectiveness as a political lobby for farmers and will further weaken its influence.

The push to establish a farmers' party is gradually succeeding. In the 1995 House of Councillors election, groups of farmers from several districts nominated candidates. However, all were unsuccessful in their bid and obtained a much smaller proportion of the vote than many in the rural sector had anticipated. This outcome contradicts the strong support for the farmers' party movement expressed by survey respondents six months earlier, and the farmers' hopes in this regard have diminished dramatically.

In the 1995 election the Agricultural Administration Alliance (Nōseiren) recommended candidates from the LDP, the Socialist Party and new parties. However, there was confusion in some prefectures where candidates from several different parties had been recommended and where there was some disparity between the Nōseiren recommendations and the local Nōkyō recommendations in a few districts. There was none of the posturing of the past over rice prices and liberalising agricultural markets. These circumstances helped further to weaken Zenchū, and the lack of any clear objectives to unify and rally agricultural interests further undermined farmers' political autonomy.

Changes in agricultural policy to liberalise the rice market and in the Foodstuffs Law to liberalise rice distribution have brought about massive changes in agricultural politics over the past two years. This situation signals the end of an era in which agricultural interests gained grand profits through political pressure from Nōkyō and Zenchū on the LDP as ruling party. Under a new electoral system, agricultural interests will continue to retain some political influence in farming districts as they usually also represent the interests of those districts at large. Nonetheless, such interests will inevitably have declining political influence in the urban areas to which former farmers have migrated for work. To ensure its survival, Nōkyō will need to respond effectively to the onerous task of building political unity among an ever-smaller and varied farming population. Recent years have seen powerful international and domestic interests over-ride those of the agricultural sector, something that may be used to unify and mobilise this currently disaffected community.

Notes

1. Zenkoku Nōgyō Kyōdō Kumiai Chūōkai Rijikai (1996) *Nōkyō sakusei hōkokusho*, Tokyo.
2. Inoguchi Takashi and Iwai Tomoaki, *Zoku giin no kenkyū* (A study of legislative tribes), Tokyo: Nihon Keizai Shinbunsha.
3. Zenkoku Nōgyō Kyōdō Kumiai (1996) *Nōkyō hōkokusho* (Nokyo Report).
4. This survey was conducted after we had obtained co-operation from Nōkyō. In December 1994, we sent questionnaires to 3,760 people randomly selected from Nōkyō membership lists from prefectures across the country. The response rate was 53 per cent, which is a particularly high rate for a survey by mail in Japan.
5. Inoguchi and Iwai, *Zoku giin*.
6. Tsujinaka has undertaken empirical work on the responses to political parties of private sector representative bodies after the 1993 LDP downfall. See Tsujinaka Yutaka (1994) *Seiken kodaiki ni okeru rieki dantai no kōdō to kōzō henka* (Changes in the behaviour and structure of profit organisations in a period of expanding political power), *Chūō chōsa shako*, p. 446.

12
Changing local politics: party realignment and growing competition

Masaaki Kataoka

Splits in the Liberal Democratic Party (LDP) and the subsequent collapse of its long-standing single-party rule in the summer of 1993 triggered structural transformation of, and revitalisation in Japan's local politics. The emergence of new parties, and the passage of legislation to reform the House of Representatives (HR) electoral system in early 1994 induced major changes at the local level, in party structure, political support networks and patterns of party competition. Some local level conservative assembly members found themselves caught between allegiance to the party that had long been their political home, and their Diet members at national level whose patronage they had long enjoyed, but who had now quit the LDP to join others. Loyalties and opportunism came into full play.

Alongside these developments, a wave of populism has engulfed local politics. The victory in the Tokyo and Osaka gubernatorial elections of 1995 of candidates who were former comedians, and who deliberately had no party support, indicated the extent of urban voters' dissatisfaction with existing parties, and their distrust of bureaucrats and professional politicians. In July 1996, a referendum on a nuclear power plant to be located at Maki township in Niigata indicated local residents' desire for self-determination through direct participation.[1] There are numerous examples signalling clearly that in the mid-1990s, Japanese politics at the local level is undergoing dynamic reorganisation and transformation.

This chapter examines this transformation underway in local politics following the downfall of the LDP, with a focus on party politics. First, I analyse the realignment of local parties, examining their reorganisation and the changing patterns of competition between them at the prefectural level. Second, I examine growing populism in local politics. I analyse how the people's distrust of political parties and their desire for a new style of politics was played out in the 1995 gubernatorial elections.

Local party realignment

The party identity crisis for conservative assembly members

The strong and sudden realignment of Japan's party political system at the national level in June 1993 was an initiative of ambitious LDP Diet members Ozawa Ichirō and Takemura Masayoshi. Dissatisfied with the LDP's leadership which had struggled to avoid, rather than pursue, radical political reform after a series of well-publicised political scandals, Ozawa and Takemura and their cohort of followers effectively deserted the LDP in parliament by supporting a no-confidence motion against Prime Minister Miyazawa Kiichi. Ozawa and Takemura created the new parties, Shinseitō and Sakigake. After the national election of July 1993, they formed a coalition with former opposition parties to take government from the LDP.

The sudden splits in the LDP and the party's subsequent fall from power at the national level dealt a serious blow to conservative politicians at regional levels. At the prefectural level, the initial fracturing of the national LDP was a source of embarrassment to LDP assembly members. For some of them, this also presented a serious dilemma in choosing the party to which they would affiliate. In many ways these tensions over party affiliation came to a head through the LDP prefectural federations (*ken shibu rengōkai*) which, by serving as both the prefectural branch of the national LDP as well as the headquarters of the prefectural party, bring together national and local organisations.

Vote-gathering activities for national elections were carried out mostly by Diet members' *kōenkai* (supporters' associations), and

208 Japanese Politics Today

this provided a conduit for LDP prefectural assembly members to cultivate political advantage at the national level as well. With the breakaway from the party of the renegade LDP Diet members, some LDP prefectural assembly members were suddenly faced with the possible loss of the advantages they had enjoyed through their patronage. Party affiliation was questioned, with significant consequences for local party formation. Let us consider the choices of party affiliation suddenly facing some LDP local assembly members, following the party's troubles.

First, under LDP rule, its assembly members could expect their demands upon the national government to be registered through a connection with their patron LDP Diet member. Because the lower house of the national parliament consisted of multi-member constituencies, these local assembly members could maintain relationships with their patron Diet members through personal ties.[2] The actions of Diet members who quit the LDP directly affected the choice of party affiliation of the assembly members for whom these Diet members had been patrons at the national level.

Affiliation to the LDP, as invariably the incumbent party, was also a benefit for local politicians. The LDP's dominant position in prefectural politics had worked to assure the influence of its assembly members on the prefectural government. These members could exert their influence in most prefectures because the party usually retained its majority at this level and controlled their assemblies.[3] Thus local assembly members whose patrons at the national level became party renegades were forced to choose between conflicting loyalties: to leave the LDP and follow their Diet member patron to the new party, or to keep faith with the LDP and cut their tie with the Diet member. Following the first choice would reduce the assembly members' influence at prefectural level, since they would no longer be representatives of the incumbent party. Following the second choice would reduce their influence at the national level by severing the dependent political connection there.

To cope with this dilemma, some of these assembly members deferred making any choice, and kept their position as ambiguous as possible, awaiting the outcome of fluid coalition politics at the national level. In some prefectures, assembly members remained in the LDP Prefectual Federation while also keeping a tie with their Shinseitō/Sakigake Diet member patron in order to keep their influence in both prefectural and national politics. Since the longer-term political consequences of the party split were still unclear, these assembly members felt the need for caution.

A second factor complicating the crisis of party identity suffered by some conservative assembly members was the result of electoral reforms: an overhaul of the HR election system. In early 1994, the introduction of a single-member district system with some proportional representation seats significantly altered the boundaries of local HR constituencies. In their new HR constituency, many conservative assembly members had lost the patron Diet member with whom they had maintained a valuable long-term relationship. Even more important, some assembly members found that they had to establish a new patron relationship with a Diet member who had been their long-time adversary under the former multimember district system.

An opinion poll of 2,000 Yamaguchi LDP members in early 1994 revealed that 31 per cent of them accepted a former rival LDP Diet member as a new patron in the new single-member constituency, while 26 per cent of them rejected him.[4] Some party members strongly opposed to their new Diet member transferred their affiliation to another party. Conservative Diet members representing new electoral districts were forced to build support organisations within their new constituencies to cope with local rivalry among party supporters nurtured under the old multimember election system.

At the time of writing, reorganisation of conservative Diet members' *kōenkai* and their linkages with local level politicians continues, in preparation for the approaching HR election under the new system. This reorganisation will not proceed smoothly because it inevitably involves the crisis of loyalty that we have just considered. Effective management of the many complex relationships to which this crisis has given rise, is also a consideration.

Breakaways from the LDP and party realignment

Conservative Diet members with affiliation to the breakaway parties took part in the HR election in summer 1993 supported by their own *kōenkai*. These new party organisations at the prefectural level were formed after the election. Leaders of the Shinseitō and the other parties that took government by forming the coalition regarded the new system as temporary, expecting a second wave of realignment. Because of this, formation of the local party organisation generally proceeded slowly, usually beginning with conversion of the Diet member's *kōenkai* into the local branch of the new party.[5] In October 1993, Shinseitō prefectural federations were established in some ten prefectures. By the end of 1993, the number of prefectures with these federations had increased to twenty-four.[6]

The LDP's loss both of powerful members and power at the national level shook the LDP local organisations. As party members with strong connections to renegade Diet members left the party, some local branches were disbanded. In Iwate Prefecture (Ozawa's home ground), the local branches in Mizusawa and Esashi halted their operations, since almost all members were supporters of Ozawa and quit the party to follow him. Among the 56 LDP local branches in Iwate, in 18 branches the LDP lost members to Shinseitō, and in 4 branches operations had ceased by early September 1993.[7]

In spite of this loss of party members and the demise of a few local branches, the damage was far from fatal to the LDP prefectural federations. As a result of the party split, by the end of 1993 the LDP had lost around 60 prefectural assembly members in 18 prefectures, which constituted only 3 per cent of the Party's representatives in prefectural assemblies. Furthermore, Shinseitō's success at the national level was not matched at the local. Shinseitō retained seats in the assembly in 14 prefectures, but with only 3.5 members on average within them.[8] Considering that it had Diet members in more than 30 prefectures, this record of performance shows that many assembly members with connections to a Shinseitō Diet member still remained in the LDP prefectural federation.[9]

In 1994, Shinseitō established prefectural federations in most areas, and gradually established a presence in the prefectural assembly by accepting more LDP renegades. However, the pace of these developments slowed in June 1994 when the LDP's return to power at the national level in coalition with the Socialist Party (SDPJ) and Sakigake made assembly members more loath to depart from the prefectural LDP.

In December 1994, when the Shinshintō or New Frontier Party (NFP) was formed as an umbrella to unify most of the then-opposition parties, Shinseitō had at least one Diet member in 35 prefectures. In the prefectural assemblies, however, Shinseitō held seats in only 23 prefectures (Table 12.1), with 6 members on average in these.[10] In 14 prefectures, Shinseitō had no party presence at the prefectural assemblies even though it had a party member representing part of the prefecture in the Diet. In many prefectures without a Shinseitō presence locally, there were nevertheless supporters of the party who remained members of the LDP or who formed a group with the LDP at the prefectural assembly to retain their political influence at the prefectural level. Thus, while Shinseitō became a serious rival of the LDP at the national level, its presence was generally weak in the prefectural assemblies. For the prefectural LDP, the party split had until then resulted in limited damage to local party organisations.

Table 12.1 Shinseitō representatives in Diet and prefectural assemblies

		Shinseitō assembly members in prefectures		
		Yes	No	Total
Shinseito Diet members in prefecture	Yes	21	14	35
	No	2	10	12
	Total	23	24	47

Source: These data are as of December 1994. They were compiled by the author from *Asahi Nenkan*, 1995 and *Asahi Shinbun*, 11 December 1994 and 1 January 1995

Integrating the New Frontier Party

In December 1994, Shinseitō joined with Kōmeitō, the Democratic Socialist Party (DSP), Japan New Party (JNP) and Social Democratic League (SDL), to establish the NFP. Because of its origins as an amalgam of former rivals, the NFP has faced a serious problem in integrating its local party organisations.

First, it should be noted that Kōmeitō kept its party organisation at the local level even after the national Kōmeitō joined the NFP.[11] Kōmeitō fought the unified local election of 1995 under its own party banner, while closely co-operating with the NFP in districts where there were no Kōmeitō candidates. Even after the assembly elections, Kōmeitō assembly members in most prefectures have maintained their own group in the assembly, separate from NFP members. At the end of 1995, the NFP and Kōmeitō formed a joint group in the prefectural assemblies in only four prefectures. On the other hand, in the prefectural assemblies in Tochigi and Nagano, former Shinseitō assembly members formed a joint group with the LDP ones.[12]

A second difficulty with integration was that the merging of parties to form the NFP sometimes triggered conflict among groups who had been in opposition to one another before this. Conflicts arose in local party organisations as some members tried to take initiatives to strengthen their position within the new party. In an extreme case, one prefectural federation was divided from the start. In Miyazaki, former Shinseitō and former DSP members formed separate NFP prefectural federations, and both federations struggled to establish themselves within the prefecture. Yet the divisions were not always so clear-cut along old party lines. In the July 1995 election, while a former DSP assembly member stood as governor with the support of former Shinseitō members, other ex-DSP members supported the incumbent governor.[13]

Efforts have been made to further integrate the NFP, though the deep divisions along former party lines cannot easily be mended. In Kanagawa Prefecture in early 1996, an integrated NFP group was formed in the Prefectural Assembly, though it disbanded a few months later due to personal distrust and antagonism among its members.[14] The group split into three, reflecting both old party loyalties and seniority. Some experienced members even left the NFP to join the LDP.[15] These experiences indicate that it will take some time to weld together a disparate collection of parties and fully integrate the NFP local party organisation.

The socialists and the local party movement

In the early 1990s, the socialists were searching for a new party identity. The SDPJ faced serious internal disputes on policy and how to achieve it. After the passage of the new HR electoral law under the Hosokawa administration, the socialists sought to form a new party through alliance with liberal politicians in a move to ensure their survival in government under the new election system. At the start of the Murayama administration in 1994, they had abandoned many of their important long-standing agendas to secure the new coalition with the LDP that finally had brought the socialists into government. This strategy saw the party accept as constitutional the Self Defence Forces, the national anthem, raising the national flag at public schools, and construction of nuclear power plants, all issues which party activists had opposed energetically for many years.

As these moves were played out at the national level of the party, at the local party level many socialist assembly members were thrown into a difficult situation. Party diehards struggled to keep their local supporters in the face of these new moves by party activists. The failure to form a new liberal party in particular drove individual assembly members to find their own ways to garner political support. At the local elections in 1995, some Left-

and Right-wing socialist assembly members quit the party to run as independent candidates. Some sought to hold on to old party platforms, while others sought support from Rengō unions or formed alliances with local liberal activists.[16]

Some socialist assembly members joined the local party movement, which aimed at forming prefectural or bloc-wide confederations of liberal politicians and citizen activists. The local party movement had become active in the early 1990s, and by the mid-1990s had gained considerable regional variety in its leading personalities and policy positions. In Kinki bloc, the movement is supported by Local Rengō, and in Hokkaido, where the socialists have retained a high level of support, it is led by retiring progressive Governor Yokomichi Takahiro and his associates. In Niigata and Saga prefectures, it is organised by citizen activists who support moves to keep the old party platforms. In Tokyo and Kanagawa, it is led by Co-op activists.[17] Some of these local parties are in a national network for mutual information exchange and co-operation, and hope to establish a new liberal party under Hatoyama Yukio.[18]

Party coalitions and competition

Coalitions in gubernatorial elections before 1993

Throughout the 1980s, gubernatorial elections were viewed as lacklustre ceremonies for installing national-level bureaucrats as governors. This was possible because a grand coalition of all major parties (except the Communists) prevailed, keeping real electoral competition to a minimum. Under this grand coalition scheme, local party branches abandoned the role of setting alternative policy agendas in prefectural politics, engaging instead in active pork barrelling serving the interests of their major supporters. Prefectural politics was regarded as mundane bureaucratic rule satisfying narrow political interests. It attracted little attention from the media.

Until the LDP lost power at the national level, it had been the key party in most prefectures. It often retained its majority in the prefectural assembly, and the DSP and Kōmeitō joined with it as junior partners. The Socialist Party lost ground to other non-LDP parties in prefectural politics from the late 1970s. In the 1980s it did not have enough popular candidates, good coalition partners nor strong public support to effectively challenge LDP candidates

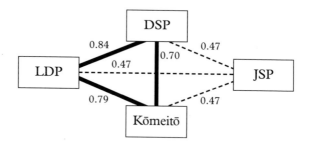

(a) May 1991–June 1993 (N = 19)

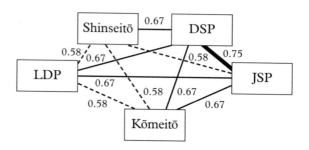

(b) July 1993–December 1994 (N = 12)

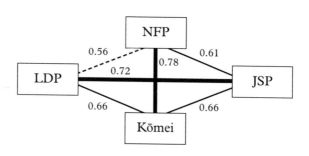

(c) January 1995–April 1995 (N = 18)

Figure 12.1   Party coalition patterns in gubernatorial elections
Source: Data compiled by the author from various issues of *Asahi Shinbun* and *Asahi Nenkan*

in gubernatorial elections. The socialists virtually gave up electoral competition with the LDP in many prefectures, tending instead towards joining LDP-centred coalitions to capitalise on party supporters' interest in prefectural politics.

This carried over to the 1990s, until the LDP's fall from power. Figure 12.1(a) shows the pattern of party coalitions at gubernatorial elections in the early 1990s. The LDP formed a coalition with the DSP and Kōmeitō in more than 70 per cent of prefectures. The socialists gave up candidate nomination in around 40 per cent of electorates. In most of the other elections, they sought a grand coalition with the LDP-DSP-Kōmeitō alliance. Gubernatorial elections were often fought by such a grand coalition, with only nominal opposition from the Communists.

Changing patterns of coalition

After the collapse of LDP rule, party coalition politics for prefectural governorships were revitalised, and gubernatorial elections again began to draw serious attention from both voters and the mass media. Table 12.2 shows a trend towards electoral competition for governorships after the 1980s. After the power swing at the national level, gubernatorial elections were fought competitively in more than 40 per cent of prefectures. Competition was cutthroat in an unprecedented 23 per cent of cases.

The collapse of the LDP nationally also altered patterns of party coalition in gubernatorial elections. But even as the party lost influence while in opposition in national politics, it kept its majority in most of the prefectural assemblies. In gubernatorial elections, the grand coalition has remained an important element of coalition politics. The new incumbent parties at the national level also began to take initiatives in prefectural politics where they had a chance of winning seats through a strong support base. The ensuing power struggle generated fierce coalition politicking and competition in some gubernatorial elections.

In such politically reactivated prefectures, the patterns of coalition and electoral competition have sometimes reflected cleavages at national level. Figure 12.1 (b) shows the pattern of coalitions at gubernatorial elections until the formation of the NFP in December 1994. It indicates that the LDP-DSP-Kōmeitō alliance was less important in gubernatorial elections at this stage.

The socialists abandoned their half-hearted attitude towards coalition competition for governorships, and participated eagerly

Table 12.2   Gubernatorial elections

Period	Number of gubernatorial elections	Competitive elections	Average voting turnout	Average number of candidates
May 1983–April 1987	47	9 (2)	55.90	2.5
May 1987–April 1991	47	14 (5)	56.30	2.8
May 1991–April 1995	49	17 (7)	52.40	3
pre-split	19	4 (0)	49.50	2.6
post-split	30	13 (7)	54.30	3.3

Note: 'Competitive elections' are defined as those in which the 'top' loser obtained more than half the votes of the winner. The number in parentheses shows the number of very competitive elections, in which a top loser obtained more than 80 per cent of the votes of the winner

Source: Data before April 1991 are taken from *Jinji Koshinroku*, Tokyo: Teikoku Data Bank, various issues, and various other Japanese sources. Post-April 1991, data are drawn from *Asahi Shinbun*.

in elections. The DSP, once a rival of the SDPJ in luring support from the labour unions, collaborated with them with the assistance of Rengō. Kōmeitō also leaned towards the non-LDP side, while remaining neutral in very competitive elections to avoid opposition status. As recently formed parties, the JNP, Shinseitō and Sakigake sometimes failed to nominate candidates because of their weak local organisations, but where they had strong support, they challenged the LDP. The LDP had to fight the election without the support of other parties in 25 per cent of electorates.

In early 1995, the coalition pattern in politicised prefectures shifted towards the pattern of the LDP-SDPJ-Sakigake coalition at national level. Figure 12.1 (c) shows that the SDPJ no longer hesitated to co-operate with the LDP, and moved to establish close ties. While Kōmeitō has kept its own local organisations, local Kōmeitō and NFP have become close allies in gubernatorial elections.

Although overall patterns of party coalition and competition in gubernatorial elections were influenced by the cleavages dividing parties at the national level, there were also many anomalies which the mass media have called 'twisted' (*nejire*) phenomena. In these prefectures, patterns of party coalitions reflected local political contexts instead of national ones. For example, in Hokkaido, the LDP and Sakigake challenged the SDPJ-NFP-Kōmeitō coalition, whereas in Mie, Sakigake sided with the NFP-Kōmeitō partnership against a former vice governor supported by the LDP-SDPJ coalition.

The grand coalition strategy still persisted in two kinds of prefectures: first, where the NFP-Kōmeitō coalition did not have enough support to compete effectively against the LDP; and second, where the parties were accustomed to joint co-ordination of policies under the multi-party system. The latter case includes urbanised prefectures such as Tokyo and Osaka.

Electoral results

With increasingly active electoral competition, by the middle of 1996 the LDP lost hold of the governorship in around one-quarter of prefectures throughout Japan, a significant development. Before the collapse of one-party rule in June 1993, only five governorships were not held by the LDP. From June 1993 to April 1995, the LDP lost an additional seven governorships. They won in Fukuoka only by forming a grand coalition.

Of the prefectures where the LDP lost, the Shinseitō/NFP won in Ishikawa, Aomori, Iwate, Miyagi and Mie. In most of these, the NFP or its predecessor parties had an influential Diet member. In Akita, an NFP candidate competed squarely with the incumbent, who was supported by the LDP. The implication of these victories for the NFP will be mainly in party politics at the national level, instead of making a difference in local policies, since the difference in policies among the parties is already minimal.

One of the biggest surprises in the 1995 gubernatorial election came from Tokyo and Osaka, where ex-comedians Aoshima Yukio and Yokoyama Nokku beat the grand coalition candidates by a considerable margin. We will analyse this surprise victory in detail later in this chapter.

Party competition and gubernatorial recruitment

Reversing the localising trend

For the 4-year period following the joint local election in April 1991, the career backgrounds of Japanese governors in 47 prefectures were increasingly those of national bureaucrats and Diet members (Table 12.3). During this period, new governors came to power in 20 prefectures, more than 40 per cent of all the Japanese prefectures. Of these 20 new governors, 9 were former national bureaucrats, and 5 were Diet members. By contrast, in the 1990s the advancement of local bureaucrats decreased. Over the same period, only 3 obtained new seats while local politicians lost 5 seats. The increasing competition among parties reversed the trend towards local political actors gaining governorships, something that had appeared in the 1980s.[19]

Throughout the post-war period, the vice-governorship has been a key position in the career development paths of aspirants to the governor's position. From 1980 to April 1991, 22 former vice-governors ran for governorship, and 17 of them were successful. Within the same period, more than half the newly-elected governors had some experience in the position. Since local bureaucrats were

Table 12.3   Career backgrounds of Japanese governors

Career backgrounds	1979	1987	1991	1995
National bureaucrats	19	21	21	25 (9)
MOHA*	14	15	15	16 (5)
Others	5	6	6	9 (4)
Local bureaucrats	5	10	9	9 (3)
National politicians	13	9	6	8 (6)
Local politicians	7	5	6	1 (0)
Amateurs	3	2	5	4 (2)
Total	47	47	47	47 (20)

*Ministry of Home Affairs
Note: The numbers in parentheses show the number of new governors since April 1991.
Source: Same as Table 12.2; data compiled by the author.

increasingly successful in winning the vice-governorship throughout the post-war period, their increasingly secure position in LDP
candidate selection politics helped assure them a greater presence
in Japanese governorships.[20]

After the LDP's 1993 downfall, however, the position of vice-
governor lost importance in gubernatorial recruitment, because
vice-governors of local bureaucratic origin began to lose elections
to challengers of national origin. Vice-governors lost the election
to former national bureaucrats in Miyagi and Iwate, and to an ex-
Diet member in Mie. In the 4-year period after May 1991, 8 former
vice-governors ran for governorship and only 5 were successful.
The degree of success of the former vice-governors seems to have
returned to that of the 1960s, when the vice-governorship was not
really an important step in eventually securing the governorship.[21]

Gubernatorial recruitment and local party politics

In terms of party politics, it should be emphasised that all the vice-
governors who were unsuccessful in their bid for the governorship
were supported by the LDP-SDPJ coalition, whereas the challengers
were backed by Shinseitō/NFP. Within the prefectures where this
outcome occurred, the LDP and SDPJ tried to protect their interest
in prefectural politics and establish policy continuity with the former
governor by nominating the vice-governor. The Shinseitō/NFP, on
the other hand, sought power by selecting a candidate from national
sources to challenge the incumbent governor.

Once the candidates who were then, or had formerly been vice-
governor faced serious electoral competition, their advantage in
the candidate selection process was wiped out by competition
among party coalitions. This indicates that the localisation of
gubernatorial career development paths that was observed in the
1980s was made possible partly by declining electoral competitiveness in gubernatorial elections during the same period.[22]

Local party politics and the voter

In spite of growing competition among parties and increasing
attention by the mass media to gubernatorial elections, the voting
turnout did not increase in these elections. The average voting turnout

in the 1990s, shown in Table 12.2, indicates that people did not go to the polls more than in the 1980s. While the elections were revitalised by competition between parties, contending candidates had similar policy packages because of the shrinking ideological difference among the parties. For the average voters in most prefectures, the choice offered by the parties was largely between candidates and party coalitions, not between policies.

In addition, the grand coalition strategy still deprived voters of a real choice in about half of the prefectures. In particular, it should be noted that the grand coalition strategy was frequently adopted in highly urbanised prefectures, in part because the multi-party setting of the prefectural assembly routinely facilitated collaboration among parties in order to satisfy their fragmented party interests.[23]

The high cost of elections in these prefectures made parties hesitate in taking on real electoral competition. The newly-introduced regulations on political fund-raising coupled with recession after the collapse of Japan's 'bubble economy' in the early 1990s prevented the parties from conducting their traditional fund-raising drives for approaching local elections. In highly urbanised prefectures, these parties favoured tactics and political manoeuvres for joint candidate selection rather than outright electoral competition.[24]

Distrust in party politics: the Tokyo and Osaka cases

In the gubernatorial elections of April 1995, the biggest surprise came from two of the most highly urbanised prefectures in Japan. In Tokyo and Osaka, former popular comedians Aoshima Yukio and Yokoyama Nokku beat national bureaucrat candidates supported by the grand coalition. Tokyo and Osaka voters rejected the jointly supported candidates by a considerable margin. Within these prefectures, major parties (except the Communists) held talks frequently, to select joint candidates for governorship. In Tokyo, the prefectural LDP took the initiative in selecting a joint candidate. With the backing of the SDPJ and DSP, the LDP lured the Kōmeitō to jointly support Deputy Chief Cabinet Secretary Ishihara Nobuo, as successor to retiring governor Suzuki Shun'ichi. The NFP initially wanted to select a candidate to compete with the LDP. However, when the Kōmeitō decided to throw its support behind Ishihara, the NFP gave up the idea and remained neutral.[25]

In Osaka, the grand coalition parties initially decided to support Governor Nakagawa for his second term. However, Nakagawa was accused by the media of illegal fund-raising activities at the previous election in 1991. When his campaign manager was found guilty in the District Court in February 1995, Rengō, Nakagawa's major supporter, withdrew its support. Nakagawa decided to retire, and the grand coalition parties looked for an appropriate candidate from national bureaucratic sources. After a series of refusals to their offers, they finally found their candidate, Hirano Takuya. He entered the run for the Osaka governorship in mid-March, just ten days before the closing date.[26]

The grand coalition was criticised for its closed selection of candidates, labelled as 'secret negotiations' (*dangō*) by the media, which insisted that voters were being deprived of their chance to choose their leader. In addition, these parties' preoccupation with selecting a joint candidate from national bureaucratic sources deeply angered voters, who expected a new style of politics at the prefectural level.[27]

In Tokyo, Aoshima Yukio declared he would run in the gubernatorial election by criticising the candidate selection of the parties as 'secret negotiation' and 'destruction of democracy'.[28] In Osaka, Yokoyama Nokku declared he would run for the same reason.[29] Backed by the major newspapers, Aoshima and Yokoyama competed strongly with the joint party candidates, and in the event won the race by a considerable margin.[30]

Considering the sharp increase in voters for independent candidates after the collapse of single-party LDP rule, the parties now face voter distrust because of their pursuit of grand coalition politics, particularly in urbanised prefectures.

Conclusion

The collapse of LDP one-party rule and the electoral reform that followed, caused Japanese local politics to begin a process of transformation. Local party organisations were shaken to their foundations, and with diminishing ideological differences among the parties, prefectural party politics has come to be driven by the ambitions of active members and their calculations of personal interest.

While the emergence of new parties led to both coalition politicking and real electoral contests in local politics, there are increasing numbers of voters for independent candidates. We can expect that the fluid situation in Japanese local party politics will continue for some time.

Notes

1. Local Government in Japan does not have a system for referenda to determine outcomes on important local issues, except for the exceptions outlined in Article 95 of the Constitution. The Maki referendum, which was conducted under local ordinance, is virtually the first policy referendum on an important local issue; see *Asahi Shinbun*, 5 August 1996.
2. Gerald L. Curtis (1988) *The Japanese Way of Politics*, Columbia University Press, Chapter 5; Wakata Kyōji (1981) *Gendai Nippon no seiji to fūdo*, Kyoto: Mineruva Shobō, Chapters 7 and 10.
3. Wakata, *Gendai Nippon*, Chapter 9; Kataoka Masaaki (1994) *Chijishoku o meguru sejika to kanryō: Jimintō no kōhosha senkō seiji*, Tokyo: Bokutakusha, Chapter 5.
4. This opinion survey was conducted by the LDP Yamaguchi prefectural federation in February 1994. The remaining 41 per cent of the members were undecided; 'Senbiki no Hazama de 4', *Asahi Shinbun*, Yamaguchi edition, 17 August 1994.
5. *Niigata Nippō*, 11 October 1993. The *Niigata Nippō* article was based on the Kyodo News Agency survey conducted nationwide in October 1993.
6. *Niigata Nippō*, 11 October 1993; *Asahi Shinbun*, 27 December 1993.
7. Shuto Yoshiyuki and Ishikawa Shigehiro, 'Jimintō ōkoku' rakujitsu no aki, *AERA*, 14 September 1993, pp. 6–7.
8. These data were compiled by the author from *Asahi Nenkan*, 1994, the Kyodo survey and *Asahi Shinbun*, 27 December 1993. The data exclude independent members with Shinseitō support.
9. Shuto and Ishikawa, *Jimintō ōkoku*, pp. 8–9.
10. These data were compiled by the author from *Asahi Nenkan*, 1995 and *Asahi Shinbun*, 1 January 1995. The data exclude independent members with Shinseitō support.
11. The Kōmeitō decided to retain its local organisations for three years after the party merger. While the DSP assembly members joined the NFP, the DSP's former party organisation still remained as a political group.
12. These data were obtained from *Asahi Nenkan*, 1996.
13. *Asahi Shinbun*, Miyazaki edition, 31 January 1995; Isobe Shūsaku, Kawamura Katsuhei and Fukuda Hiroki, 'Saihen no ashimoto', *Asahi Shinbun*, 8 March 1995.
14. At a party meeting, the group leader, a former Shinseitō member, was severely criticised by former DSP members for the group's clumsy strategy in assembly sessions. The criticisms voiced by these former DSP members were so emotional and harsh that mutual distrust developed among the NFP assembly members. This antagonism, however, appeared not to have had policy connotations; *Kanagawa Shinbun*, 25 July 1996.
15. *Kanagawa Shinbun*, 10, 16 and 25 July 1996.
16. *Asahi Shinbun*, 9 March 1995.

17. *Asahi Shinbun*, 5 February 1995 and 8 August 1996; 'Taiketsu no teiryū', *Asahi Shinbun*, Hokkaido edition, 2 February 1995; Hatayama Toshio and Sumizawa Hiroki (eds), *Chiiki o koeru rōkaru pāti: Tsukurō, watashitachi no seiji*, Tokyo: Asu Sakyureshon Shuppanbu, 1995.
18. *Asahi Shinbun*, 8 August 1996.
19. Kataoka, *Chijishoku o meguru seijika to kanryō*, Chapter 9.
20. Kataoka (1994) 'Chijishoku o meguru chūō kanryō to chiho kanryo: ken-reberu no seifunai ni okeru kyaria keisei no henka' in Kataoka Hiromitsu (ed), *Gendai gyōsei kokka to seisaku katei*, Tokyo: Waseda Daigaku Shuppankai, pp. 186–88.
21. These data were compiled by the author. For an account of the increasing importance of the vice governorship as a prerequisite for gaining the position of governor see Kataoka, 'Chijishoku o meguru chuo kanryo to chiho kanryo'.
22. Kataoka, *Chijishoku o meguru seijika to kanryō*, Chapters 7 and 9.
23. *Asahi Shinbun*, Osaka edition, 9–12 March 1996; 'Gendai kunitori monogatari: '95 Chijisen no kozu' 4', *Asahi Shinbun*, 12 March 1996.
24. *Asahi Shinbun*, 1 and 5 February, 1996.
25. 'Kensho: Tochijisen kohosha erabi', *Asahi Shinbun*, 15–17 March 1996.
26. *Asahi Shinbun*, Osaka edition, 10–12 March 1995; 'Gendai kunitori monogatari: '95 chijisen no kozu', *Asahi Shinbun*, 13 March 1996; "Yoto' to iu na no mikoshi', 1 and 2, *Asahi Shinbun*, Osaka edition, 18 and 19 March 1996.
27. *Asahi Shinbun*, 10 April 1995; *Nokku chiji tōjō*, 3, *Asahi Shinbun*, Osaka edition, 13 April 1995.
28. *Asahi Shinbun*, 10 March 1995.
29. "Yoto' to iu na no mikoshi', *Asahi Shinbun*, Osaka edition, 21 March 1996.
30. Tōkyō Shinbun Shaikabu Tosei Shuzaihan (1996) *Mutoha chiji no hikari to kage*, Tokyo: Tokyo Shinbun Shuppankyoku, pp. 50–54; *Asahi Shinbun*, 10 April 1995; Omae Ken'ichi (1995) *Omae Ken'ichi haisenki*, Tokyo: Bungei Shunju, pp. 30–34. Discussion of Aoshima's successful approach to the mass newspapers is taken up in Omae's book.

13
The 1996 general election: status quo or step forward?

Purnendra C. Jain and Maureen Todhunter

On 20 October 1996, the Japanese electorate passed judgement on its leaders under the newly reformed electoral system. In some ways this election was a post-war record-setter, with more candidates than ever to choose from but fewer voters who actually chose. In other ways, the election was more of the same. Attempts to flush out entrenched corruption involved much old-style politicking, despite the introduction of long-awaited electoral reforms. No party was expected to gain a simple majority and none did. The LDP was returned to lead a minority government, and in the immediate aftermath of the election (November 1996) uncertainty and political jockeying prevail. The 1996 general election has, however, set the stage for the next phase of re-organisation, as Japan's political players transform the political life of the nation from long-standing single-party conservative rule into a more fluid, and seemingly more democratic form.

When the seven-party coalition of Hosokawa Morihiro took government in August 1993, few analysts expected that the next general election would be held more than three years later. Indeed, as we have seen across the previous chapters, the intervening time was full of intense politicking under four different coalition governments and four different prime ministers. All were carried along by the heady rhetoric of reforming the political system, and actual attempts to achieve this. At the same time, they clutched desperately at their residual power. This interlude saw major shifts in personal and party coalitions. It also saw the demise of ideology as a motivating, and therefore distinguishing factor. Political opportunism continued to thrive, driving forward the reconfiguration of the party landscape after the single-party rule of the LDP.

At the beginning of 1996, numerous signs indicated that an election would be called before the four-year term of the House of Representatives was due to end, in mid-1997. With the LDP two years into a coalition with the Socialists and Sakigake, LDP Prime Minister Hashimoto Ryūtarō was positioned to extol the coalition's achievements and further consolidate this tripartite arrangement by establishing a second Hashimoto coalition government, should the LDP fail to win a majority of seats in the next election. But politics got in the way. Hashimoto was beset by scandal, with allegations ranging from misdemeanour and corruption to illicit romance, and his second-in-charge, LDP Secretary General Katō Kōichi, faced corruption charges. Hashimoto favoured a 'smoke-screen' dissolution rather than risking floundering in the Diet. He announced the general election for 20 October.

It was the first to be held under the new rules introduced in 1994, and so was a portentous election. It highlights not just the change, but also the continuity in Japan's electoral politics after the 1993 watershed, when the LDP was voted from government. The election also serves as a report card by the Japanese people on the coalition governments and their attempts to institutionalise political reform. In this concluding chapter we examine the results of the October election and offer some explanations. We highlight some of the main features and major electoral issues. We identify change and continuity in electoral styles, and conclude with some observations about future directions in Japanese politics, based on the results of this election and its immediate aftermath. We need to begin with a brief review of the new electoral rules, on paper and in action.

The new electoral rules

The October 1996 election was the first to be held under the new electoral rules, established by (and, it can be argued, at the expense of) the first non-LDP government under Hosokawa Morihiro, and in the face of intense opposition. The new rules passed into law in January 1994, details were negotiated in the following months, and the new electoral districts were adopted in November 1994.[1] Radical reform of the Lower House electoral system had for years been urged by many as fundamental to political reform. The final result was inevitably a product of compromises made by the ruling and opposition parties that pushed, self-servingly, for specific rules. The new system was designed to encourage campaigns based on policies and parties rather than individuals.

There are 500 lower house members in the revised system, 300 elected from single-member districts (SMD) in a 'first-past-the-post' system, and the remaining 200 elected by proportional representation (PR) from eleven blocs nationwide. Each voter has two ballots, one to choose a specific candidate in an SMD and the other to choose the voter's preferred party in their PR district. In PR districts, seats are distributed according to the proportion of votes each party obtains. Where there are more candidates nominated by a party than the number of seats that the party gains via proportional representation, winners are chosen by the ratio of the candidate's votes in the single-seat district to the votes won by the district winner. The new system allows candidates to run in both districts. If a candidate fails in an SMD, s/he might be elected in a PR district if placed high enough on the party list. In the October 1996 election all parties except Shinshintō and the Japan Communist Party registered most of their candidates for both contests.

The new rules in action

A post-war record of 1,503 candidates stood for election, 1,261 running in the 300 single-seat districts, 808 running for PR, and 566 running in both districts. In many instances, the PR seats were used as a 'safety net' for high-profile politicians who were unsure of their competitive power in a single-member district. For example, 260 (more than 90 per cent) of single-seat LDP candidates ran as dual candidates. 32 LDP candidates who lost in single-seat districts won a seat under proportional representation. Across all parties the dual system of candidacy allowed 84 losers in the 300 single-seat districts to 'win' by being placed high on the PR list of their parties.

Many observers speculate that a hierarchy will emerge among parliamentarians as a result of the new electoral system. Those elected in a single-seat district without a safety net in PR candidacy will be classified as 'gold medallists'. Those listed in both but elected in a single-seat district will be 'silver medallists'. Those elected from proportional districts who did not run in SMD will be 'bronze medallists', and those who secured a place through PR after failing in SMD would rank lowest, as 'brass medallists'. The way that most parties used the system to rescue their losers has drawn some opposition, yet when we turn to the performance of the smaller parties we see that PR has also delivered the desired results: to provide some representation for the small parties that would mostly be denied this in a system with only 'winner-takes-all' SMDs.

The single-member districts, as expected, intensified competition between the two major parties, the LDP and NFP. Together these parties won close to 90 per cent of single-seat places. The LDP won 56.4 per cent of seats with only 38.6 per cent of votes and the NFP won 32 per cent of these seats with 27.9 per cent of the votes. Only 11.6 per cent of SMD seats went to other parties. On the other hand, the LDP and Shinshintō could win only 35 and 30 per cent of PR seats respectively, with the other 35 per cent going to smaller parties. These results were in line with political orthodoxy: that SMD generally produce competition between the two major parties while PR allows small parties to compete effectively in an election.

The results

Results of the election are set out in Table 13.1. The figures indicate that in a political system requiring majority rule, no party emerged as the clear winner with a majority of the 500 seats. The LDP won the largest number of seats (239), building on its pre-electoral strength of 211, though this was 12 short of an outright majority. The number was insufficient to secure the 265 seats necessary to occupy all the top posts in the lower house standing committees. After failing to woo any other party into coalition, the LDP formed a minority government. This status in the parliament will present problems for the party in passing legislation, especially since it does not hold a majority of seats in the upper house. Though the LDP has not regained its majority, its electoral performance could be seen as strong, given that this election secured a return to government for a party ousted from power only one election before.

The other major party, the New Frontier Party (NFP, or Shinshintō) gained the second highest number of seats, at 156. The NFP was unable to retain its pre-electoral strength of 160 seats,

Table 13.1   The 1996 House of Representatives election results (by party seat numbers)

Party	Single-member	Proportional representation	Total	% of Total	Pre-election strength	% of total
LDP	169	70	239	47.8	211	41.3
NFP	96	60	156	31.2	160	31.3
DPJ	17	35	52	10.4	52	10.2
JCP	2	24	26	5.2	15	2.9
SDP	4	11	15	3	30	5.9
Sakigake	2	0	2	0.4	9	1.8
Independents	9	0	9	1.8	10	2
Other	1	0	1	0.2	6	1.2
	300	200	500	100	493*	100

Source: Asahi Shinbun, 21 October 1996
*Vacancies: 18; under the old system the House of Representatives consisted of 511 members
LDP: Liberal Democratic Party
NFP: New Frontier Party (Shinshintō)
DPJ: Democratic Party of Japan (Minshutō)
JCP: Japan Communist Party
SDP: Social Democratic Party

let alone increase that number. This was a poor performance for the party, set against its dramatic success in the 1995 upper house election, and given the unmistakable confidence of NFP leader, Ozawa Ichirō, that his party would take government this time. Its weak performance suggests that voters could already see cracks in party unity, and weaknesses derived from its formation as an amalgam of as many opposition parties as possible were already surfacing. In fact, the NFP was on the verge of disintegration as soon as the election results were announced. Two high-ranking politicians, Hata and Hosokawa (both former Prime Ministers), threatened to leave the NFP and form a new party, to protest Ozawa's reluctance to accept responsibility for this poor performance, and resign as NFP leader.[2]

The newly established Democratic Party (DPJ, or Minshutō), under the leadership of Kan Naoto and Hatoyama Yukio, came a distant third, with 52 seats. This party had been launched on September 28, just days before campaigning began. It united a number of reformist-minded LDP and Socialist Party renegades, and was expected to fare well in urban areas where voters were disenchanted with established parties. It campaigned on the grounds that coalition governments had been ineffective in wiping out the corruption of traditional politicians hunting for concessions from the bureaucratic-led decision-making system. It also targeted voters born post-war. The DPJ's popularity derived largely from former Health and Welfare Minster Kan Naoto, who publicly unveiled the cover-up of the HIV scandal. The party was, however, only able to maintain its pre-electoral strength of 52 seats.

The Japan Communist Party (JCP), the only party that has not joined the throng of party realignments since 1993, increased its seats from its pre-electoral strength of 15, to 26.

The results of the election were disastrous for the LDP's two pre-election coalition partners. The Social Democratic Party (Shamintō, SDP) won just 15 seats, only half its pre-electoral number. Used and wasted by the LDP through a two year partnership in government, the SDP could see what was happening, but could do nothing to halt the decline, especially after more than half its lower house ranks defected to the newly established Democratic Party of Japan. A last-ditch attempt to salvage the party by changing its leadership from the crusty former Prime Minister Murayama Tomiichi back to the one-time charismatic leader, Doi Takako, did nothing to save the socialists from near-extinction.[3] Sakigake's decline was even more marked. Of the 9 seats the party held in the lower house prior to the election, it could save only 2, neither through proportional representation.

With no clear mandate through a majority of seats, and hampered further by its lack of numbers in the upper house, the LDP made an all-out effort to get other political parties, groups and independent politicians to form a partnership.[4] LDP leader Prime Minister Hashimoto favoured keeping the previous coalition with the SDP and Sakigake. One major reason is that the SDP controls 33 seats in the upper house, which would have ensured the LDP smooth parliamentary management in passing legislation. Nevertheless, Socialist Party leader Doi Takako was wary of a coalition with the LDP, favouring a loose alliance with policy consultation groups outside Cabinet. Sakigake, with only two seats in the lower house, is peripheral on this issue. The Democratic Party agreed to discuss some individual issues with the LDP, but insisted on staying on the opposition bench to assert the party's policy goals 'instead of cozying up to political power'.[5]

Features of the election

Results of the election also tell us about voters and candidates. The tallies indicate how political players have responded (and failed to respond) to changes resulting from the 1990s coalition governments. We begin with voters.

First, we can note the particularly low voter turnout rate, 6 per cent lower than for the 1993 general election and, at 59.6 per cent, a post-war nadir.[6] As in most democratic nations, voting is not compulsory in Japan. In most Japanese elections for the past fifty years, the voter turnout rate has been relatively high when compared with circumstances in other industrialised democracies. Nonetheless, in national elections in the 1990s the turnout rate has been declining rapidly.[7] Politicians offer the defensive reason that abstention means tacit approval of their work. Yet we surely can interpret some of this abstention as default voting, with voters deliberately shunning the polls rather than supporting untrustworthy politicians who they see as mired in corruption, switching parties after election, or not fulfilling election promises.

Second, we see how some voters chose to split their votes under the 'two ballots' system. Exit polls revealed that a significant proportion of voters chose a candidate from the LDP or NFP in the single-seat district, and a candidate from another, smaller party in the PR district.[8] The results in Table 13.1 confirm this finding. In most PR candidacies, the LDP won 10 to 30 per cent less votes than in the single seat constituency. Vote-splitting has complicated the task of campaign planners, psephologists and politicians themselves in trying to predict which way votes will go. Yet this was surely part of the reason why the 'two district' system was introduced: to enable voters to support at least two different political parties so that small parties would not be swallowed by an SMD system.

Next we turn to the candidates who were voted into the lower house. First, we find that compared with pre-election, a higher percentage of lower house representatives are women. This suggests some significant advance when we consider that Japan has the worst record among industrialised nations for the proportion of women holding political office. In this election 23 women won seats (4.6 per cent of seats), up from the 1993 election result of 14 (2.7 per cent of seats) in a 511-member house. The 1996 result unambiguously brings more women than before the election into parliament. Yet women's representation is still below the 1946 peak of 39 women in the Lower House. Only 7 of the 23 women elected this time are in SMDs, since it is much more difficult for women than men to be put forward by their party as a candidate in the single-member district.[9]

The results also suggest the possibility of a generational shift among the elected representatives, not simply from Taishō to Shōwa but from pre-war to post-war generations. Certainly the age of political leaders has been a source of contention for some years; in a general election in 1996 the generation issue will inevitably be important. In this election 181 successful candidates (36 per cent) were born post-war, up 35 (7.6 per cent) from the 1993 election. The Democratic Party states in its manifesto that even though post-war generations already account for 70 per cent of the Japanese population, the ratio is still reversed in Nagatachō, the heartland of Japan's political institutions in central Tokyo. The Democratic Party proclaimed itself the party of those born after the war, to endear itself to young urban voters, and 27 (52 per cent) of its successful candidates were born post-war. The LDP and NFP (marked by factions that are pro and anti-1942-born Ozawa) have their own internal generational feuds. The 1996 election data make it clear that the post-war generation is making its presence felt in parliament, with the fresh outlook that this trend foreshadows.[10]

We can observe clustering in the career backgrounds of successful lower house candidates. Thirty per cent of the 500 candidates have backgrounds in local politics, 15 per cent are from the national bureaucracy (20 per cent in the LDP) and 13 per cent are former Diet member's secretaries. These data tend to confirm that in Japan as elsewhere, politics is a rather incestuous business. They also provide an indication of the life experience and possibly the world views that these people bring with them to their position as national representatives.[11]

Then there is the rural/urban split between parties. The election reconfirms a geographical divide in targeted constituencies. The LDP has fortified its rural stronghold as the party of farmers and business interests in the provincial urban centres. The DPJ and NFP present themselves as principally parties for urban dwellers, competing for the urban vote mainly in metropolitan outskirts.

Policy issues

Policy issues have not been a major concern in most post-war Japanese general elections. Japan's politicians have rarely depended for votes on articulating clear policy visions, or rigorously debating issues of national concern.[12] Under the multi-member constituency system, what drew most votes and therefore mattered most to electoral candidates, was ability to deliver a range of services and favours (pork) to constituents. But political pork-barrelling is expensive and has too often attracted corrupt practices. In the 1993 election, as the mountain of graft rose around key political figures, this became a major issue. Most opposition parties campaigned on promises of 'political reform', though mostly in sketchy terms. Nonetheless, 'corruption' and the systemic reasons for it became crucial to the election's outcome, and were instrumental in sweeping the LDP from office.

As we explained earlier, the new election system was intended to foster policy debate in the electoral arena, to put 'real' politics back into elections. The plan was to wipe out as much as possible the 'spoils of pork' that were contaminating the democratic aspirations of the electoral system. The new system would, it was thought, encourage voters to base their decisions on candidates' policy skills rather than their skills in delivering political pork. The electorate's anger at political corruption during the 1993 election suggested a climate ready for this change. To some extent it was. And to some extent policy discussion entered the fray in the lead-up to the October 1996 election. Two issues in particular became a focus of debate for most political parties: taxation and administrative reform.

In early 1989, the LDP government forced into law a new and unpopular 3 per cent consumption tax, despite stiff opposition from the socialists and other opponents. This tax has remained a festering sore. The Hosokawa government in 1994 proposed to raise it to 7 per cent, claiming it was to meet the demands of Japan's ageing population. Very soon, however, it dropped the proposal under intense political pressure. The LDP-Socialist-Sakigake coalition decided in 1995 to raise the consumption tax rate from 3 to 5 per cent, from April 1997. The Democratic Party also gave its support for an increase, justifying it as a way to deal with the country's huge fiscal deficit. The new leader of the SDP, Doi Takako, refused to give her unqualified support to the coalition decision. NFP championed a freeze, at 3 per cent, even though NFP leader Ozawa Ichirō had suggested in his popular 1994 book raising the consumption tax from 3 to 10 per cent.[13] Inside the NFP, dissension was rife; some members maintained that the tax increase was inevitable, while others suggested eliminating the tax altogether. Ozawa also promised a drastic tax reduction, amounting to 11 trillion yen (US $160 million), without providing sufficient detail as to how this would be achieved. The tax debate presented the NFP's inconsistencies rather than its policy expertise and party unity.

Meantime the weight of accumulated government debt (both at national and local levels) is estimated in October 1996 to be 443 trillion yen. According to some calculations, this is equivalent to 90 per cent of Japan's GDP and the worst national record in the industrialised world.[14] Yet none of the parties presented a concise, practicable plan for servicing the nation's debt. Meanwhile unlike usual electoral outcomes in industrial democracies, where parties calling for a tax hike do *not* win many votes, the LDP emerged as winner of the election.

Another central focus of all major parties' campaigns was administrative reform. Each party's platform seeks to merge some of the central ministries and restructure their functions. The LDP favoured reducing the number of ministries from 22 to 13 or 14 by 2010. Shinshintō, on the other hand, promised to trim the ministries and agencies to just 10. The Democratic Party argued for reducing the role of the most powerful, the Ministry of Finance, and establishing a system of checks and balances to decentralise political power. There seems to be a general agreement developing in Japanese political circles that the power balance between the bureaucracy and politicians needs to be changed, with politicians needing to become more active in formulating policy. Yet opinions vary on how far and how soon these reforms will be carried out.

Now that it has been elected, the LDP may be held to account by voters, who now have a precedent. Their vote can deliver a change of government and prompt it to be more responsive to the electorate. In the case of bureaucratic restructuring, unlike the promises of the NFP and DPJ, the LDP's stated goal appears achievable. It will not, however, be easy for the LDP to eliminate some of those in the bureaucracy with whom it has shared a long and often comfortable relationship, especially when the party may still perceive a need for their co-operation.

Foreign policy issues did not figure prominently in the election. It is likely that the LDP under Hashimoto will maintain a moderate line. An amicable and strong relationship with the United States appears sure to remain a top priority for the LDP, as the September 1996 arrangements on stationing American troops in Okinawa would indicate. Among the opposition members, Ozawa is a proclaimed internationalist who is likely to push for a pro-active role for Japan in international affairs, especially as a regional leader in Asia. The Democratic Party raised as an issue in the election campaign the need to reconsider the Japan-US Security Treaty. However, no major foreign policy shift is likely following the October general election since the new Hashimoto administration appears set to keep a fairly consistent approach to managing international relations. Existing institutional frameworks will continue to provide channels for liaison, alliance strengthening and strategic planning.

The new government

After about two weeks of post-election negotiations with most parliamentary actors, the LDP took the helm as a minority government. An agreement was reached between the LDP and SDP that the latter would support an LDP minority government from outside the Cabinet. Thus, in one election turnaround, and little more than three years after losing power to a disparate group of opposition parties, the LDP is back in power single-handedly. There is no doubt, however, that the LDP will be walking a tightrope, dependent as it is on support from opposition parties over which it has no control, but who will be keenly seeking leverage. Despite their partnership in two previous coalition governments, the LDP and the socialists remain divided on some major policy issues, most importantly the immediate issues of taxation and Japan-US security relations. It is likely that under Doi's leadership, the socialists will co-operate with the LDP issue by issue, rather than giving blanket support, and of course with an eye out for return favours.

The LDP may have regained power in its own right, but with a minority in both houses of parliament, it is far from being back in its dominant pre-1993 position. The party has fewer members and more opponents. A good few of these are turncoats, and are now experienced in running government outside the LDP. Before the LDP's 1993 ouster none of the opposition parties had experience of running government or interacting as ruling party members with the national bureaucracy. Between mid-1993 and mid-1996, however, most former opposition parties and their leaders gained invaluable experience of running government. A few made a remarkable difference and gained valuable public support for their ministerial initiatives, without simply falling back on bureaucratic support.[15] If the NFP and DPJ, respectively the largest and second largest opposition parties in the lower house, maintain a shared front and pursue effective policy debate, the LDP will be under pressure to perform effectively. If opposition parties cannot work towards shared interests and co-operate to some extent in the parliament, the LDP will be able to consolidate its position further and reaffirm its support from the electorate.

Radical reform under the LDP is unlikely. But early indications are that Hashimoto means business. This is his second administration and he has appointed some veteran reform campaigners to key posts. The appointments of seasoned politicians Mitsuzuka Hiroshi as Finance Minister and Mutō Kabun as Director-General of the Management and Co-ordination Agency are one indication of this government's giving high priority to administrative and fiscal reform.

Future directions

The October 1996 election has given the LDP a four-year mandate to govern in the lower house. The verdict that voters as a bloc delivered on 20 October under the new electoral rules was a cautious vote of support for the LDP. It was not a firm embrace, and if not appropriately reciprocated it may be withdrawn in the next election. Voters appear to have been frustrated with 'reformist' politicians who claimed they would introduce political reform if voted to power. They have included former LDP politicians like Hosokawa, Ozawa and Hata, socialist politicians and others who finally had an opportunity to demonstrate their political skills and concern for the electorate inside a coalition government. But in the eyes of many in the electorate, their performance was less than impressive, since their quest for personal influence and power appeared to eclipse the important policy matters concerning Japanese voters.[16]

The election outcome also suggests a call from the electorate for stable government, a preference for some degree of predictability rather than the politically unknown and unstable. It appears, then, that the LDP now has a golden opportunity to run a government that broadly serves the interests of the community at large, rather than the narrow interests of a few privileged groups. It is highly likely voters will withdraw their support if the LDP fails to present itself as a 'reformed' party that has moved beyond the corruption and nepotism of its rule during the late 1980s and early 1990s.

The New Frontier Party did not attract the level of support it had anticipated for various reasons. It did not espouse policies that were both attractive to voters *and* deliverable. Neither did it convince voters that it would present a united front itself. In fact, voters' doubts about party unity may well have been verified when a few key politicians in the party threatened to leave after a minor disagreement.[17] But beyond these shortcomings there was always the questionable and to some observers, offensive style of its redoubtable leader, Ozawa.[18] How far and how fast the NFP may be able to consolidate itself as a reliable party is an open question. One important imperative for internal cohesion is that this party now effectively constitutes the oppositional flank that will allow for future alteration between ruling parties. This was one long-awaited outcome that political reform helped to produce, something that had been absent in post-war Japanese political life. The key to the NFP's survival is its unity.[19] Unless the party stands for some distinct and appealing sets of policies, and speaks with a single voice, it will ride a rough and destabilising political course.

The Democratic Party's future is also uncertain. The DPJ's co-leaders are progressive, reformist-minded and experienced politicians, who have broad-based community support. As Minister for Health and Welfare in the Hashimoto Cabinet, Kan Naoto has gained immense popularity because of his fight against the bureaucracy in support of HIV-infected patients in Japan. Hatoyama Yukio and his brother Kunio are well known because of their family background. Dubbed the Kennedy Family of Japan, Hatoyama's grandfather was a Prime Minister and their father a high-profile politician and minister. In November 1996 the party is barely two months old. The DPJ clearly has potential to grow into a stronger and more effective political force.

The Social Democratic Party, in spite of its name and leadership change, appears a spent force. It has lost its optimism and its relevance in the face of successive departures. It is likely to remain either as a small party or merge with other progressive parties. Unlike the Socialist Party, the Japan Communist Party will probably remain unchanged; it has not lost its *raison d'être*, nor its ideological core, nor the bulk of its membership. The JCP will most likely continue to take part in electoral politics by registering an alternative voice to the mainstream, but its impact on policy decisions will most likely, as in the past, be minimal.

Because there are so many doubts across the board about Japan's political future, it is difficult to say with precision what form the opposition parties will take, and thus how individually, or *en bloc*, they will function in the party system. Some in Japan hold out for a much-touted two-party system along the lines of the British or the American systems. The formation of the NFP in 1994 was originally a step in that direction, by default, if not design. With the introduction of SMD and PR, the electoral climate appears to be more conducive to the emergence of at least two major parties and some smaller ones.

On the basis of just one election and in the early days after that election, it is difficult to identify what the engines of Japan's political machine will be as it drives the nation into the twenty-first century. Policy issues may surface more significantly in the future. However, the October 1996 election reveals that old habits, entrenched social, political and economic structures, and long-held loyalties die hard. In many of the single-seat districts in this election, candidates' ability to serve their constituencies and use their personal networks seem still to have played a greater role than their party leaders' stated policy. We cannot be surprised that a firmly embedded political culture has failed to undergo instant conversion merely with changes in electoral laws — especially when the system has served its political masters so well. Why would it change?

Conclusion

Politics in Japan will doubtless remain volatile, since the October 1996 general election did not deliver a tight outcome. There appears to be no real anchor in Japan's political party system, and therefore still considerable leeway for individual and party realignments. Reform is now firmly fixed on the nation's domestic political agenda, as action as well as rhetoric. Prime ministers and party leaders who attempt to override serious reform efforts are likely to pay for it at the expense of their political futures. This presents an interesting contrast to successive governments of the early 1990s, that lost their mandate not because of failure to implement reform but failure to hold it back. The October 1996 general election tells us that the rhetoric of political reform that marked Japanese politics in the first half of the 1990s is now taking shape as an overdue and powerful political reality. The incessant political wrangling of recent years is not about to stop. Nor are politicians who have been absorbed in wily manoeuvring about to change their style in favour of adherence to party doctrine or policy. It will take much more than adjustment of the electoral system and a few brief years of coalition governments to overhaul entrenched institutions and understandings of how politics are to be carried out.

Notes

1. For details on background of the new election system, see Purnendra Jain, 'Electoral Reform in Japan: Its Process and Implications for Party Politics', *Journal of East Asian Affairs*, Summer/Fall 1995, pp. 402–27, and Raymond V. Christensen, 'The New Japanese Election system', *Pacific Affairs*, Spring 1996, pp. 49–70. Also see Stockwin's chapter in this book.
2. The party avoided the imminent danger of disintegration when Hata and Hosokawa decided to remain in the party. Since then, at least three members of the NFP have resigned and now sit as independents in the lower house; see *Asahi Shinbun*, 7 November 1996. Many Shinshintō members dislike Ozawa's dictatorial leadership style and his close ties with the Kōmeitō that were so important for unifying a disparate membership into one party in 1994.
3. Doi Takako was the charismatic leader of the Socialist Party in the late 1980s and early 1990s. Under her leadership the party gained substantial electoral strength, but the Doi 'boom' was short-lived in the face of intra-party manoeuvring. Following the 1993 general election and the formation of a non-LDP government, Doi was elected Speaker of the Lower House and left the SDP in accordance with Diet tradition. On Doi's leadership, see J. A. A Stockwin (1994) 'On Trying to Move Mountains: The Political Career of Doi Takako', *Japan Forum* 6: 1, pp. 21–34.
4. *Yomiuri Shinbun*, 22 October 1996.
5. Party leader Hatoyama's words to news reporters, *Yomiuri Shinbun*, 2 November 1996.
6. See Masumi Ishikawa's Chapter 3 in this book.
7. Ibid.
8. *Yomiuri Shinbun*, 22 October, 1996

9. *Nihon Keizai Shinbun*, evening edition, 21 October 1996.
10. Ibid.
11. Ibid.
12. See chapters in Scott C. Flanagan *et al.* (1991) *The Japanese Voter*, New Haven: Yale University Press.
13. Ichiro Ozawa (1994) *Blueprint for a New Japan: The Rethinking of a Nation*, Tokyo, Kodansha International.
14. *Mainichi Shinbun*, 6 October 1996.
15. Mention may be made of Kan Naoto's contribution as the Minister for Health and Welfare under the Hashimoto coalition government.
16. For an informative overview on reformist groups, see Otake Hideo, 'Forces for Political Reform: The Liberal Democratic Party's Young Reformers and Ozawa Ichirō', *Journal of Japanese Studies* 22: 2, 1996, pp. 269–94.
17. Immediately after the election results were announced, Hosokawa, Hata and a few other Shinshintō politicians were about to leave the party and form a new one. The party averted an imminent crisis by convincing Hosokawa and Hata to stay: *Asahi Shinbun*, 21 October 1996.
18. The party suffered a further blow when in the Okayama gubernatorial election held a week after the general election (27 October) the Shinshintō-supported candidate, Eda Satsuki, lost to an LDP-supported candidate, Ishii Masahiro: *Asahi Shinbun*, 28 October 1996.
19. The NFP depends heavily on Kōmeitō, which is supported by a Buddhist organisation, Sōka Gakkai. Shinshintō's strong performance in the 1995 upper house election was partly attributed to the powerful vote mobilisation machine of Sōka Gakkai. By contrast, reports suggest that Sōka Gakkai was not very effective in the Lower House election: *Nihon Keizai Shinbun*, 22 October 1996 and *Asahi Shinbun*, 29 October 1996. Some NFP members who were not formerly in Sōka Gakkai are uncomfortable with this religious body's political principles, its close relationship with Ozawa, and therefore its influence on the party to which they belong.

Index